"In the evenings, my wife and I read to each other, and during the last two years or so, we have read around thirty books on near-death experiences. We both independently reached the conclusion that *Imagine Heaven* is in the top two or three books we have ever read on the subject. It was a sheer joy to read, it is solidly biblical, and it contains several exciting and convincing NDE accounts. Burke has managed to write this book like a detective novel—it's very hard to put the book down—yet he fills it with important content that answers the questions a typical person would have on this subject. In all honesty, this is now the go-to book on the subject. Ideal for the layman, it should also be required as a text in seminaries and Christian colleges. I urge you not only to read this book, but to urge your Christian friends to do the same."

J. P. Moreland, distinguished professor of philosophy, Biola University; author of *The Soul: How We Know It's Real and Why It Matters*

"In his engrossing book, my friend John Burke surveys the vast literature on NDEs, examining them in light of the Bible and showing how they can help us live with an eye on eternity. It's a creative and compelling approach to a controversial yet crucial topic."

Lee Strobel, bestselling author of *The Case for Christ* and *The Case for Grace*

"It's been a long time since I have enjoyed a book as much as this one. *Imagine Heaven* by John Burke is clearly reasoned, makes use of the best sources for near-death cases, works carefully through some appropriate inferences, and draws relevant applications for our lives. It has always seemed to me that there should be a direct connection between a well-anchored concept of the afterlife and one's practical commitment to life in this world. This work develops that link well. I recommend this volume highly."

Gary R. Habermas, PhD, distinguished research professor and chair of the department of philosophy, Liberty University

"John Burke brings the mind of an engineer, the heart of a pastor, and the discipline of a journalist as he tackles the subject of Heaven. If you have ever wondered about the afterlife or longed for a thoughtful investigation into the possibility of a Heaven, then this is your next book."

Erwin Raphael McManus, lead pastor of
Mosaic church; author of *The Artisan Soul*

"John Burke's *Imagine Heaven* masterfully combines the surprisingly large amount of 'data' from interviews with people who have had near-death experiences (NDEs) with 'data' from the Scriptures to create a remarkably believable picture of what life after death will be like. He then shows how this picture should significantly impact the way we live our lives today. As a scientist, I particularly appreciated John Burke's careful analysis of the significant amount of raw 'data' from NDE interviews with people of very different ages, cultures, religious beliefs, and physical challenges (such as blindness) to find the common elements that emerge to give a vibrant picture of what life after death will likely entail."

Walter Bradley, PhD, materials science;
author of *The Mystery of Life's Origins*

"*Imagine Heaven* is a comprehensive compilation of inspiring life-after-death experiences—grounded in the author's solid Bible teaching. Extensively researched yet enjoyable to read, John Burke's book is a must-read for those wanting a thorough understanding of Heaven."

Captain Dale Black, author of *Flight to Heaven*

IMAGINE
HEAVEN

IMAGINE HEAVEN

NEAR-DEATH EXPERIENCES,
GOD'S PROMISES,
AND THE EXHILARATING FUTURE
THAT AWAITS YOU

JOHN BURKE

BakerBooks

a division of Baker Publishing Group
Grand Rapids, Michigan

© 2015 by John Burke

Published by Baker Books
a division of Baker Publishing Group
P.O. Box 6287, Grand Rapids, MI 49516-6287
www.bakerbooks.com

Printed in the United States of America

Library of Congress Cataloging-in-Publication Data
Burke, John, 1963–
    Imagine heaven : near-death experiences, God's promises, and the
    exhilarating future that awaits you / John Burke.
        pages cm
    Includes bibliographical references.
    ISBN 978-0-8010-1526-7 (pbk.)
        1. Heaven—Christianity. 2. Future life—Christianity. 3. Near-death
    experiences—Religious aspects—Christianity. I. Title.
    BT848.B78 2015
    236.24—dc23   2015023210

Unless otherwise indicated, Scripture quotations are from the Holy Bible, New International Version®. NIV®. Copyright © 1973, 1978, 1984, 2011 by Biblica, Inc.™ Used by permission of Zondervan. All rights reserved worldwide. www.zondervan.com

Scripture quotations labeled ESV are from The Holy Bible, English Standard Version® (ESV®), copyright © 2001 by Crossway, a publishing ministry of Good News Publishers. Used by permission. All rights reserved. ESV Text Edition: 2007

Scripture quotations labeled NASB are from the New American Standard Bible®, copyright © 1960, 1962, 1963, 1968, 1971, 1972, 1973, 1975, 1977, 1995 by The Lockman Foundation. Used by permission.

Scripture quotations labeled NLT are from the Holy Bible, New Living Translation, copyright © 1996, 2004, 2007 by Tyndale House Foundation. Used by permission of Tyndale House Publishers, Inc., Carol Stream, Illinois 60188. All rights reserved.

Scripture quotations labeled NLV are from the New Life Version copyright © 1960 and 2003. Used by permission of Barbour Publishing, Inc., Uhrichsville, Ohio 44683. All rights reserved.

List of permissions is found on pages 345–46.

21 22 23 24 25 26 27   28 27 26 25 24 23

To Mom and Dad.

I love you.

I miss you.

And I'm so grateful for the touch of Heaven

you gave me growing up.

Now you know what Heaven is really like,

and I can't wait until our whole family

is together forever!

Contents

Contents

Foreword

I MAGINE HEAVEN . . . imagine understanding it! I've found that people all over the world will show up to hear someone talk about Heaven. They will read books about Heaven. Whether they would admit it or not, everyone wants to know if there is life after death. After all, the death rate is 100 percent!

Since the release of my book *90 Minutes in Heaven: A True Story of Death and Life*—in which I describe how I was crushed by an 18-wheeler, pronounced dead for ninety minutes, and visited Heaven—people have often asked why I did not write more about Heaven. I shared what I experienced while there and nothing more. To add to my personal experiences would have been disingenuous and fanciful. What I experienced reflects what the Bible says about Heaven. Many other devoted Christians have experienced and shared similar glimpses of the afterlife. They have received every imaginable response to their personal stories—from pharisaical diatribes to blind acceptance. Some pundits have been condescending, smug, and even mean-spirited in their responses to near-death experiences.

So what is the truth about Heaven, and who is telling it?

The Bible has numerous accounts of people who died and came back to life. Should we really be surprised that modern medical science affords even more such miracles? With the avalanche of people who have come forward in recent years to relay heavenly experiences, someone passionate about the Scriptures should examine those experiences. John Burke has taken up the challenge. Rather than arriving at conclusions based on personal biases, he tests whether or not these firsthand reports of life after death are legitimate and accurate.

Finally, someone has written a book that clearly examines Heaven and hell, or what happens after we die. Across an amazing group of diverse individuals, Burke skillfully considers each near-death experience. And he concludes that these folks don't reveal such intimate life-and-death details indiscriminately. Indeed, they often do so with great difficulty. Many are reluctant witnesses, but witnesses nonetheless. All were astonished and transformed by what they saw, smelled, felt, and heard.

Three cheers for John Burke and his willingness to tackle this twenty-first-century hot-button issue head-on. He's done it with compassion, understanding, and an attitude of reaching out to all who are seeking truth.

It was my privilege to be interviewed by TV/radio host Sean Hannity a few years ago. He wanted to know about Heaven. I shared my thrilling visit to the gates of Heaven following my catastrophic car crash. Hannity seemed extremely interested. Then he posed this question: "Is Heaven boring?" His other guest on the program that evening was pastor of Saddleback Church and bestselling author Rick Warren. Warren laughed out loud at Hannity's question. "You can't be serious. Heaven is a glorious place. Never boring!" He went on to share the extraordinary activities of God's home.

Heaven is a real place. The more we know about it, the more we should anticipate it. As I have often suggested, Heaven is a prepared place for prepared people. After presenting research combined with incisive commentary and critique, Burke asks the ultimate question: Are you prepared for life after death? It's last breath here, next breath somewhere else! Burke celebrates what happens next, if you are ready to go. He comments that people "can't imagine Heaven, so they don't live for it." How stunningly true! Experiencing Heaven is the most real thing that's ever happened to me. I did not want to come back. If you've been there, you don't want to be here. But when I did come back here, I intensified my efforts exponentially to help people understand the free gift of Heaven offered through Christ.

It is my fervent prayer that many will read this balanced, relevant, and penetrating analysis of the Bible's report of Heaven and these stories of the fortunate few who have experienced Heaven during a temporary separation from earth, and will embrace the utterly urgent need to prepare for their own entrance into eternity.

Now, *Imagine Heaven* . . .

Don Piper,
June 2015

Introduction

THE DOCTORS TOLD US my mom had only days to live. As she lay in the hospital for two weeks on her deathbed, I read the unedited manuscript of *Imagine Heaven* out loud to my sister and mom. I don't know if Mom heard it from her comatose state, but by the end my sister's comment was, "I want to go with her." I felt the same—not in a death-wish, morbid kind of way, but with a Christmas-morning, childlike excitement for the exhilarating life to come. I hope this book does the same for you. Although all of us face death, not all of us have an expectant hope for the future beyond this life. I believe that is because we just can't seem to imagine it. *Imagine Heaven* will undoubtedly help you do just that.

Heaven and near-death experiences (NDEs)—when people clinically died, were resuscitated, and claimed to have gotten a peek into the afterlife—have been a hot topic of late. Usually we're asked to take a person's word for it, but I've never been one to gullibly believe every story of seeing Heaven. As a result, this book has been slow coming. Over the past thirty-five years, I've read or heard close to 1,000 near-death stories (there are millions out there). I started seeing amazing commonalities across stories—intriguing, detailed descriptions by doctors, professors, commercial airline pilots, children, people from around the globe. Each gave a slightly different angle to what started to look like a very similar picture.

During that same thirty-five-year time frame, I went from a career in engineering to full-time ministry. The more I studied the Christian Scriptures, on my own and in seminary, the more intriguing and confusing reading about NDEs became. *Intriguing* because so many of them described the picture of the afterlife found in the Scriptures. *Confusing* because individuals' interpretations of their experiences could wildly vary and even seem at odds with the Scriptures.

After reading hundreds of NDE accounts, I started to see the difference between what they *reported* experiencing and the *interpretation* they might give to that experience. While interpretations vary, I found the shared core experience points to what the Scriptures say. In fact, the more I studied, the more I realized that the picture Scripture paints of the exhilarating Life to come is the common experience that NDErs describe.

Some Christians say that NDEs should be rejected because these tales of the afterlife deny the sufficiency of Scripture and therefore add to God's revelation. I respectfully disagree, and I've included Scriptural references throughout the book to show how aligned the Scriptures actually are with the common experience. Do these experiences add color and detail that help us vibrantly imagine the Life to come? Absolutely!

Think about it this way. The Scriptures tell us that all creation declares the glory of God (see Psalm 19:1). But if you actually witness a glorious sunset of explosive colors, where the bluest Hawaiian ocean crashes into the majestic mountain-lined beaches of gold—now you've experienced the black-and-white words of Scripture in a color-saturated way that can glorify God even more. Near-death experiences do not deny or supplant what Scripture says, they add color to Scripture's picture. But of course, like any gift from God, people can miss what God wants them to understand, misinterpret the experience, or even worship the gift instead of the gift Giver.

I include well over one hundred stories of people who were clinically dead or near death, were revived, and had amazing details to report. Some of them I personally interviewed, but most I compiled from reading about their experiences. Given this, I cannot vouch for each individual's authenticity or credibility. Some NDErs I will quote because their reported experience correlates with other experiences and Scripture, yet I do not agree with their interpretations or conclusions. And even if some turn out to be fraudulent (like the boy who made up a near-death story for attention), this does not concern me, because the stories I've chosen could be replaced with many others describing much of the same things. I also do not advise forming a worldview of the afterlife from a few people's interpretations. But what I am trying to do is show you something amazing that I think God is showing me.

I'm writing from the perspective of a convinced Christian, but I was not always convinced. I've studied the world's religions, and as a former skeptic, my passion is helping skeptical people consider the many reasons that keep me believing. If you're still skeptical about God, the afterlife, or even religious leaders—this is the book for you. You will get a thorough understanding of the picture of Heaven from the Bible, but don't worry, this isn't like a theology textbook—it reads more like a novel. If nothing else, it will open your eyes to the millions of accounts out there that have convinced skeptical doctors, atheistic college professors, and many others (all whose stories you'll read) that Heaven is real.

Could people make up stories or fabricate detail to sell more books? Yes. For this reason, I've tried to choose stories from people with little to no profit motive: orthopedic surgeons, commercial airline pilots, professors, neurosurgeons—people who

17

probably don't need the money but have credibility to lose by making up wild tales. I've also included children; people from predominately Muslim, Hindu, and Buddhist countries; and people who did not write books. Amazingly, they all add color to a similar, grand picture of the afterlife. And that's my main motive in writing this book—to help you *Imagine Heaven* so you'll see how wise it is to live for it, plan for it, and make sure you're prepared for a safe arrival someday.

Two days after reading this book to my mom and sister in the hospital, my mom breathed her last. My sister and I were in the room, hugging, blessing my mother, and celebrating with her—because we knew in that moment, she had come alive. Alive like she hadn't been in years; alive like she'd never been before! Alive like you've never imagined.

So join me on this journey, and let's . . . *Imagine Heaven.*

1

If You Only Knew
What Awaits You!

I SAT UP WITH A START. What time was it? I looked at the bedside table but they had taken the clock away. In fact, where was any of my stuff? The train schedules. My watch! I looked around. I was in a tiny little room I had never seen before."[1]

It was 1943 in Camp Barkley, Texas, and George Ritchie had enlisted to fight the Nazis. In the middle of boot camp, he got word that the Army would send him to medical school—his dream come true! The weather and training both took their toll, and Ritchie got double pneumonia the week he was supposed to ship out to Richmond for school. The morning he'd planned to catch the train, he woke up at midnight in a sweat, heart pounding like a jackhammer, with a 106-degree fever. During X-rays, he passed out.

"Where was I?" Ritchie pondered.

And how had I gotten there?

I thought back trying to remember. The X-ray machine—that's right! They had taken me to the X-ray department and . . . and I must have fainted or something.

The train! I would miss the train! I jumped out of bed in alarm, looking for my clothes. . . .

I turned around, then froze.

Someone was lying in that bed.

I took a step closer. He was quite a young man, with short brown hair, lying very still. But, [this] was impossible! I myself had just gotten out of that bed! For a moment I wrestled with the mystery of [the man in my bed]. It was too strange to think about—and anyway I did not have time.

The ward boy! Maybe my clothes were in his room! I hurried out of the little room and looked around. . . .

A sergeant was coming along [the corridor], carrying an instrument tray covered with a cloth. Probably he did not know anything, but I was so glad to find someone awake that I started toward him.

"Excuse me, Sergeant," I said. "You haven't seen the ward boy for this unit, have you?"

He didn't answer. Didn't even glance at me. He just kept coming, straight at me, not slowing down.

"Look out!" I yelled.

The sergeant walked right past George without knocking him down or spilling the tray—but how? Ritchie didn't care; his mind was fixed on not missing his train to Richmond. Medical school wouldn't wait. Determined to find some way to get to Richmond, even if he had missed his train, George headed down the hallway and out the door.

Almost without knowing it I found myself outside, racing swiftly along, traveling faster, in fact, than I had ever moved in my life. It was not as cold as it had been earlier in the evening—felt neither cold nor hot, actually.

Looking down I was astonished to see not the ground, but the tops of mesquite bushes beneath me. Already Camp Barkley seemed to be far behind me as I sped over the dark frozen desert. My mind kept telling me that what I was doing was impossible, and yet . . . it was happening.

A town flashed by beneath me, caution lights blinking at the intersections. This was ridiculous! A human being could not fly without an airplane—anyhow I was traveling too low for a plane. . . .

An extremely broad river was below me now. There was a long, high bridge, and on the far bank the largest city I had come to yet. I wished I could go down there and find someone who could give me directions. . . .

. . . I caught a flickering blue glow. It came from a neon sign over the door of a red-roofed one-story building with a Pabst Blue Ribbon Beer sign propped in the front window. Café, the jittering letters over the door read, and from the windows light streamed onto the pavement. . . .

Down the sidewalk toward the all-night café a man came briskly walking.

At least, I thought, I could find out from him what town this was and in what direction I was heading. Even as the idea occurred to me—as though thought and motion had become the same thing—I found myself down on the sidewalk. . . .

"Can you tell me, please," I said, "what city this is?"

He kept right on walking.

"Please sir!" I said, speaking louder. "I'm a stranger here and I'd appreciate it if—"

We reached the café and he turned, reaching for the door handle. Was the fellow deaf? I put out my left hand to tap his shoulder.

There was nothing there.

Disturbed that his hand had passed right through the man, George leaned up against a telephone pole wire to think. . . .

There for the first time it dawned on him that he might possibly be dead. The sergeant who had not run into him . . . that man's body in his bed . . .

He decided to try to get back to his body. As soon as his mind was made up, he was leaving the city by the river and speeding even faster than before back the way he came. He got back to the base and began a frantic search for his body, room to room throughout the army hospital. He had been unconscious when they put him in the room. The loneliness he had felt in the unfamiliar city was now a mounting panic as he was unable to get anyone's help in his frantic search for himself.

Something was strange about time, too, in this world where rules about space and speed and solid mass all seemed suspended. He had lost all sense of whether the experience was taking a split second or lasting for hours. Finally, he came upon a man in a bed with a ring on his left hand, a small gold owl on an oval of black onyx. It was his ring! And the sheet was pulled way up over his head!

George had felt so alive, so himself, he had not really let it sink in that he was dead. Now it hit him. In despair, he sunk down on the bed.

The light in the room started to grow brighter and brighter.

I stared in astonishment as the brightness increased, coming from nowhere, seeming to shine everywhere at once. . . . It was impossibly bright: it was like a million welders' lamps all blazing at once. And right in the middle of my amazement came a prosaic thought, probably born of some biology lecture back at the university: "I'm glad I don't have physical eyes at this moment," I thought. "This light would destroy the retina in a tenth of a second."

No, I corrected myself, not the light.

He.

He would be too bright to look at. For now I saw that it was not light but a Man who had entered the room, or rather, a Man made out of light. . . .

The instant I perceived Him, a command formed itself in my mind. "Stand up!" The words came from inside me, yet they had an authority my mere thoughts had never had. I got to my feet, and as I did came the stupendous certainty: You are in the presence of *the* Son of God.

He thought about Jesus, the Son of God, whom he had learned about in Sunday school—gentle, meek, kind of a weakling. But this person was Power itself fused together with an unconditional love that overwhelmed him.

An astonishing love. A love beyond my wildest imagining. This love knew every unlovable thing about me—the quarrels with my stepmother, my explosive temper, the sex thoughts I could never control, every mean, selfish thought and action since the day I was born—and accepted and loved me just the same.

When I say He knew everything about me, this was simply an observable fact. For into that room along with His radiant presence—simultaneously, though in telling about it I have to describe them one by one—had also entered every single episode of my entire life. Everything that had ever happened to me was simply there, in full view, contemporary and current, all seemingly taking place at that moment.

How this was possible I did not know. . . .

. . . Transfixed, I stared at myself standing at the blackboard in a third-grade spelling class. Receiving my Eagle badge in front of my scout troop. Wheeling Papa Dabney onto the verandah at Moss Side. . . .

There were other scenes, hundreds, thousands, all illuminated by that searing Light, in an existence where time seemed to have ceased. It would have taken weeks of ordinary time. . . .

Every detail of twenty years of living was there to be looked at. . . .

What have you done with your life to show Me? . . .

The question, like everything else proceeding from Him, had to do with love. How much have you loved with your life? Have you loved others as I am loving you? Totally? Unconditionally?

. . . Why, I had not known love like this was possible. Someone should have told me, I thought indignantly! A fine time to discover what life was all about. . . .

I did tell you.

But how? Still wanting to justify myself. How could He have told me and I not have heard?

I told you by the life I lived. I told you by the death I died. And, if you keep your eyes on Me, you will see more.[2]

Life After Life

George Ritchie did claim to see much, much more, which we will explore in the following pages. Beauty surpassing earth's favorite vacation destinations, people alive and active in a world not unlike ours, yet so infused with such exhilarating love, purpose, and belonging that it made earth seem merely a shadow of the real Life to come. As the loving Being of Light sent him back after his tour of another dimension, George said, "From that loneliest moment of my existence I had leaped into the most perfect belonging I had ever known. The Light of Jesus had entered my life and filled it completely, and the idea of being separated from Him was more than I could bear."[3]

After being clinically dead for nine minutes, George found himself back in his earthly body, but with a sheet over his head. Dr. Francy signed a notarized statement of his death that George would later produce whenever he talked about his experience.[4] Several years later, George and his friends were driving back to Texas from Virginia. George had never driven through Vicksburg, Mississippi, yet he began to recognize it. He insisted the driver follow his directions, leading them right to the red-roofed all-night cafe with the Pabst Blue Ribbon sign in the window! George had indeed been to this very place, but somehow from another dimension of reality.

In *Return from Tomorrow* he says, "I have no idea what the next life will be like. Whatever I saw was only—from the doorway, so to speak. But it was enough to convince me totally of two things from that moment on. One, that our consciousness does not cease with physical death—that it becomes in fact keener and more aware than ever. And two, that how we spend our time on earth, the kind of relationships we build, is vastly, infinitely more important than we can know."[5]

After this life-altering experience, George finally made it to medical school, worked for thirteen years as a medical doctor, and eventually formed what would be the precursor to the Peace Corps. At age forty, George Ritchie earned his doctorate in psychiatry. Years later, Dr. Raymond Moody heard Dr. Ritchie lecture at the University of Virginia about his experience. Moody had never heard of such a thing, but had studied Plato's works on immortality while getting his PhD in philosophy.

Dr. Moody began having his philosophy students read theories on postmortem survival and found to his amazement that about one out of every thirty students came up to report something similar to Dr. Ritchie's story. Moody started "collecting" these accounts, and in 1975 coined the term "near-death experience" (NDE), publishing his findings in the international bestseller *Life After Life*. Moody wrote that he hoped his book would shine light on these mysterious experiences, which are more common than they may appear.[6]

Four years later, I saw *Life After Life* on my parents' bedside table and picked it up. My father was dying of cancer at the time, and even though I didn't have much interest in God or the afterlife or anything beyond the next party, death's reality was knocking on our family's door. I read the book cover to cover that night, skeptical yet awestruck that so many people had these near-death experiences. Moody had interviewed hundreds of people who had stories of a near-death experience. While no two stories were identical, many shared common core traits. Moody described what was commonly reported, which generally followed a certain sequence.

It begins with a dying man (or woman) reaching a climax of intense physical anguish, even hearing the attending physician announce his death. Immediately, he finds himself no longer in his physical body, yet often still in the immediate surroundings. He is now merely observing his own body from a distance, and even witnessing efforts to resuscitate his body. At first, he is confused and unaware that he has died, but shortly, he becomes somewhat adjusted to this new state of being. He takes note that he seems to still have a body, but one that is very different than his previous physical body in nature and ability. Eventually, others also show up to offer support in various ways. He sees the spirits of deceased family and friends. Then a being of light appears, brighter than the sun, who is described as uniquely and supremely warm and loving. This loving being asks questions communicated through thoughts, leading him to examine his actions, often including a living replay of his entire life.

Afterward, he encounters some sort of boundary, seemingly the border between earth life as he knows it and eternal life. But at the edge, he discovers he must return to earth because it is not yet his time to die. He protests and does not want to return due to the powerful feelings of peace, joy, and love enveloping him. But even though he is resistant, he finds himself back in his physical body and continues to live.[7]

I sat on my bed, stunned, after I finished reading the book. I remember thinking, *If there's even a shadow of a chance that this is true, I had better find out—nothing's more important.*

Funny how it usually takes imminent death or tragedy to think about life in light of eternity, but that's what got me willing to explore. Over the next few years while studying engineering,

I also put my analytical mind to work studying about God. I discovered there really are good, rock-solid reasons to believe for those who want to find them.

Since that time, I've gone from a career in engineering to starting a church for doubters like me, because I've become convinced that God loves each of us like no other, and that most people are just like I was—they just don't realize how great life with God can be: starting in this life, but even more so in the Life to come.

A Boring Heaven?

I find that most people, whether Christ-followers or not, have a horrible view of Heaven. At best it's a cloudy, ethereal, disembodied, nonphysical experience—yeah, maybe with love, joy, and no suffering sprinkled in, but if we're honest, we don't really get *excited* about it. We can't imagine actually *liking* it. At worst, people think of it as an endless, boring church service, singing songs you're not excited about—forever! That sounds horrible to me, and I'm a pastor!

How you think about Heaven affects everything in life—how you prioritize love, how willing you are to sacrifice for the long term, how you view suffering, what you fear or don't fear. I'm convinced we can't even begin—but we should try—to picture how magnificent, how spectacular, how much fun Heaven will be—how much of what we love about this life and more awaits us in eternity. As the Scripture says, "No eye has seen, no ear has heard, and no mind has imagined what God has prepared for those who love him" (1 Corinthians 2:9 NLT). But that doesn't mean we shouldn't push our imaginations to the limit trying to understand.

For the past thirty years, I've studied the Bible, the major world religions, philosophy, and multitudes of near-death experiences. I've concluded that the core common elements of near-death experiences (NDEs) are a gift from God to color in the picture revealed by the prophets and Jesus. I'm convinced a main reason many people (Christian or not) live materialistic, self-centered lifestyles is their poor view of the life to come. They can't imagine Heaven, so they don't live for it. But all the great heroes of faith "were looking for a better place, a heavenly homeland. That is why God is not ashamed to be called their God, for he has prepared a city for them" (Hebrews 11:16 NLT). Imagining and living for Heaven is not optional to God—it's the hope God wants us to hold in our mind's eye.

We have the ability to *Imagine Heaven* like never before, not only by using our God-given imagination based on Scripture, but also our earthly experience (because God created this life too—his abode is not less spectacular). And now modern medicine is bringing more and more people back from near death to give exciting details that can color in our picture of Heaven and motivate us to live with eternal perspective. That's why I'm writing this book.

Loving Life

My hope is that you will begin to see with this God-given gift called imagination that Heaven is not imaginary, but more Real than the world we know. Maybe you're skeptical about God and the afterlife or you're not a Christian. In full disclosure, I'm writing as a convinced Christian. But I wasn't always convinced. I will try to show you what the Bible says about Heaven and how that lines up with what most near-death experiences report (not always with what they *interpret*, but with the core experience they *report*). I'm not seeking to add content to what the Scriptures already teach, but rather, help you imagine it, so I've included scriptural references throughout. Like watching a movie in high-def, 3-D, surround sound instead of black-and-white: you get the same content in a richer sensory experience.

Although I'm writing from a Christian worldview, we will also consider the stories of people from other religious perspectives. I hope you'll travel these pages with an open mind, no matter what your background, because I'm convinced your Creator loves you more than you can imagine—and you will love life with him!

Hazeliene from Singapore discovered experientially the truth of this statement when she blacked out, hit her head, and apparently "died." She explains in English (not her native language),

> I suddenly was in the very dark tunnel going up, up, up. . . . After passing through from that very dark tunnel, it has changed to very bright light. I had seen a very bright light, I thought it was sun, but it was not. I don't have an idea where that light came from. Someone spoke to me for a while, I heard, and that voice came from that light. You know what I felt when I saw that light? When I saw that bright light, I felt that someone loves me very much (but no idea who it was). I was very overwhelmed with that bright light. And while I was there, I felt the love, and that love I never felt before. That light welcoming me very warmly and loves me very much. My words to the light before I [revived] was this: *I wanted to stay here, but I love my two kids.* When I said this, I suddenly woke up. . . . Was it true that the light was GOD? Reason why I felt very overwhelmed? I felt that only that light ever love me and no one does. All people know only to beat me, hurt me, criticized me, offended me and many more. Nobody love me like that kind of love before. How I wish, my two kids and me could go there and feel that love forever.[8]

I hope you become convinced that your Creator has crazy love for you. But he won't force himself on you; he gave you a free will. He lets us decide if we will seek to know him and love him back, as you will see. I hope you will at least take time to discover what modern medicine and those revived from near death are revealing.

If you consider yourself a Christian, I hope this book gives you a better picture of Heaven than you've ever imagined. Jesus implored us not to live for earthly treasures and material junk that won't last, but to live every day with an eye on eternity. C. S. Lewis once said, "If you read history, you will find that the Christians who did most for the present world were just those who thought most of the next. . . . Aim at Heaven and you will get earth 'thrown in': aim at earth and you will get neither."[9]

In the Western world, we live for retirement. We have a vision, a mental picture in our imaginations, of what retirement will be like—a house on a beautifully manicured golf course, or maybe in the mountains or on the beach, with time to play golf, garden, boat, or do that favorite hobby, and time to spend with the people we love. Because we can picture it, we will work for it, save for it, sacrifice for it. There's nothing wrong with retirement, but it only lasts a few decades at best.

What if we became people who have a vision for the ultimate Life to come? What if it's true that this life is merely a tiny taste on the tip of our tongues of the feast of Life yet to come? What if Heaven is going to be better than your wildest dreams? And what if how you live really does matter for the Life to come? That would change how we live, work, love, sacrifice—wouldn't it? That's what I pray will happen for you as you get a clearer picture of Heaven. But first, what evidence is there that these near-death experiences are not just hallucinations or the last flicker of a dying brain? What convinced so many skeptical medical doctors? Let's find out.

2

Skeptical Doctors and the Afterlife

NO LIGHT, NO SHADOWS, NO NOTHING," Vicki explained.
Kenneth Ring, a professor at the University of Connecti-
cut, was conducting a study on the near-death experiences of blind people.[1] Both optic nerves were so severely damaged, Vicki had never visually seen anything during her twenty-two
years of life. As Vicki explains, "A lot of people ask me if I see
black. No, I don't see black. I don't see anything at all. And in my
dreams I don't see any visual impressions. It's just taste, touch,
sound, and smell. But no visual impressions of anything."[2]

That is . . . until one fateful night at age twenty-two.

Vicki occasionally sang at a Seattle nightclub. Unable to catch
a taxi after closing time, her only resort was to hitch a ride with
two inebriated patrons in a van. Not surprisingly, they crashed.
Vicki was hurled from the van and suffered a basal skull fracture
and a broken back and neck.

The next thing Vicki knew, she found herself above the scene
of the accident, "looking" down at what she realized must be
a crumpled-up van. Having never "seen" anything as a blind

person, Vicki recalls, "It was hard to adjust to, and . . . [seeing] was scary at first. Then, I liked it, and it was OK. I had trouble relating things to one another—what I was seeing and perceiving versus what I had touched and known."[3]

Vicki doesn't remember the ambulance ride to Harborview Medical Center, but the next thing she recalls is that she left her body again and floated up near the ceiling, from where she watched a male doctor and a woman working on a woman's body. "I was quite tall and thin at that point," Vicki recalls. "And I recognized at first that it was a body, but I didn't even know that it was mine initially. Then I perceived that I was up on the ceiling, and I thought, *Well, that's kind of weird. What am I doing up here?* I thought, *Well, this must be me. Am I dead?*"[4] She could overhear the doctors as they discussed their fear that possible damage to her eardrum could lead to deafness, in addition to her blindness. Vicki tried to tell them that she was fine, but the doctors didn't respond.

Vicki recognized her hair, which was down to her waist, and her wedding band, which had orange blossoms engraved on it.

> And I thought: *Is this my body down there? And am I dead or what?* They kept saying, "We can't bring her back, we can't bring her back!" And they were trying to frantically work on this thing that I discovered was my body, and I felt very detached from it and sort of "so what?" And I was thinking, *What are these people getting so upset about?* Then I thought, *I'm out of here, I can't get these people to listen to me.*
>
> As soon as I thought that, I went up through the ceiling as if it were nothing. And it was wonderful to be out there and be free, not worry about bumping into anything, and I knew where I was going. And I heard this sound of wind chimes that was the most incredible sound that I can describe.[5]

Vicki experienced a sense of upward motion as she traveled through the ceilings of the hospital and up above the roof of the building itself. She had a brief panoramic view of the hospital roof below her, as well as the streets, the other buildings around the hospital, and the city lights. As Ring reports, she felt "very exhilarated during this ascension and enjoyed tremendously the freedom of movement she was experiencing."[6]

Vicki noticed that she was fully herself, and had a distinct form and a nonphysical body she said "was made of light." Then she found herself going up through a dark enclosure, "like a tube." She was being pulled up into this tube or tunnel headfirst. She had no fear as she found herself moving toward a pinpoint of light getting brighter and brighter. As she reached the opening of the tube where the light was, she heard sublimely beautiful and exquisitely harmonious music that she had heard earlier. It transitioned into songs of praise to God.

As she reached the opening of the tube, she "rolled out" to find herself lying on grass. Trees and flowers and a vast number of people surrounded her. She found herself in a place of tremendous light, and the light, Vicki says, "Was something you could feel as well as see." Even the people she saw were bright. "Everybody there was made of light. And I was made of light. What the light conveyed was love. There was love everywhere. It was like love came from the grass, love came from the birds, love came from the trees."[7]

"It was incredible, really beautiful, and I was overwhelmed by that experience because I couldn't really imagine what light was like. It's still . . . a very emotional thing when I talk about this."[8] Vicki goes on to explain that in this other World she was welcomed by some acquaintances. As Ring notes,

> There are five of them. Debby and Diane were Vicki's blind schoolmates, who had died years before, at ages eleven and six, respectively. In life, they had both been profoundly retarded as well as blind, but here they appeared bright and beautiful, healthy and vitally alive. They were no longer children, but, as

Vicki phrased it, "in their prime." In addition, Vicki reports seeing two of her childhood caretakers, a couple named Mr. and Mrs. Zilk, both of whom had also previously died. Finally, there was Vicki's grandmother—who had essentially raised Vicki and who had died just two years before this incident.[9]

Vicki relates, "I had a feeling like I knew everything. . . . This place was where I would find the answers to all the questions about life, and about the planets, and about God, and about everything."[10]

Ring notes, "As these revelations are unfolding, Vicki notices that now next to her is a figure whose radiance is far greater than the illumination of any of the persons she has so far encountered. Immediately, she recognizes this being to be Jesus."[11]

"I was real close to him," Vicki explains.

He actually hugged me. He embraced me, and I was very close to him. And I felt his beard and his hair. . . . He actually enveloped me—that's the only word I can think of to describe it. He enveloped me with so much warmth and love . . . [and his eyes] were piercing eyes. It was like they permeated every part of me, but . . . not in a mean way. It was like you couldn't lie about anything, and he just looked everywhere and he could see everything. Yet I wanted to reveal everything to him.[12]

He communicated to her mind: "Isn't it wonderful? Everything is beautiful here, and it fits together. And you'll find that. But you can't stay here now. It's not your time to be here yet, and you have to go back."[13]

Vicki reacted with extreme disappointment and protested vehemently, "No, I want to stay with you." The Being reassured her that she would come back, but for now, she "has to go back and learn and teach more about loving and forgiving. . . . But first, watch this," he said. And what Vicki then saw was "everything from my birth" in a complete panoramic review of her life, and as she watched, the Being gently commented to help her understand the significance of her actions and their repercussions. The last thing Vicki remembers, once the life review had been completed, are the words, "You have to leave now." She then experienced "a sickening thud" like a roller-coaster going backward, and found herself back in her body, feeling heavy and full of pain.[14]

Seeing Is Believing

As a former skeptic, I would have had lots of counterarguments forming in my head about now. It all seems too good to be true. Yet the testimonies of people like Vicki have convinced many skeptical doctors, professors, and researchers that life continues after death.

Dutch cardiologist and researcher Dr. Pim van Lommel notes that Vicki's story and those of other blind people who have experienced NDEs are prompting researchers to reconsider the relationship between consciousness and the brain. "Vicki's reported observations could not have been the result of sensory perception or of a functioning (visual) cerebral cortex," says van Lommel. Considering how many details of Vicki's story are verifiable, van Lommel notes, her reported observations clearly were not imagined either.[15]

For instance, Kenneth Ring, who is not a Christian, says, "We asked [Vicki] a number of probing questions about exactly how [Jesus] looked to her and how she could be certain of his identity."[16] She described a bearded man with shoulder-length hair and piercing eyes, wearing a robe with a sash but barefooted, and she said brilliant light came out of him.

Ring notes, "On the one hand, Vicki, as a deeply religious person, even as a child, would certainly be familiar with descriptions of Jesus. On the other hand, she maintains that, because of her blindness since birth, these descriptions never had formed any coherent pictorial image in her mind of Jesus. If we take her avowal not only to be sincere but truthful, the fact that her portrait of him accords so well with tradition is surely a puzzle worth pondering."[17]

Ring also points out several fascinating "visual" descriptions made by Vicki. First, during the life review, Vicki "saw" a playback of her earthly life with her two friends, Debby and Diane. She was later able to describe to the researchers how her childhood friends looked and even walked (one moved with great difficulty). These were observations looking back on her childhood friends that Vicki could not have seen at the time but claimed to "see" in the life review. The researchers confirmed the observations with the housemother who raised all three of the girls.

Ring also points out that "when asked to describe the color of a flower, all she can say is: 'It was different brightnesses . . . different shades. . . . But I don't know. Because I don't know how to relate to color.'" He concludes, "The fact that she was unable to discriminate colors in that [heavenly] realm (and was also unable to do so in the physical world) only adds plausibility to her account."[18]

Blind people claim to see, deaf people claim to hear. And in this new "spiritual" existence, before passing through the tunnel, many claim to see and hear what's happening in our world. The types of things they say and report display corroborative evidence (claims that can be checked out and verified).

In Kenneth Ring's study published in 2008, he interviewed twenty-one blind people (fourteen blind from birth) who reported an NDE. He subjected his research to peer review, and "the reviewers tended to agree on the main conclusions of the researchers, that (1) the near-death experience is the same for sighted persons and blind or vision impaired persons, (2) blind and visually impaired descriptions of the experience show visual, or 'visual-like' perceptions, and (3) some of these reports have been validated by outside witnesses. So (4) there is preliminary evidence that the visual information can be corroborated."[19]

Modern Medicine and the Afterlife

With the advent of modern medicine and superior resuscitation techniques, the prevalence of people being brought back from clinical death has soared. In 1982, "a Gallup poll reported that 8 million people have had near-death episodes," according to the *New York Times*.[20] In the forty years since Moody coined the term, studies in the United States and Germany suggest approximately 4.2 percent of the population has reported a near-death experience (NDE). That's one out of every twenty-five people, or nearly 13 million Americans![21]

Skeptical medical doctors became some of the first researchers after *Life After Life* was published. Dr. Michael Sabom is a cardiologist who heard a presentation on Moody's book but thought it was nonsense. None of the patients he'd resuscitated had ever conveyed such an imaginative story. Challenged by the presenter to *ask* his patients, he did. As he expected, most had nothing to report . . . except Jane. Dr. Sabom recalls,

> When I asked Jane if she had had any unusual experiences during these brushes with death, the tone of her voice fell reverent. Beneath her words rose powerful emotions. I became quickly aware that she was entrusting to me a story deeply personal. That story unfolded like the pages of Moody's book. I was flabbergasted, but tried to maintain a sense of professionalism as I listened. . . . I started to believe there might be something to the stories that Moody reported. But all he had was a collection of stories; there was no science in his book. I decided to take the near-death experience to its next logical step—I wanted to see if

it would pass scientific muster. It did. After five years of research, I published my findings in the book *Recollections of Death*.[22]

Shocked into Belief

Dr. Sabom discovered hundreds of stories like Jane's when he began to sincerely ask. What convinced Dr. Sabom and other skeptical doctors of life beyond death were patients claiming they had left their physical body and observed their own resuscitation. Here was corroborative evidence—some verifiable way to substantiate whether these tales were more than hallucination or reactions of a dying brain. Dr. Sabom records multiple stories like that of Pete Morton.

> [Pete] told me he had left his body during his first cardiac arrest and had watched the resuscitation. When I asked him to tell me what exactly he saw, he described the resuscitation with such detail and accuracy that I could have later used the tape to teach physicians. Pete remembered seeing a doctor's first attempt to restore his heartbeat. "He struck me. And I mean he really whacked me. He came back with his fist from way behind his head and he hit me right in the center of my chest." Pete remembered them inserting a needle into his chest in a procedure that he said looked like "one of those Aztec Indian rituals where they take the virgin's heart out." He even remembered thinking that when they shocked him they gave him too much voltage. "Man, my body jumped about two feet off the table."

"Before talking with Pete, and scores like him," Sabom says, "I didn't believe there was such a thing as a near-death experience. . . . These people, like Pete Morton, saw details of their resuscitation that they could not otherwise have seen. One patient noticed the physician who failed to wear scuffs over his white, patent-leather shoes during open-heart surgery. In many cases I was able to confirm the patient's testimony with medical records and with hospital staff."[23]

Suspecting "familiarity with procedures" as an explanation, Sabom went on to conduct a study comparing resuscitation descriptions of people claiming to have NDEs with a control group of seasoned heart patients. This type of study has now been duplicated multiple times with similar conclusions. In a five-year prospective study of NDEs in the United Kingdom, Dr. Penny Sartori tested the "good guesses hypothesis." She asked seasoned cardiac patients who did *not* claim to see their bodies to guess what happened during their resuscitation. Sartori reports,

> Twenty-eight of these patients were unable to even guess as to what procedures had been performed. Three reported scenarios based on things they had seen in popular hospital dramas on TV and two guessed about the scenario. All had errors and misconceptions of the equipment used and incorrect procedures were described. Many guessed that the defibrillator had been used when, in fact, it had not. . . . This contrasted significantly with the surprisingly accurate accounts made by patients who claimed to be out of their bodies and observing the emergency situation.[24]

Scientific Research of Thousands

Dr. Jeffrey Long, a radiation oncologist, read about Dr. Sabom's near-death research published in the prestigious *Journal of the American Medical Association* (*JAMA*). He had never heard of such a thing, but as one who has to face death with cancer patients every day, he read Moody's book and was impressed by it, as well as by the work of other early NDE researchers. Still, he admits he was surprised by the lack of more extensive research, especially considering the fact that one of humankind's most pressing questions is whether there is life after bodily death. Just as Dr. Long began to wonder if he should pursue the study of NDEs himself, something happened that helped him decide.[25]

He and his wife went out for dinner with another couple. During dinner, their friend Sheila mentioned having severe allergies, so severe that she once had an allergic reaction during surgery and coded (her heart stopped beating).

Dr. Long decided to probe. He asked Sheila if anything had happened to her when she coded on the table. She responded immediately and emphatically, "Yes!" And it was then that Dr. Long heard his first in-person near-death experience story.[26]

Sheila's Joyous Reunion

Immediately after her heart stopped, Sheila quietly explained,

I found myself at ceiling level. I could see the EKG machine I was hooked to. The EKG was flatlined. The doctors and nurses were frantically trying to bring me back to life. The scene below me was a near-panic situation. In contrast to the chaos below, I felt a profound sense of peace. I was completely free of any pain. My consciousness drifted out of the operating room and moved into a nursing station. I immediately recognized that this was the nursing station on the floor where I had been prior to my surgery. From my vantage point near the ceiling, I saw the nurses bustling about performing their daily duties.

After I watched the nurses a while, a tunnel opened up. I was drawn to the tunnel. I then passed through the tunnel and became aware of a bright light at the end of the tunnel. I felt peaceful. After I passed through the tunnel, I found myself in an area of beautiful, mystical light. In front of me were several of my beloved relatives who had previously died. It was a joyous reunion, and we embraced. I found myself with a mystical being of overwhelming love and compassion. "Do you want to go back?" He asked. I responded, "I don't know," which was just like my old indecisive self at the time.

Sheila sensed the choice to return was hers. "It was a most difficult decision. I was in a realm of overwhelming love. In this realm I knew I was truly home."

A day later, Sheila awoke in the ICU, wires and tubes protruding from her body. She found herself unable to talk about her profound experience. Later, after she had returned to the floor where she'd been before surgery, she confided in one of the nurses, who seemed shocked and even afraid to hear about Sheila's NDE. When a nun was sent to speak with Sheila about her experience (it was a Catholic hospital), the nun reacted negatively as well, declaring Sheila's NDE to be the "work of the devil." From that point on, Sheila was extremely hesitant to share the details of her NDE with anyone.

Dr. Long recalls vividly, "When Sheila finished her story, there was silence around the table. . . . I remember thinking these experiences could change my views about life, death, God, and the world we live in."[27]

Since then, Dr. Long has collected and scientifically studied thousands of accounts from around the world, some of which we will explore in this book. Dr. Long's extensive study led him to conclude: "NDEs provide such powerful scientific evidence that it is reasonable to accept the existence of an afterlife."[28]

If the Shoe Fits

Numerous repeated cases in which someone is apparently unconscious in a hospital bed and reported seeing things they could not have seen from that bed prompted many doctors and professors to take these stories seriously. Kimberly Clark Sharp, a noted NDE researcher in Seattle, Washington, reported a case study in which a woman named Maria was rushed to the hospital with a severe heart attack. After successful resuscitation, Maria told Sharp about her near-death experience, including detailed out-of-body observations of her resuscitation. Then she went one step beyond. She claimed to travel outside the hospital, she said, where she observed a tennis shoe on the third-story window ledge of the hospital. Maria provided detailed information about the shoe. It was a man's shoe, she said, left-footed, and dark blue with a wear mark over the little toe and a shoelace tucked under the heel. Sharp went window to window on the hospital's third floor looking on the ledges. Finally, she found the shoe, exactly as Maria had described it. As Dr. Long points out, this account offers substantial evidence, despite the attempts of some skeptics to discredit it.[29]

The Lancet, one of Europe's most prestigious medical journals, published the account of a patient who had experienced cardiac arrest and was brought into the hospital comatose and not breathing. As a tube was placed in the patient's airway in order to ventilate him, it was noted by the medical staff that the patient wore upper dentures. The dentures were removed and tucked into the drawer of a nearby crash-cart while the patient was in a deep coma. After resuscitation, the patient was moved to another room where he remained unconscious. A week later, the patient regained consciousness. When the nurse came in he exclaimed, "Oh, that nurse knows where my dentures are." The nurse was very surprised as the patient explained: "Yes, you were there when I was brought into the hospital and you took my dentures out of my mouth and put them onto that cart, it had all these bottles on it and there was this sliding drawer underneath and there you put my teeth." The nurse reported in *The Lancet*, "I was especially amazed because I remembered this happening while the man was in a deep coma and in the process of CPR. When I asked further, it appeared the man had seen himself lying in bed, that he had perceived from above how nurses and doctors had been busy with CPR."[30]

J. M. Holden, a professor of psychology, studied ninety-three NDE patients who claimed to make multiple verifiable observations while out of their physical bodies. "Of these out-of-body perceptions, 92 percent [of these observations] were completely accurate, 6 percent contained some error, and only 1 percent was completely erroneous."[31]

The Logical Conclusion

Many studies have now been done, convincing many former skeptics that these people truly pass from death into some new state of existence. Miller notes the amount of scholarly, peer-reviewed literature now available since Moody wrote *Life After Life*: "Over 900 articles on NDEs were published in scholarly literature prior to 2011, gracing the pages of such varied journals as *Psychiatry, The Lancet, Critical Care Quarterly, The Journal for Near-Death Studies, American Journal of Psychiatry, British Journal of Psychology, Resuscitation* and *Neurology*."[32] *The Handbook of Near-Death Experiences* chronicles fifty-five researchers or teams who have published at least sixty-five studies of over 3,500 NDEs.[33] Many have come to the conclusion there is life after death. Alternative explanations have been proposed over the years, but none make as much logical sense of the evidence as the simple conclusion: there *is* life after death! (Appendix B gives an overview of alternate explanations and why researchers find them lacking.)

But what will that life be like? Every experience is unique, and each should be filtered with a measure of skepticism. However, when thousands of people of all ages across the globe report the same core elements over and over, we need to consider what this means.

3

The Common NDE Experience

SEVEN-YEAR-OLD KATIE was found floating facedown in a swimming pool. A pediatrician resuscitated her in the emergency room, but she remained profoundly comatose—massive swelling of the brain, no gag reflex—with an artificial lung breathing for her. He gave her a 10 percent chance of surviving. Astonishingly, she made a full recovery within three days.

When she returned for a follow-up appointment with the pediatrician, Katie recognized Dr. Morse. She told her mom, "That's the one with the beard. First there was this tall doctor who didn't have a beard, and then he came in. First I was in a big room, and then they moved me to a smaller room where they did X-rays on me." She explained the way the doctors put a tube down her nose—all accurate, but "seen" while her eyes were shut and her brain was deeply comatose. Morse asked her what she remembered about her near drowning. After all, if it resulted from a seizure, she might have another one. Katie responded, "Do you mean when I visited the Heavenly Father?"

"That's a good place to start," Morse said, skeptical yet intrigued. "Tell me about meeting the Heavenly Father."

"I met Jesus and the Heavenly Father," she said. Perhaps it was his shocked expression. Perhaps her natural shyness kicked in. Whatever the reason, that's all she'd say for that appointment. The next week, Katie was more talkative. She remembered nothing of the drowning, but recalled an initial darkness, then a tunnel through which Elizabeth came. She described her as "tall and nice," with bright, golden hair. Elizabeth (her angel) accompanied Katie through the tunnel, where she met several people, including her late grandfather, two young boys named Mark and Andy, and others.

During those days lying comatose, Katie reported having other near-death episodes where she followed her family home (while out of her physical body) and claimed she saw her brothers pushing a GI Joe in a jeep. She reported watching her mom cook roast chicken and rice. She even knew what clothes each member of the family wore that night. Her parents were shocked at the detailed accuracy. Finally, Elizabeth took Katie to meet the Heavenly Father and Jesus. The Father asked if she wanted to go home. She wanted to stay. Jesus asked if she wanted to see her mother. She said, "Yes," and then woke up. Katie's story opened Dr. Morse's eyes.[1]

Dr. Morse conducted the first systematic study of NDEs in children at Seattle Children's Hospital. He interviewed 121 children who had been near death and found similar accounts to Katie's. He also interviewed a control group of "37 children who had been given potentially mind-altering drugs, but none of these reported an NDE."[2]

When studies done on hundreds of children report the same core elements to their NDEs, you have to stop and ponder how so many children, completely oblivious to NDE stories, could confirm the same common elements as adults from around the world.

The Core NDE Experience

Although no two experiences are alike, and some outlying details should be skeptically questioned, there are amazingly common elements to the core near-death experience described by young and old, across cultures, in different languages. Researchers and individuals do not all agree on the interpretation of the experience (who, for instance, is this Being of Light?), but they agree on the core experience. Dr. Long reports on the percentage of each core element described in his study of 1,300 NDEs from around the world.

1. Out-of-body experience: separation of consciousness from the physical body (75.4%)
2. Heightened senses (74.4% said "more conscious and alert than normal")
3. Intense and generally positive emotions or feelings (76.2% "incredible peace")
4. Passing into or through a tunnel (33.8%)
5. Encountering a mystical or brilliant light (64.6%)
6. Encountering other beings, either mystical beings or deceased relatives or friends (57.3%)
7. A sense of alteration of time or space (60.5%)
8. Life review (22.2%)
9. Encountering unworldly ("heavenly") realms (52.2%)
10. Encountering or learning special knowledge (56%)
11. Encountering a boundary or barrier (31%)
12. A return to the body (58.5% were aware of a decision to return)[3]

After thirty years of research as a practicing oncologist skeptically looking at all alternative explanations, Dr. Long concludes there is no chance, with a flat EEG, that electrical activity in the lower parts of the brain could account for the kind of highly lucid and ordered experience described by NDErs. "Lucidity coupled with the predictable order of [core] elements establishes that NDEs are not dreams or hallucinations, nor are they due to any other causes of impaired brain functioning."[4]

At first, I was skeptical of adults telling these stories, especially when they had something to gain by selling books. Dr. Long's collection of what's grown to over three thousand testimonies on his website is important for two reasons. First, none were paid—they were not benefiting by selling a book—and it takes close to thirty minutes to complete his extensive questionnaire. There's not much to gain personally and it actually costs time. Second, the reports come from all over the globe—verifying the similarities of the core experience.

A Global Phenomenon

In Holland in 1969, cardiologist Pim van Lommel resuscitated a patient whose response shocked him. The doctor recalls that the patient expressed deep disappointment after he was revived. He was extremely emotional as he talked about the tunnel, the colors, the light, and the beautiful landscape and music he had experienced. "The term near-death experience (NDE) did not yet exist, and I had never heard of people remembering the period of their cardiac arrest," says Dr. van Lommel. "I was taught that there is a reductionist and materialist explanation for everything. And up until that point, I had always accepted this as indisputably true."[5]

He read Dr. Ritchie's book in 1986 and started asking his patients who had been resuscitated about their experience. What he discovered is that people don't tell unless asked. They don't want to be labeled "crazy."

One of Dr. van Lommel's Dutch patients described an NDE that had taken place when she was five years old, after she had contracted meningitis and fallen into a coma. She recalled that after she died, she was free of fear and pain, and actually felt quite at home in the place she found herself. At one point she saw a young girl who looked to be about ten years old. "I sensed that she recognized me," she remembered. After the two girls embraced, the other girl said, "I'm your sister. . . . I was named after your grandmother. Our parents called me Rietje for short." After kissing her, Rietje said, "You must go now," and in a flash, the young girl with meningitis returned to her body and, to the relief of her parents, opened her eyes. She excitedly told her parents about her experience, and even drew them a picture of the sister who had welcomed her. "My parents were so shocked that they panicked," she recalled. "They got up and left the room." When they returned, her parents confirmed that they had indeed once had a daughter called Rietje who had died of poisoning. They had decided not to tell their other children about Rietje until they felt they were old enough to understand the meaning of life and death.[6]

Dr. van Lommel, who has studied numerous childhood accounts, notes that if an NDE was based on wishful thinking, one would expect children to say they met living family members, such as their father or mother. Instead, they were more likely to encounter their favorite childhood pets who had died. Dr. van Lommel also found that very young children rarely experience a life review (it seems those begin around age six). And, like adults, children find it difficult to talk about their experience.[7]

Not All Good

But not every NDE is positive. Dr. Maurice Rawlings did not believe in God or the afterlife when he had a harrowing experience one evening in 1977. While doing a stress test, a forty-year-old man had a cardiac arrest and dropped dead in his office. Three nurses rushed in and began CPR while Dr. Rawlings started external heart massage, but the heart would not maintain its own beat. Dr. Rawlings recalls,

> I had to insert a pacemaker wire into the large vein. The patient began "coming to." But whenever I would reach for instruments or otherwise interrupt my compression of his chest, the patient would again lose consciousness, . . . stop breathing, and die once more. Each time he regained heartbeat and respiration, the patient screamed, "I am in hell!" He was terrified and pleaded with me to help him. I was scared to death. In fact, this episode *literally* scared the hell out of me! After several resuscitations, the man pleaded, "Don't you understand? I am in hell. Each time you quit I go back to hell! Don't let me go back to hell!" I dismissed his complaint and told him to keep his "hell" to himself . . . until I finished getting this pacemaker into place. But the man was serious.
>
> "How do I stay out of hell? Pray for me!" He begged.
>
> Pray for him! *What nerve!* I told him I was a doctor, not a preacher.
>
> "Pray for me!" He repeated

It was a dying man's request, so Dr. Rawlings drew on the little bit of Sunday school he remembered. Even if he didn't believe it himself, he had the man repeat after him while he continued working: "Lord Jesus, I ask you to keep me out of hell. Forgive my sins. I turn my life over to you. If I die, I want to go to Heaven. If I live, I'll be 'on the hook' forever." The patient's condition finally stabilized. A couple of days later, Dr. Rawlings asked his patient to explain what he saw in hell. The patient could not recall *any* of the unpleasant events—only pleasant ones when he again flatlined after the prayer! Rawlings reflects,

> Apparently, the experiences were so frightening . . . they were subsequently suppressed far into his subconscious. He does recall standing in the back of the room and watching us work

on his body there on the floor. He also recalls meeting both his [deceased] mother and stepmother during one of these subsequent death episodes. This experience was very pleasurable, occurring in a narrow valley with very lush vegetation and a brilliant illumination by a huge beam of light. He saw his [birth] mother for the first time. She had died at age 21 when he was 15 months old.[8]

This event changed Dr. Rawlings's beliefs, and after doing his own research, he writes in *Beyond Death's Door*, "Not all death experiences are good. . . . The unpleasant experiences in my study have turned out to be at least as frequent as the pleasant ones."[9] We will explore what this means and Rawlings's theory of blocked memories in later chapters.

Interpreting the Experience

While studying the Scriptures and reading more and more about NDEs, I've become convinced that the core elements that people report add color to the sketch already drawn by the Jewish prophets and Jesus. Yet many Christians have reacted negatively to NDEs, considering them either New Age tales or satanic deception. In part, I believe this is because some early researchers (who had not had these experiences, but simply studied them) advocated occultic practices like contacting the dead or transcendental out-of-body experiments. But I hope to show these *interpretations* do not fit the core experience *reported* as well as a biblical interpretation does, so we shouldn't throw out a possible gift from God because of misinterpretations of the data.

As theologian R. C. Sproul says, "It shouldn't shock the Christian when people undergoing clinical death and being revived come back with certain recollections. I've tried to keep an open mind, and I hope that this interesting phenomenon will get the benefit of further research, analysis, and evaluation.

Too many of these experiences have been reported for us to simply dismiss them as imaginary or hoaxes."[10] We will explore what these experiences mean, discover how they line up with the Bible, and see what an amazing future God wants for all the people he created.

But a word of warning is needed. These stories are *interpretations* of an experience. The core elements stay amazingly true to Scripture, but we should remain skeptical of outlier details. After reading close to one thousand NDEs, the most common thing I've heard is how impossible it is to put into words. Listen to the expressions of struggle:

There are no human words that even come close.[11] —Crystal

There are no words to express His divine presence.[12] —Gary

What I saw was too beautiful for words.[13] —Dutch patient

The kind of love that I experienced there cannot be expressed in words.[14] —Suresh

One person summed it up well by recounting his thoughts during the experience in relation to what he had been taught in geometry. He had always accepted the existence of only three dimensions, but now he knew his teachers were mistaken—there are more. He concluded that this was the reason retelling his experiences was so difficult, because, "I have to describe it to you in words that are three-dimensional. That's as close as I can get to it, but it's not really adequate."[15]

So every individual near-death story is actually an *interpretation* of an experience that's beyond our finite, earthly language. That doesn't mean it's completely foreign; actually, you'll be pleasantly shocked to find Heaven vastly more "earthy," "physical," and "real-life like" than you ever imagined, yet so beyond earth as well. But we must be cautious to avoid building a theology (or view of God and eternity) around individual stories or details that go beyond the framework of Scripture or the core elements found in most NDEs.

So What's Heaven Like?

As Katie said when her pediatrician kept giving her a skeptical look, "Don't worry, Dr. Morse, Heaven is fun!"[16] That's what you're going to discover as we turn our attention to imagine Heaven. I'm convinced God has prepared a future for you filled with more exhilaration and excitement, more breathtaking beauty, more love and relational depth with friends and family than you've ever experienced on this great big rock. The most common denominator of those who've had a glimpse: they don't want to come back!

So let's begin our imaginative journey. Maybe fifty years from now, maybe tomorrow, when you leave this earthly body behind, you'll get a better body! No more body image hang-ups or painful ailments. The deaf will finally hear, the blind will finally see. Imagine what that body will be like . . .

4

A Better Body

D<small>R. MARY NEAL</small>, an orthopedic spine surgeon, was on a white-water kayak trip in Chile when she plunged over a waterfall. The nose of her kayak lodged between two boulders, trapping her beneath a cascading torrent of water. Mary and her boat were completely submerged under ten feet of rapids. "I very quickly knew that I would likely die,"[1] Mary told me when I interviewed her about her near-death experience. In spite of the fact that she could feel the intense pressure of the water as she lay bent at the waist over the front of the kayak, her bones breaking and her ligaments tearing, she didn't panic.

> At that point I completely surrendered the outcome to God's will. The moment I asked that God's will be done, I was immediately and very physically held by Christ and reassured that everything would be fine. I grew up in the water. I grew up swimming, boating, doing everything in the water, and I love the water still but I'd always, always feared a drowning death. So, the irony was not lost on me that I was drowning. I always thought that would be a terrible and frightening way to die, but

at no point did I ever have fear. I never felt air hunger. I never felt panic. I'm a spine surgeon. I certainly tried to do those things that would free me or free the boat, but I felt great. I felt more alive than I've ever felt.[2]

The very moment I turned to Him, I was overcome with an absolute feeling of calm, peace, and of the very physical sensation of being held in someone's arms. . . . I knew with absolute certainty that I was being held and comforted by Jesus, which was initially surprising . . . as I am just an ordinary person . . . but at the same time I understood perfectly how Jesus could be there holding and comforting me and would similarly be present for any other person who called for His help at the same time, anywhere in the world.[3]

As Jesus held her, he took Mary through a review of her life. After fourteen minutes under water, Mary's body finally broke free from the kayak, and as she began to tumble through the rapids, she experienced a feeling of release. "It felt as if I had finally shaken off my heavy outer layer, freeing my soul."[4] Mary felt her soul break through the surface of the water and rise above the river, where a welcoming committee (she likened to the great cloud of witnesses described in Hebrews 12:1) was there to joyously greet her.

I was immediately greeted by a group of . . . people, spirits, beings. I'm never really quite sure what word to use because those names mean different things to different people. They were wearing robes of a sort but they were absolutely exploding with a pure, pure love. It was a welcoming committee. I absolutely knew that they were there to welcome me and greet me and make me feel loved and comfortable. . . . They had physical bodies. . . . They had heads, arms, legs. I knew without any doubt that I had known them and loved them as long as I've existed. I knew that they knew me and loved me as long as I existed.[5]

It was joy at an unadulterated core level. . . . My arrival was joyously celebrated and a feeling of absolute love was palpable as these spiritual beings and I hugged, danced, and greeted each other. The intensity, depth, and purity of these feelings and sensations were far greater than I could ever describe with words and far greater than anything I have ever experienced on earth. Don't get me wrong . . . I have been very blessed in my life and have experienced great joy and love here on earth. I love my husband and I love each of my children with great intensity. It's just that God's world is exponentially more colorful and intense. . . .

My companions and I began to glide along a path, and I knew that I was going home. My eternal home. . . . As I was drinking in the beauty and rejoicing with my companions, I glimpsed back at the scene on the river bank. My body [which after fourteen minutes underwater had now been recovered] looked like the shell of a comfortable old friend, and I felt warm compassion and gratitude for its use. I looked at Tom and his sons [close friends kayaking with Mary], and they seemed so terribly sad and vulnerable. I heard them call to me and beg me to take a breath. I loved them and did not want them to be sad, so I asked my heavenly companions to wait while I returned to my body, lay down, and took a breath.[6]

A Spiritual Body

Just imagine, that point of life you feared most—the death of your earthly body—suddenly frees you in a way you never anticipated. You feel alive! In fact, so much yourself and so alive that you have to adjust. It takes a little time to realize you're no longer in your earthly body. You still have a body—arms, legs, fingers, and toes—but you begin to realize that something's different as well. It's the same, but different. An upgrade!

Imagine, no more aches and pains, those ailments and impairments are gone, and the limitations of movement in your earthbound body do not seem to apply to this new, upgraded spiritual body. You still have your senses intact; in fact, all your senses seem turbocharged and multiplied. You sense and experience in a way that feels more "real," more "alive" than ever before. All anxiety fades into an astounding sense of peace. So many people who fear death are afraid of the pain of death. Yet many who describe it don't recall the pain at all; instead they speak of what Paul called "the peace of God, which transcends all understanding" (Philippians 4:7).

Paul the apostle apparently had a near-death experience. "They stoned Paul and dragged him outside the city, thinking he was dead. But after the disciples had gathered around him, he got up" (Acts 14:19–20). I believe Paul's talking about this experience when he writes, "I know a man in Christ who fourteen years ago was caught up to the third heaven. Whether it was in the body or out of the body I do not know—God knows. And I know that this man—whether in the body or apart from the body I do not know, but God knows—was caught up to paradise and heard inexpressible things, things that no one is permitted to tell" (2 Corinthians 12:2–4).

Some things people can't express or are not allowed to tell, but other things God wants us to know. He wants Heaven to fire up our imaginations, and I believe that's why he's giving us more and more evidence and insight into the life to come—so we will live for it. Most people don't realize this, but this new spiritual body is a promise from God conveyed in the Scriptures. Paul may be reflecting on his own near-death experience when he explains,

> For we know that when this earthly tent we live in is taken down (that is, when we die and leave this earthly body), we will have a house in heaven, an eternal body made for us by God himself and not by human hands. We grow weary in our present bodies, and we long to put on our heavenly bodies like new clothing. For we will put on heavenly bodies; we will not

be spirits without bodies. While we live in these earthly bodies, we groan and sigh, but it's not that we want to die and get rid of these bodies that clothe us. Rather, we want to put on our new bodies so that these dying bodies will be swallowed up by life. . . . And we would rather be away from these earthly bodies, for then we will be at home with the Lord. So whether we are here in this body or away from this body, our goal is to please him. (2 Corinthians 5:1–4, 8–9 NLT)

Paul reiterates, "It's going to be so much better in this new, upgraded spiritual body, I'd rather put on the new body, but either way, I'm going to live to please God." Mary felt herself in a new body, but could also see her old body. Yet the fear and pain of that old body went away as she transitioned into the spiritual body Paul talked about. So what's this new, spiritual body going to be like according to the Scriptures? Amazingly, just what people of all ages from around the world describe when on the brink of clinical death.

Forever Young

Not only will we be free of the pains and worries of this earthly body, we will feel young again! Remember what it was like to have endless energy as a child? Recall the strength and stamina of those teen years? Imagine a new body that feels even better than that! Paul mentions this when writing to the church in Rome: "For all creation is waiting eagerly for that future day when God will reveal who his children really are" (Romans 8:19 NLT). Jesus said, "Let the little children come to me, and do not hinder them, for the kingdom of God belongs to such as these" (Mark 10:14). What if we're going to feel like kids again—with all the energy and excitement of life?

Marv Besteman, a retired bank president, had surgery at the University of Michigan Medical Center to remove a rare pancreatic tumor called an insulinoma. It was after visiting hours, and his family had gone home for the night. Marv recalls,

> I was alone and racked with pain and more than a little bit grumpy as I tossed and turned; more than anything, I just wanted to sleep and escape the misery and discomfort for just a little while. I had no idea I was about to get an escape beyond my wildest dreams. . . .
>
> Suddenly, two men I had never seen before in my life walked into my hospital room. Don't ask me how I knew, but immediately I had a sense that these men were angels. I wasn't the least bit anxious, either. Once they had detached me from my tangle of tubes [which he later reflected was unnecessary, but probably for his benefit as a high-control banker], the angels gathered me in their arms and we began to ascend, on a quick journey that felt light and smooth through the bluest of blue skies. I was deposited on solid ground, in front of a monumental gate. And no, I don't remember it as being "pearly."
>
> Standing in a short line of people, I observed the other thirty-five or so heavenly travelers, people of all nationalities. Some were dressed in what I thought were probably the native costumes of their lands. One man carried a baby in his arms. I saw color-bursts that lit up the sky, way beyond the northern lights I had seen once on a trip to Alaska. Simply glorious. . . . The music I heard was incomparable to anything I had ever heard before. . . . My [old] geezer body felt young and strong and fantastic. The aches and pains and limitations of age were just gone. I felt like a teenager again, only better.[7]

I know it sounds like science-fiction fantasy, which is why I've mostly chosen the testimonies of professors, medical doctors, wealthy professionals, or children, who don't seem to have anything to gain (and credibility to lose) by such amazing stories. Yet as you'll see, thousands of people from all walks of life, saying much the same thing, makes you start to wonder . . . Could it be?

Maybe the reason we never feel fully satisfied in this life is because we were created for the life to come. As Paul said, "Our present sufferings are not worth comparing with the glory that will be revealed in us. . . . We know that the whole creation has been groaning as in the pains of childbirth right up to the present time" (Romans 8:18, 22). What if this life is merely a birth canal into true Life? Imagine—to live again, forever young, but with wisdom too!

Whole and Healthy

I've been blessed with amazing health. However, as I type this, I'm wearing a cast on my leg from playing soccer with college students—a broken fibula now reminds me that I'm not that young anymore! When I consider the prospect of a new, improved body, I think about how right that sounds. Not just for me, but especially for those who never had the blessing of a healthy body.

I think about my good friends Rich and Arden Seggerman. Their oldest daughter, Naomi, was born with a condition preventing her from ever walking or talking. They've spent twenty years loving and serving Naomi. They know God's promise, that just like Vicki and her friends, one day the blind will see, the deaf will hear, and Naomi will run and laugh and talk—and it will all be worth it. As Mother Teresa said, "In light of heaven, the worst suffering on earth, a life full of the most atrocious tortures on earth, will be seen to be no more serious than one night in an inconvenient hotel."[8]

Gary Wood had a car accident and was killed instantly. He states, "I turned to see what the matter was. There was an explosion, then a sharp, instant pain seared across my face. There was a brilliant light that engulfed me, and I remember being free from all pain. I slipped out of my body. . . . I was above the car now. . . . As I began to ascend up through this tunnel of light, I felt such a tranquil feeling of peace wash over me. . . . All around me I could hear angels singing."

Gary found himself at the edge of an incredible city (which we will explore in a later chapter). As he entered, he found an unexpected reunion.

> An angel nodded and I was granted access to the city. The first person I saw when I entered the city was my friend John who had been decapitated in an accident in high school. His death had been a haunting memory for me. When I saw him, I was overwhelmed with joy. He was just as I remembered him only so much more complete. He ran and embraced me. It was a glorious reunion. When he wrapped his arms around me, they went all the way through me—we went into one another. This hug was so much deeper than hugs on earth.

Gary revived after being pronounced "dead" for twenty minutes. Due to his injuries, he had no vocal cords. Yet he believes as a sign of what's to come, God did something the doctors still say is impossible. Gary says, "I have an X-ray that shows that I have no vocal cords, yet I talk and sing."[9] God's promise to those who love him is that "there will be no more death or mourning or crying or pain, for the old order of things has passed away" (Revelation 21:4).

Real Bodies or Bodies of Light?

"But someone may ask, 'How will the dead be raised? What kind of bodies will they have?'" Paul asks and addresses this question: "There are also bodies in the heavens and bodies on the earth. The glory of the heavenly bodies is different from the glory of the earthly bodies" (1 Corinthians 15:35, 40 NLT). Paul explains later in that chapter that one day our earthly physical bodies will be resurrected just like Jesus's body was resurrected. But this doesn't happen right when we die.

In essence, when we die we get an upgrade from our temporal, earthly bodies (version 1.0) to a spiritual body (version 2.0) that has a far greater "glory." Yet it's still not the final version. When all is said and done, and God wraps up human history as we know it, Scripture says all original earthly bodies will be resurrected just like Jesus's body was resurrected. Jesus is the prototype of how our upgraded spiritual body will be united with our resurrected earthly body (version 3.0). Jesus could be physically touched, eat fish, walk down the Emmaus road talking with his disciples in his resurrected body, yet he also displayed the spiritual body's shining brilliance, ability to pass through walls, and move with thought.

What most people don't realize is that God plans on making everything new—including the earth and our bodies—and uniting Heaven and earth as one. "Then I saw 'a new heaven and a new earth,' for the first heaven and the first earth had passed away" (Revelation 21:1). Randy Alcorn, in his extensive theology of Heaven, notes, "The present, intermediate Heaven is in the angelic realm, distinctly separate from Earth (though . . . likely having more physical qualities than we might assume). By contrast, the future Heaven will be in the human realm, on Earth."[10]

But the present Heaven, or intermediate Heaven, is the primary concern of this book. What's it going to be like? Recall that every NDEr is describing something hard to put into words.

Body Parts

One woman told Dr. Moody that while she was out of her body, even though she was weightless, she could still feel an entire form to her body, including arms and legs.[11] Another lady who watched the resuscitation attempt on her body from a point just below the ceiling describes herself as still being in a body that was extended as she was watching the events below. She remembers moving her legs and taking note that one leg felt warmer than the other.[12] So this spiritual body feels the same as our physical body, and yet many notice it is translucent or in some cases a body of light.

Dr. Long reports what seventeen-year-old Valerie recalled when she "died" during surgery: "I remember looking at my hands, and they were translucent. Then an angel appeared; she had such a radiant glow to her beauty to behold. She comforted me, telling me I was safe. I remember telling her I wasn't ready to die. She said she knew that. Then she pointed down, and I could see the doctors doing CPR on a little girl. Not really understanding that was me, I watched my whole operation, CPR and all."[13]

Doctors like Mary Neal and Richard Eby seemed to notice more about the body. Richard Eby and his wife were helping clean out a relative's Chicago apartment. Richard leaned against a second-story railing to drop boxes down. He did not know termites had destroyed the wood anchoring the railing. The railing gave way. Richard plunged two stories to the cement sidewalk below—headfirst! Dr. Eby recalls, "The eggshell of my skull completely broke apart and broke the large blood vessel in my brain; my eyes popped out. . . . I was dead on impact." He miraculously revived in the morgue. While "dead," Dr. Eby noticed,

> I was the same size, the same shape, as the person I had seen in the mirror for years. I was clothed in a translucent flowing gown, pure white, but transparent to my gaze. In amazement I could see through my body and note the gorgeously white flowers behind and beneath me. This seemed perfectly normal, yet thrillingly novel. . . . My feet were easy to see. No bifocals needed. I had instantly noted that my eyes were unlimited in

range of vision; ten inches or ten miles—the focus was sharp and clear. . . . There were no bones or vessels or organs. No blood. I noted the absence of genitals. . . . The abdomen and chest were organless and transparent to my gaze, though translucent to my peripheral vision. Again my mind which worked here in Heaven with electric-like speed answered my unspoken query: they are not needed; Jesus is the Life here. He is the needed energy.[14]

So we get this picture of real bodies that still feel physical and can sense things in this new dimension of life, yet are unable to make contact with anything on earth. We have a translucent body that's able to "do" all we used to do, including touch, feel, and even hug, all with a heightened level of awareness. If it's a real body, will we wear real "clothes" too?

What Clothes Will I Wear?

Jesus said in the book of Revelation, "They will walk with me, dressed in white, for they are worthy. The one who is victorious will, like them, be dressed in white. I will never blot out the name of that person from the book of life, but will acknowledge that name before my Father and his angels. Whoever has ears, let them hear" (Revelation 3:4–6). John the apostle said of his experience of Heaven, "There before me was a great multitude that no one could count, from every nation, tribe, people and language, standing before the throne and before the Lamb [Jesus]. They were wearing white robes and were holding palm branches in their hands" (Revelation 7:9). According to NDErs, other types of clothing get worn in heaven besides the translucent robe of white Dr. Eby wore.

Bank president Marv Besteman said he looked down and noticed he no longer wore his hospital gown; he was dressed in what he might normally wear to take his wife out—a light-brown golf shirt, tan slacks, and shoes. He later noticed that those he met in Heaven seemed to be dressed in what they felt most comfortable in on earth. "The smiling people who stood in that line were from all over the world and wore all kinds of different clothing. I saw many different nationalities represented, including Scandinavian, Asian, African, and Middle Eastern . . . [as well as] primitive African tribes; they were wearing loose, flowing tribal gowns and toga-like garb with sandals on their feet."[15]

After reading so many of these accounts, I have a theory. It's just a theory, but follow me. I think we will find we can clothe ourselves in what feels natural, so people from different times and cultures will wear what felt comfortable to that time. However, many NDErs report people dressed in robes of white. Reading this I thought, *I don't want to wear a white robe forever!* Then I contemplated what this "white robe" might signify to make it so special.

When Jesus was on earth, he took Peter, James, and John alone with him and they saw him transfigured in "glory." Scripture says, "The appearance of his face changed, and his clothes became as bright as a flash of lightning. Two men, Moses and Elijah, appeared in glorious splendor, talking with Jesus" (Luke 9:29–30). When Jesus lets these three disciples see his "glory," he and these two Old Testament prophets are clothed in brilliant light. So glory and light seem to go together.

Dr. Mary Neal confirms the brilliant glory of the people she called her welcoming committee. "They were radiating a brilliance that was indescribable," Mary explained during our interview. "It was as though they were like the Northern Lights in that they were of a physical form, but their edges were a little indistinct. It's sort of translucent, pearlescent, shimmery. A brilliance of light—just exploding in it, and the light was not just something you would *see*. If you look at the sun, you see light and it's blinding. This was really a light born out of love. I don't know quite how else to explain it."[16]

Paul tells us, "Now if we are children [of God], then we are heirs—heirs of God and co-heirs with Christ, if indeed we share in his sufferings in order that we may also *share in his glory*" (Romans 8:17, italics mine). So here's my theory. Maybe people want to wear the white, translucent "robes" you'll hear so many describe because it shows off how much they share in God's "glory." We dress on earth to show off our physical "glory" or the physical attributes we want noticed. What if in Heaven, what we want noticed is how much the light/glory of God shines through us? NDErs note this translucent body seems to be able to "shine" or radiate a light that comes from within, and different people radiate different degrees of brilliance. Maybe the "white" robe isn't white at all, or even a "robe" as we know it, but what it means to be clothed in God's glory.

Dean Braxton's heart stopped for an hour and forty-five minutes during kidney surgery. He revived, claiming he saw Jesus: "Jesus is pure light! His brightness was before me, around me, part of me, and in me. He is brighter than the noonday sun, but we can still look at him in Heaven. . . . I was in Jesus, and Jesus was shining out of me. I would see the brightness. The brightness was around me. I was part of the brightness, and brightness was shining out of me. All of it was life."[17]

The Jewish prophet Daniel, writing from Babylon around 550 BCE, was told by an angel, "Everyone whose name is found written in the book—will be delivered. Multitudes who sleep in the dust of the earth will awake: some to everlasting life, others to shame and everlasting contempt. Those who are wise will *shine like the brightness of the heavens*, and those who lead many to righteousness, like the stars for ever and ever" (Daniel 12:1–3, italics mine).

Will You Reflect the Glory of God?

Jesus reiterates this idea that we will reflect God's glory in Heaven: "Then the righteous will shine like the sun in the kingdom of their Father. Whoever has ears, let them hear" (Matthew

13:43). God asks Job, "Have you seen the gates of the deepest darkness? . . . What is the way to the abode of light?" (Job 38:17, 19). And God tells Job, "The wicked are denied their light" (Job 38:15).

It is fascinating that thousands around the world who have these near-death experiences report seeing spiritual bodies that are somewhat translucent, but may shine with a light that comes from within. Different people seem to have different luminosities. Kenneth Ring asked Vicki, the blind woman, "Was there a brightness associated with Jesus?" Vicki responded, "Much more than anybody there. He was the brightest of anybody there at all . . . but it was incredibly beautiful and warm. It was very intense. I know I couldn't have stood it if I were myself ordinarily."[18] Notice, Vicki distinguishes different "brightnesses," with Jesus being the "brightest" (most glorious).

We marvel at celebrities' glorious dresses on the red carpet and the glory of buffed bodies on TV. Imagine sharing in God's glory! Maybe the more "open" and "available" you are now to allow God's Spirit to work in and through you (despite the sufferings it requires), the more God's glory shines through you in Heaven! Apparently, we will have the ability to wear different clothes, whatever feels comfortable, but what an honor to be clothed in God's glory—a light that feels like love and life.

That must be what Paul meant when he encouraged us to become "'children of God without fault in a warped and crooked generation.' Then you will shine among them like stars in the sky. . . . [And he] will transform our lowly bodies so that they will be like his glorious body" (Philippians 2:15; 3:20–21).

But for some of us, it still feels a bit scary. Translucent? Shining with light? What will it feel like? Will I actually be myself? That's critical to understand. You haven't fully been yourself yet! As one NDEr put it, you'll be shocked to find "the first person you meet in Heaven, will be you!"

5

You'll Be Yourself... Finally!

CRYSTAL STRUGGLED WITH GOD. Struggled with her identity. Struggled with shame... and for good reason. The sexual abuse had started at age three at a babysitter's house. At five, it happened again, in the home of a different babysitter, but Crystal didn't tell her mother about the molestation because she wanted to shield her from more pain and suffering.

Crystal knew her mom had endured one divorce, and now, after marrying Hank, things got even worse. Hank had anger issues, was always drunk, and became physically abusive to Crystal's mom. One night while trying to scare her mom, Hank threatened to kill little Crystal. Pointing a shotgun at Crystal's head while she slept, he pulled the trigger. He barely missed.

By age six, Crystal had watched two marriages fall apart and endured horrific sexual abuse. Her mom started partying each week upstairs in the home of friends, while downstairs, Crystal and her brother were left alone. For five straight years, Crystal was sexually abused during these weekly escapades. While it didn't happen every time, she remembers, it happened a lot, yet she didn't tell a single person. "The shame and the dirtiness and the brokenness that I felt became my identity," she says. That shame-based identity clung to Crystal like wet, smelly clothes. For years, she acted out of this false identity.

Until age thirty-three, when she died.

Crystal went to the hospital for pancreatitis, and due to complications, she coded. During a nine-minute span, she left her body and went to Heaven, where she stood before God. Crystal says the experience profoundly transformed her to the very core of her being, yet she kept the story to herself, afraid she would be seen as crazy, judged, shunned, or even fired from her job as a teacher. Although God had clearly instructed Crystal to tell others what she remembered from her near-death experience, she still hesitated.

Crystal questioned why God had chosen her. Although she had grown up in the heart of the Bible Belt, been baptized, and attended church regularly in her youth, after all that happened to her, she turned far from God and claims she broke every one of the Ten Commandments—"all ten," she emphasizes. Again and again she challenged God to prove his existence, and when he did, she constructed a new obstacle or challenge for him to overcome, she explains. "I saw the hardships in my life as evidence that God had no interest in protecting me from harm." Crystal questioned and cursed God. She was determined to cut him out of her life.[1]

That day in the hospital, Crystal's lips started turning blue, her mom called the nurse, and the nurse called for Code Blue. Not everyone goes through a tunnel when they die clinically; some just wake up in a new world, and that was Crystal's experience. After she told her mother she loved her, closed her eyes, and drifted off, Crystal awoke to find herself in Heaven with God.

> The first thing I remember becoming aware of was that I was still me. And I was still the me who had just told my mother

that I loved her and died. And I was very aware of the fact that I had just died. But I also was the me that had existed from the moment that God had created me. Unlike on earth, where I was plagued by doubts and fears, in heaven there was nothing but absolute certainty about who I was.[2]

Crystal felt infused with a complete and total self-understanding and self-knowledge. All the baggage and abuses that had muddied her identity on earth instantly evaporated, revealing, for the first time, her true, essential self. "'Before I formed you in the womb, I knew you,' God says in Jeremiah 1:5. And now," says Crystal, "I knew myself. Imagine that—the first person we meet in heaven is ourselves."[3]

Uniquely You

"Who defines who you are?" This is such a critical question, but so few of us have really stopped to answer it. Who has the right to define who you are? What you're worth? What your purpose is? Whether you succeed or fail? How you define your identity is ultra-important. What you believe about yourself is what shapes all your decisions and actions.

Most of us end up believing things about our identity that are not grounded in God's reality—who God created us to be, what God created us to do. We believe lies about our identity that the evils of this world inflict on us. We constantly worry about the opinions or approval of others. We experience intense anxiety when we're not succeeding or are not recognized for our accomplishments. We feel sick inside when the stock market drops or we don't get promoted. We find ourselves lowering our standards to new levels, then justifying it in order to prove our worth or get someone to love us. We feel the need to control our spouse or our kids because our identity has somehow gotten wrapped up in what others think or do.

When we base our worth or identity on what we do or what was done to us, we will struggle with fear of failure, feel the need to prove ourselves, or manipulate others who get in the way of our success. We will become self-consumed. That's because God never created us to get our identity from what we do or what others did to us, but from *who we are* to God.

Van Lommel notes that many NDE survivors he's interviewed attach less importance on acquiring status, power, and material things like expensive cars or big houses after an NDE.[4] We often try to perform, accomplish, or gain notoriety to make a name for ourselves. What we will see in Heaven is that life is not about all that.

Uniquely Loved

When Dr. George Ritchie had his life review, this matter became evident:

> Every detail of twenty years of living was there to be looked at. The good, the bad, the high points, the run-of-the-mill. And with this all-inclusive view came a question. It was implicit in every scene and, like the scenes themselves, seemed to proceed from the living Light beside me.
>
> *What did you do with your life?*
>
> It was obviously not a question in the sense that He was seeking information, for what I had done with my life was in plain view. . . . Hadn't I ever gone beyond my own immediate interests, done anything other people would recognize as valuable? At last I located it, the proudest moment of my life: "I became an Eagle Scout!"
>
> Again, words seemed to emanate from the Presence beside me: *That glorified you. . . .*
>
> I saw myself walking forward at a church service at age eleven, asking Jesus to be Lord of my life. But I saw how quickly that first excitement turned into a dull routine of church-on-Sunday. . . .

I started to point out my premed courses, how I was going to be a doctor and help people. But visible alongside the classroom scenes was that Cadillac car and that private airplane—thoughts as observable as actions in that all-pervading Light.

And all at once rage at the question itself built up in me. It was not fair! Of course I had not done anything with my life! I had not had time. How could you judge a person who had not started? The answering thought, however, held no trace of judgment. *Death*, the word was infinitely loving, *can come at any age.*

George thought about the insurance policy he had just taken out with the military—guaranteeing him money at age seventy. Before he could pull the thought back, it was out in the open. If he wondered if the Lord had a sense of humor, now he found out.

The brightness seemed to vibrate and shimmer with a kind of holy laughter—not at me and my silliness, not a mocking laughter, but a mirth that seemed to say that in spite of all error and tragedy, joy was more lasting still. And in the ecstasy of that laughter I realized that it was I who was judging the events around us so harshly. It was I who saw them as trivial, self-centered, unimportant. No such condemnation came from the glory shining round me. He was not blaming or reproaching. He was simply loving me. Filling the world with Himself and yet somehow attending to me personally. . . .

What have you done with your life to show Me?

Already I understood that in my first frantic efforts to come up with an impressive answer, I had missed the point altogether. He was not asking about accomplishments and awards. The question, like everything else proceeding from Him, had to do with love. *How much have you loved with your life? Have you loved others as I am loving you? Totally? Unconditionally?*[5]

God never intended you to base your identity on accomplishments or performing. No one knows what you were created to *do* and *be* except your Creator. Look what God says about your true identity: "Bring my sons from afar and my daughters from the ends of the earth—everyone who is called by my name, whom I created *for my glory*, whom I formed and made" (Isaiah 43:6–7, italics mine). God made you for himself—not to prove your glory, but to *be his glory*. His pride and joy. His beloved son or daughter. What he wants you to do is learn to *be* secure in his love, in who he made you to be, and from that place of security, you can *do* what he created you to do. And first and foremost, this is to love those you uniquely can love.

Paul explained, "For now we see only a reflection as in a mirror; then we shall see face to face. Now I know in part; then I shall know fully, even as I am fully known. And now these three remain: faith, hope and love. But the greatest of these is love" (1 Corinthians 13:12–13). Heaven will be that place where you realize how uniquely loved you are. He doesn't want you to wait until Heaven to realize this.

He Knows My Name

Dr. Richard Eby, who plunged two stories headfirst to the cement sidewalk below, recounts how personal the experience of life was following his "death":

> I was dead on impact. Instantly, with a thud, I arrived at a place that was so ecstatically loaded with love, I knew it was Heaven. . . . I looked to see what I landed on. My feet were the same size and shape. I recognized myself by the conformity to my earthly self. . . . Suddenly I had a mind that thought with a speed incomputable on earth. The first time I heard the Lord's voice, He said, "Dick, you're dead!" Though I heard the voice within me. . . . That He called me by my name showed me the intimacy He has with my existence. I asked, "Why did you call me Dick?" [It was a name used only by close friends and family.] He said, "When I died for you on the cross, it was a most intimate thing."[6]

After ten hours as a bloodless, lifeless corpse, Richard miraculously revived, but he never forgot how personally he is known and loved.

Think about it: we all want to make a name for ourselves. But why? We want our lives to count, to matter, to be worth something. Yet, apart from God, your name will not be remembered. Try something—quickly. What are the names of your *great*-grandmother and grandfather? Great-great-grandmother or grandfather? Most of us don't know. That's only three or four generations removed from us, and we owe them our lives—yet they've already been forgotten. Even if *they've* been remembered, most names will be forgotten within a hundred years, and all will be forgotten eventually. Yet we *all* want to be remembered.

Wise King Solomon said it's because God has "set eternity in the human heart" (Ecclesiastes 3:11). We want our lives to count. We want to be remembered. We want a name that will last, because God made us for himself for eternity. Jesus taught that God the Father wants us to live in the security of knowing how valuable we are to him. "Are not two sparrows sold for a penny? Yet not one of them will fall to the ground outside your Father's care. And even the very hairs of your head are all numbered. So don't be afraid; you are worth more than many sparrows" (Matthew 10:29–31).

God knows you better than you know yourself (bet you don't know how many hairs you have—or once had!). He alone knows how valuable you are. "Everything about Him is love. Yes, love for you; and it seemed as if the love is only for you," Dean reminisced after his NDE. "Yet you know in yourself that he loves all, but the love for you is so personal it seems as if it is only for you. You know He has cared for you forever and will [continue to] care for you forever."[7]

No one else has the right or ability to say what you're worth except the One who created you. He alone knows your name. In

the book of Revelation Jesus says, "To everyone who is victorious . . . I will give to each one a white stone, and on the stone
will be engraved a *new name* that no one understands except
the one who receives it" (Revelation 2:17 NLT, italics mine).
The promise of Heaven is that one day, you will truly know who
you were created to be. To God, you are already one of a kind.
No one else can have the unique relationship with God that he
created you to have. Imagine in Heaven when you finally realize
how special you are to the most important Being in the universe!

Gary Wood, who died in the car accident, said, "A radiant,
beautiful light came from Him. When He looked at me, His
eyes pierced me, they went all the way through me. Just pure
love. . . . His words came as the same sound as the water flowing
over Niagara Falls. . . . 'Tell people they are special and unique,
each one. God made every one of His children to have a divine
purpose, which only they can accomplish in the earth.'"[8]

A Unique Purpose

We don't feel fully known, understood, or valued by others
or even ourselves—that's why we labor to prove ourselves, get
people to notice us, make a name for ourselves, or try to be
someone else. Imagine how in Heaven, all this gets replaced
with an unbelievable clarity of who God created you to be—
fully yourself, fully unique, for a unique relationship with your
Creator.

We won't lose our earthly identity; it will finally be known to
us fully. We won't lose our humor, our unique personality, our
unique look, our emotions, or our history and memories—we
will finally be ourselves, fully. We will be all this—without all the
confusion and wounds and lies that clouded our true identity.

He alone knows who he created you to be. He alone knows
what a successful life uniquely means for you—not compared to
others, compared to what he had in his mind before he created

74

anything! I believe the reason people having NDEs say "I feel like I'd been here before," or "I feel like I had always existed," is because you did exist in the mind of God eternally! In Heaven, we get clarity on who he intended us to be before we were born.

Knowing how God sees you sets you free to accomplish things God created you to accomplish. It sets you free to use your unique gifts, time, and resources to make an impact that lasts for eternity—not to prove you're worth something, but because you're worth *everything* to God. "God saved you by his grace when you believed. And you can't take credit for this; it is a gift from God. . . . For we are God's masterpiece. He has created us anew in Christ Jesus, so we can do the good things he planned for us long ago" (Ephesians 2:8, 10 NLT).

You are his masterpiece. His one-of-a-kind work of art. But we're all damaged masterpieces in need of restoration. He wants everyone to receive his gift—salvation, being "set right" with God. When you know you're right with God—not because of what you have or have not done, but because of what God has done for you—then you don't need to prove your identity. Then you're free to accomplish the things God planned for you before you were born. People having an NDE get a clear message—God has a purpose for you still.

A man in Dr. Long's study wrote that he didn't want to return to his earthly life, but was told "by a man in light" that he had not yet completed what he had to do in his life. Subsequently he returned to his body "with a sudden lurch."[9]

A thirteen-year-old girl who died in surgery recalls, "I heard a voice that seemed soft yet authoritative tell me, 'My child, go back, for you have much work left to do!' I was instantly back in my body. Instantly!"[10]

While recovering from surgery, Mark's weakened heart stopped. As the doctors worked feverishly to bring him back, Mark took a journey down "the most beautiful road I have ever seen," one that took him through a mountain paradise. Mark began to hear a voice that seemed to be "from nowhere, yet everywhere. . . . 'Mark! You must go back!' 'Go back? No! No! I can't go back!' Again the voice said, 'You must return; I have given you [a] task; you have not finished.' 'No, no, please, God, no! Let me stay.' . . . The voice of the Supreme Being seemed to emanate from nowhere but at the same time from everywhere."[11]

What's My Unique Purpose?

But what is my purpose? How am I supposed to know what God has me uniquely here to do? I think often we make it complicated because we want our purpose to give us identity, but God means it to work the other way around. Moses said it and Jesus reiterated it—to love God is the first and greatest command (our purpose). To love our neighbors (those he puts in our lives) as much as we love ourselves—that's second. Do those two, Jesus taught, and you fulfill the intent of all the other commands of the Bible (Matthew 22:34–40). Even those who don't know the Bible bring back this same message from the other side. God has us uniquely here for a purpose—and love is central to that purpose—whatever else we accomplish.

Howard Storm, an art professor who had an NDE, believes that God brought him and his wife together for a specific reason, to learn how to love. He says this is our main job to accomplish on earth; to love the people we are with.[12] It might not be our only job, but it's clearly our first job.

Steve Sjogren was the pastor of a large church doing lots of good serving Cincinnati in thousands of ways. No doubt that was part of God's purpose for Steve, but Steve's brush with death reminded him of God's priorities for us. Steve humbly recalls,

> God got me good. I was hovering over the operating table as close to the ceiling as I could get without actually leaving the

room. . . . I knew intuitively that God was the one who was addressing me. It was like the voice of a hundred friends talking in harmonious unison. It was a voice that was familiar and comforting and drew me near. . . . In all my years of seeking God, I had never before heard Him speak audibly (nor have I since that time). . . . We did not communicate just with words, but also with memories and images. God let me know how much He valued me. It's almost impossible to describe the perfect sense of acceptance that surrounded me, yet even in the midst of this very personal embrace, part of me knew that not everything in my life had matched what God had intended for me.

The doctors were in emergency mode and God was calmly quizzing me. "Do you know the names of your children's friends?" He asked. This was not a daydream. God wanted to know the answer, but I couldn't list a single one! I was caught dead to rights. The realization struck me like a bolt of lightning. I hadn't taken the time to get to know my children's best friends and long-term buddies. . . . These friends often visited our house. They were always welcome, but I was anything but hospitable. When they came, I was usually fixated on one project or another. Many times, I just wasn't there. My job was important, after all.[13]

How do we know our unique purpose? It always starts with loving and seeking God, then following his lead to love the people closest to us, and then using the gifts and passions he's put in us to serve humanity. You don't need to worry about not fulfilling your purpose; if you seek God and his will, you will live it. But we can't forget, it's all about love.

Come Home!

Reflecting on her experience of Heaven, Crystal—who had been baptized but never felt loved due to her abusers—admits that it's challenging to find the right words to describe all she experienced in Heaven, simply because human language doesn't even come close. Words like "beautiful," "brilliant," and "amazing" fall far short, she says. "What I experienced in heaven was so real and so lucid and so utterly intense, it made my experiences on Earth seem hazy and out of focus—as if heaven is the reality and life as we know it is just a dream." Crystal describes being immersed in a feeling of complete and utter purity, perfection, unbrokenness, and peace, a kind of assurance she's never experienced on earth. "It was like being bathed in love," she remembers. "It was a brightness I didn't just see, but felt. And it felt familiar, like something I remembered, or even recognized. The best way to put it is this: I was home."[14]

Jesus traveled the countryside of Israel teaching, feeding, healing, and restoring dignity to people. He demonstrated the unconditional love of God, who values the most sin-stained human like a uniquely precious runaway child. As a result, the Crystals of the world flocked to Jesus. Luke tells us, "Tax collectors and other notorious sinners often came to listen to Jesus teach. This made the Pharisees and teachers of religious law complain that he was associating with such sinful people— even eating with them! So Jesus told them this story" (Luke 15:1–3 NLT).

Jesus tells these self-righteous religious people the story of a father (representing God the Father) who had a prodigal younger son and a "good" older son. The prodigal son demands an early inheritance, flips off his father, and moves to Vegas where he blows everything partying and using prostitutes (this is obviously my paraphrase, but accurate to the story).

Jesus tells us the son finally hit rock bottom, came to his senses, and said, "I will go home to my father and say, 'Father, I have sinned against both heaven and you, and I am no longer worthy of being called your son. Please take me on as a hired servant'" (Luke 15:18–19 NLT).

The religious leaders would have expected the father to punish him and teach the son a lesson, but Jesus shocks them: "While [the prodigal son] was still a long way off, his father saw him coming. Filled with love and compassion, he *ran to his son*, embraced him, and kissed him. His son said to him, 'Father, I have sinned against both heaven and you, and I am no longer worthy of being called your son.' But his father said to the servants, 'Quick! Bring the finest robe in the house and put it on him. Get a ring for his finger and sandals for his feet. . . . We must celebrate with a feast, for this son of mine was dead and has now returned to life. He was lost, but now he is found.' So the party began" (Luke 15:20–24 NLT, italics mine).

Finally Home

Reading through hundreds and hundreds of NDE stories, I'm awestruck by how everyone who experiences this Being of Light describes a love that *would* run toward them, embrace them, value them, no matter what—and simply want them home. And *home* is what they describe!

Jeff left the scene of a fiery car accident to find he "was in a different place. This was a place of joy. It was familiar. It was home. I felt real, but I was not injured. I was not a floating orb. I was myself."[15] Samaa, who grew up in the Middle East, found herself in the presence of Love: "He radiated an amazing love that contained deep acceptance. I felt neither condemnation nor shame. At first I hardly dared to look at Jesus, but after a time I felt my body being lifted up. Then I was standing before Him. As He smiled at me, relief poured over my soul. 'Welcome home, Samaa,' He said in a voice sweet and gentle, yet also powerful, like the sound of many waters. He opened His arms to me. His beautiful eyes were like blazing fires of consuming love that overwhelmed me."[16]

While Don Piper spent ninety minutes clinically dead, he said, "I saw colors I would never have believed existed. I've never, ever felt more alive than I did then. I was home; I was where I belonged. I wanted to be there more than I had ever wanted to be anywhere on earth."[17]

Jesus claimed that the heart of God for all people is that of a loving Father who would do anything to have his kids come home. "Christ suffered for our sins once for all time. He never sinned, but he died for sinners to bring you safely home to God" (1 Peter 3:18 NLT). One day he wants to welcome you home, too!

And home is the place where you are finally known and loved, and surrounded by family and friends. If you've ever feared being lonely in Heaven, think again.

6

With Friends and Loved Ones

I DON'T RECALL THE EXACT DETAILS of the next few moments. And maybe I don't want to know. There were strong cross-winds that day and a small red pickup truck driving er-ratically through that stretch of freeway. I may have dozed off at the wheel and swerved off the road, but for whatever reason, our vehicle, traveling at seventy-five miles per hour, abruptly went off the shoulder of the freeway."

Time slowed as Jeff woke up to a father's worst nightmare. Four-year-old Spencer and fourteen-month-old Griffin, asleep in the back, startled as his wife Tamara screamed and reached for the steering wheel. Jeff overcorrected and their SUV rolled seven or eight times down the asphalt. Jeff felt himself slip out of his body.

> I was encircled with light, a bright-white light that seemed to be energized with pure, unconditional love. I was calm. Peace infused this almost tangible light. I realized all the pain was gone. I was fine. . . .

81

Then I felt a familiar touch. I opened my eyes. Tamara was right next to me. She was real too. I could feel her. She was alive. . . . I looked at her. I could feel everything. She was crying and upset. Why? Where were we? Was the crash a bad dream now? Or had I died? Had we both died? And where were the boys?

I had read about experiences like I was having. Many people describe passing through a tunnel toward a bright light. That wasn't happening to me. I felt like I was in some kind of protective bubble. And I felt alive, not dead.

"You can't stay here," Tamara said. "You have to go back. You can't be here."

Why was she crying?

"You can't come. You cannot stay here."

What did she mean I couldn't stay? I belonged there.

"You have to go!"

She was as real as ever. The thought of our boys raced through my head. Where were they? Were they here too? If I stayed, would Spencer be left orphaned? Where was Griffin?

"You have to go!" Tamara insisted. But I didn't want to go anywhere. It seemed odd to me that in that glorious bubble she would be upset. Was it heaven? I didn't know, but it made my earthly existence seem like a foggy dream. What I was experiencing was far more real, far more tangible, and far more alive than anything I had ever known. I pulled Tamara to me tightly. She was tangible as well. I even felt her wet tears on my skin. I kissed her. That was real. I smelled her hair. Not in the earthly sense, but with senses that seemed to be tenfold what I had experienced before.

"You can't be here. You have to go," she sobbed.

It almost felt as if my course was set. I didn't want to go, but I also knew she was right. I was not meant to stay. I felt I had a choice, but something deep within me knew I had to get back to Spencer. . . . I looked into Tamara's eyes, those crystal, sky-blue eyes. Everything in the universe was calling me back to Spencer, but I wanted to stay with her. And where was Griffin? I felt a warm tear roll down my face and fall from my upper lip.

"I have to go."

"I know."

I looked at her one more time, the love of my life, and the wife of my dreams. I leaned forward, putting my forehead onto hers. . . .

"I love you."

"I know."

The next thing Jeff heard was the haunting reality of Spencer crying in the backseat of the crashed SUV. Tamara and Griffin were dead. As he came to, Jeff heard a question, "echoed into every cell of my being. The question was simply, 'To what degree have you learned to love?'"[1]

Love God, Love People—Forever

One of the biggest struggles people have with Heaven is the thought of being separated from the ones they love most. Yet it's not Heaven, but the effects of a fallen earth that separate us. God created us for a love that lasts forever. Love has always been God's central theme, and as you'll see in the coming chapters, love is the only thing that makes sense of why God allows so much hurt and pain in the meantime.

Jesus was once asked, "Teacher, which is the most important commandment in the law of Moses?" Jesus replied, "'You must love the Lord your God with all your heart, all your soul, and all your mind.' This is the first and greatest commandment. A second is equally important: 'Love your neighbor as yourself.' The entire law and all the demands of the prophets are based on these two commandments" (Matthew 22:36–40 NLT). To love God first, and then to let him help us love those around us as much as we love ourselves—that sums up the Scriptures and the point of every command.

Those who get a glimpse of Heaven agree on one thing more than anything—love is the point of it all. In the presence of

God, they experience a love that words cannot explain, and the people of Heaven seem to be filled with a light that is love. So if love and relationship is the goal of life on earth, why would we think God wants to tear that apart or take relationship from us in Heaven? Nothing could be further from the truth.

Everything God claims to have done through the prophets and through Jesus is for the sake of love—to restore people to a love relationship with God, so he can teach us to love one another as he loves us. He intends those relationships to last in Heaven, and even more, to find their fulfillment in Heaven. The greatest love we feel for children, a spouse, friends, or family on earth amounts to a teaspoon of love compared to the oceans we will experience together for eternity. The Old Testament prophets foretold it, Jesus demonstrated it, and those who have had a peek behind the veil consistently say the same thing—God is love, and Heaven will be the greatest reunion ever.

The Greatest Reunion Ever

Don Piper was coming back from a pastors' conference when an 18-wheeler lost control on a rainy bridge and hit Don head-on, running over the top of his car. When EMS arrived several minutes later, Don was pronounced dead. For ninety minutes his dead body lay trapped in the car while EMS waited for the Jaws of Life to cut him out of the squashed wreckage.

> Simultaneous with my last recollection of seeing the bridge and the rain, a light enveloped me, with a brilliance beyond earthly comprehension or description. Only that. In my next moment of awareness, I was standing in heaven. Joy pulsated through me as I looked around, and at that moment I became aware of a large crowd of people. They stood in front of a brilliant, ornate gate. I have no idea how far away they were; such things as distance didn't matter. As the crowd rushed toward me, I didn't see Jesus, but I did see people I had known. As they

surged toward me, I knew instantly that all of them had died during my lifetime.

Their presence seemed absolutely natural. They rushed toward me, and every person was smiling, shouting, and praising God. Although no one said so, intuitively I knew they were my celestial welcoming committee. It was as if they had all gathered just outside heaven's gate, waiting for me. The first person I recognized was Joe Kulbeth, my grandfather. He looked exactly as I remembered him, with his shock of white hair and what I called a big banana nose. He stopped momentarily and stood in front of me. A grin covered his face. I may have called his name, but I'm not sure. "Donnie!" (That's what my grandfather always called me.) His eyes lit up, and he held out his arms as he took the last steps toward me. He embraced me, holding me tightly. He was once again the robust, strong grandfather I had remembered as a child. . . .

The crowd surrounded me. Some hugged me and a few kissed my cheek, while others pumped my hand. Never had I felt more loved. One person in that greeting committee was Mike Wood, my childhood friend. Mike was special because he invited me to Sunday school and was influential in my becoming a Christian. Mike was the most devoted young Christian I knew. He was also a popular kid and had lettered four years in football, basketball, and track. . . . When he was nineteen, Mike was killed in a car wreck. It broke my heart when I heard about his death. . . . Now I saw Mike in heaven. As he slipped his arm around my shoulder, my pain and grief vanished. Never had I seen Mike smile so brightly. I still didn't know why, but the joyousness of the place wiped away any questions. Everything felt blissful. Perfect.

More and more people reached for me and called me by name. I felt overwhelmed by the number of people who had come to welcome me to heaven. . . . I saw Barry Wilson, who had been my classmate in high school but later drowned in a lake. Barry hugged me, and his smile radiated a happiness I didn't know was possible. He and everyone that followed praised God and told me how excited they were to see me and to welcome me to heaven and to the fellowship they enjoyed. Just then, I spotted two teachers who had loved me and often talked to me about Jesus Christ. As I walked among them, I became aware of the wide variety of ages—old and young and every age in-between. Many of them hadn't known each other on earth, but each had influenced my life in some way. Even though they hadn't met on earth, they seemed to know each other now.[2]

Your Welcome-Home Party

Jesus said, "Use your worldly resources to benefit others and make friends. Then, when your earthly possessions are gone, they will welcome you to an eternal home" (Luke 16:9 NLT). Many who have had NDEs felt like they had a "welcoming committee" there to greet them just like Jesus described. Real people and real relationships do not end when this life ends, they go on to new depths. Paul told those he helped find faith in Thessalonica, "For what is our hope, our joy, or the crown in which we will glory in the presence of our Lord Jesus when he comes? Is it not you? Indeed, you are our glory and joy" (1 Thessalonians 2:19–20).

Like Don Piper, bank president Marv Besteman recalls a welcome party consisting of close relatives, those who had spiritually influenced him, or those he spiritually encouraged. "Both of my friends were prayer warriors, and we had spent many hours praying together. I'm not sure if this is why God chose these two guys for me to see—they were significant to me and my spiritual life. Everyone I saw had been influential in shaping my life in some way."[3]

Just imagine what God wants for you. Your temporal life on earth will transition into the most joyous, exciting, celebratory party, welcoming you into Real Life. Deceased relatives and friends who also loved God, all the people you've loved and served and helped spiritually, all gather because they just can't wait to show you around. You're still you, and they're still them—those relationships don't die, they go deeper than ever into the exploration of eternity with God and each other. That is God's design and desire, but not everyone experiences it.

Dr. Mary Neal and others have mentioned a protective role of the angels or their welcoming committee: "I knew they were sent to guide me across the divide of time and dimension that separates our world from God's. I also had the unspoken understanding that they were sent not only to greet me and guide me, but also to protect me during my journey."[4]

Dr. Moody writes about a woman who died giving birth who said almost the exact same statement: she recounted seeing her grandmother, as well as a girl she had known from her school days. She also saw numerous other friends and relatives, whom she realized "had come to protect or guide me. It was almost as if I were coming home."[5]

This struck me after reading multiple NDEs that said the welcoming committee was there both to guide *and protect* along the journey. As we will see in later chapters, protection may be needed, because not every NDE "welcoming committee" turns out to be as benevolent as it may first appear.

But Scripture makes it very clear that God's desire is that we would all trust God, let him into our lives, and let him adopt us as his own children. What he wants is to usher us into one big, happy eternal family! In fact, the whole point of this life is the creation of a spiritual family for God.

The Family of Families

In the early years of our family, my wife didn't like to think about Heaven. It made her sad to think our loving little family might not be as special or close. I would always ask, "What makes you believe that?" She would say something like, "Well, Jesus said we won't be married. And we'll love all people equally, so we won't feel that special bond we had." I've since convinced her that her fears were unwarranted, but I know this is the fear of many.

What Jesus said was in response to the Sadducees, a group of antagonistic religious leaders who did not believe in life after death. They asked Jesus a trick question: "If a woman is married and her husband dies, she remarries and it happens again . . . seven times, which of the seven will she be married to in Heaven?" Jesus replied, "You are in error because you do not know the Scriptures or the power of God" (Matthew 22:23–30, my paraphrase). He goes on to say God told Moses, whom they claimed to follow, that he is the God of Abraham, Isaac, and Jacob (who were all dead). Jesus says, God isn't the God of the dead, but of the living—God's people live on by God's power! And the power of God can unite people in ways that overcome our relational squabbles and concerns, and that's what he will do for all his children.

Then Jesus says, "At the resurrection people will neither marry nor be given in marriage; they will be like the angels in heaven" (Matthew 22:30). Jesus did not say we will not be with our spouse or loved ones. He said there won't be new individual marriages—there won't need to be because there will be no procreation or new families. But our family relationships will not be less special or less close in eternity, they will be closer and deeper. We might love all our new brothers and sisters, but that does not mean we will have the same special relationship, history, memories, or bonds with all people equally.

In fact, our earthly families seem to be really important in Heaven. All throughout the Old Testament, when a person would die, the Scriptures would say, "Then Abraham breathed his last and died at a good old age . . . and he was *gathered to his people*" (Genesis 25:8, italics mine). "Then [Isaac] breathed his last and died and was *gathered to his people*" (35:29, italics mine). God created love, relationship, and family, and they remain important to him in Heaven.

Interestingly, the Kelly Study, conducted in 2001 at the University of Virginia, found that 95 percent of the people encountered on the other side during NDEs were deceased relatives, while only 5 percent were friends. Only 4 percent of the NDErs in the study claimed they saw people who were alive at the time of the NDE.[6] Dr. Long points out that in dreams or hallucinations, usually people claim to see recently encountered *living* people. On the other hand, a study of five hundred Americans and five hundred Indians found that the vast majority of the human figures seen in visions of the dying were deceased close relatives.[7]

Imagine Heaven—the greatest reunion ever—with friends, family, even distant relatives you never knew. Ancestry.com can't come close to giving you a sense of your heritage like it will be when you actually meet your relatives! Little kids report meeting deceased relatives during their NDEs—even ones they never knew! Imagine the family you've had but never known.

7

The Family You Never Knew

OUR-YEAR-OLD COLTON BURPO had a brush with death and claimed to visit Heaven. Several months later, he and his dad, Todd, were driving across the Nebraska cornfields. Colton asked his dad if he had a grandpa named Pop. Todd said he did and told Colton that Pop had passed away when Todd was about Colton's age.

Colton replied, "He's really nice."

Todd almost drove off the road. He later relates, "It's a crazy moment when your son uses the present tense to refer to someone who died a quarter century before he was even born." As Todd and Colton continued to talk, Colton explained that he not only met Pop in Heaven, but he got to stay with him.[1]

Not long after they got back from their road trip, Todd pulled out the last picture of Pop he had. Pop was sixty-two, with white hair and glasses. Todd asked if Colton recognized him. Colton squinched up his face, shook his head, and said, "Dad, nobody's old in heaven . . . and nobody wears glasses." It bothered Todd that Colton didn't recognize Pop, so he had his mom send a younger picture of Pop when he was twenty-nine, standing with his wife (Colton's great-grandmother) and two other people. He showed it to Colton, who said, "Hey! How did you get a picture of Pop?"[2] Colton's great-grandmother (now in her eighties), whom Colton had recently seen, was also pictured next to Pop. Colton didn't recognize his great-grandmother in her twenties, yet he recognized his twenty-nine-year-old great-grandfather he'd never met!

Later that October, Colton gave his family another surprise as they were all gathered in the living room working on different projects. "Mommy, I have two sisters," Colton said. His mom, Sonja, corrected him, reminding him he only had one sister. Colton repeated himself, insisting that he had two sisters. Sonja replied that Cassie is his only sister, and then asked if he meant his cousin, Traci.

"No!" Colton insisted adamantly. "I have two *sisters*. You had a baby die in your tummy, didn't you?"

Time stopped in the Burpo house. Shocked, Sonja asked her son who it was that told him she had a baby die in her tummy.

"She did, Mommy," Colton explained. "She said she died in your tummy." Sonja was overcome with emotion. They had never told Colton about the miscarriage.

"It's okay, Mommy," Colton said. "God adopted her."

Todd said he could hear the effort it took for Sonja to steady her voice as she asked Colton what his sister looked like.

Colton explained that in Heaven, a girl who looked a lot like Cassie, but with dark hair, ran up to him and wouldn't stop hugging him. He clearly didn't like a *girl* hugging him so much.

Sonja asked him what her name was.

"She doesn't have a name. You guys didn't name her."

"You're right, Colton," Sonja said, dumbfounded. "We didn't even know she was a she."

Colton said, "Yeah, she said she just can't wait for you and Daddy to get to heaven."[3]

King David lost his infant son at birth. He had fasted, prayed, wept, and wailed for healing, but when his son died, he stopped. His friends were confused. David explained: "Why should I fast when he is dead? Can I bring him back again? I will go to him one day, but he cannot return to me" (2 Samuel 12:23 NLT). David knew he would see his son again in Heaven.

Imagine all the family hurts and pains, finally redeemed by the love of God. Imagine all the little babies, finally reunited with their families, all the brothers and sisters, moms and dads, grandparents and even distant relatives, joined together as a family inside God's great Family. That's what God is doing: "In bringing many sons and daughters to glory, it was fitting that God . . . should make the pioneer of their salvation perfect through what he suffered. Both the one who makes people holy and those who are made holy are of the same family. So Jesus is not ashamed to call them brothers and sisters" (Hebrews 2:10–11).

Imagine this new Family of families God has in store for all who love him. Imagine meeting relatives from hundreds of years past, joined as this family you never knew. But that brings up other relational questions, like what age will we be? And how will there not be sibling rivalry and family feuds?

Ageless Ages

What age will we be in Heaven? The more I've pondered what the Scriptures say and what the NDErs report, it's unclear. My best theory is that we will be ageless, yet we will have the ability to appear to others as the age they knew us best. I say this as a theory, because Scripture seems silent on the topic, though it does tell us time in Heaven doesn't work like it does on earth. "With the Lord a day is like a thousand years, and a thousand years are like a day" (2 Peter 3:8). Listen to some of the things NDErs note about age.

From some accounts, people appear to be all ages. Gary Wood said as he walked through the City of God with his best friend, John, "I saw a playground with children and teenagers—those who died prematurely." At another point he saw his grandmother and grandfather sitting on the front porch of a three-story house, talking to people walking by, but he was not allowed to talk to them for some reason.[4]

Marv, the bank president, noticed outside the City gate, "Most of the men in line were between fifty and seventy years of age, and most of the women were between seventy and ninety years of age. There were three children in line, each of them around four or five years of age. These little ones were not standing still, but moving around, wiggling in their spots in line, like children do. They all had big smiles on their faces. . . . [An Indian man] was carrying a tiny baby for . . . a young [Indian] woman standing in front of him."[5]

Marv came to a barrier (which we will see is common) that he could not cross. He described it as a crystalline barrier, but sixty yards inside and waving him to come were his grandma and grandpa. "Both of them were wearing clothing similar to what they wore on earth, and they appeared to be the age they were when they died. Still, Grandma and Grandpa looked like no other eighty-five-year-olds I have ever seen walking around here. I kid you not. Had I thrown a [football] pass at them, both of them gave the impression they could've easily jumped up and snatched it."[6] So even though people may look the ages when we would best recognize them, they also seem young and vibrant, or in some cases, older.

"I saw a bright, bright light very quickly," another NDEr relates, "and then a beach, and then I saw my mom and daughter [who died at age two] standing on the beach; my daughter was grown up."[7] Others seem to indicate that even though people in Heaven looked their age, somehow they also appeared age-less, or in their prime. Dr. Long reports how Bob fell out of a

93

building and landed three stories below. During his NDE he met many relatives:

> My relatives (all deceased) were there, all at their prime in life. They were dressed (I would say 1940's style which would have been prime years for most). Relatives I knew of, such as my grandfathers, but never knew in life were there as well as uncles/ aunts who passed before I knew them. The unconditional love was overwhelming and permeated all of us genuinely and richly. There was no element of time and no verbally spoken word . . . everything was open thought communication.[8]

Another NDEr notes, "Suddenly I recognized all these relatives. They were all around thirty-five years old, including the little brother I'd never known, because he had died during the war when he was two years old."[9] Doctors tell us our earthly bodies grow and develop until sometime in our late twenties or early thirties; then we begin our slow decay. Maybe that's our heavenly age. Or perhaps in Heaven we will be known for our true identity and our projected form can be perceived or "seen" in different ways.

Airline captain Dale Black noticed that he "saw them for who they were. None were skinny, none overweight. None were crippled, none were bent or broken. None were old, none were young. If I had to guess, I would say they appeared to be some-where around thirty years old. . . . Although some form of time does seem to exist in heaven, no one aged."[10]

Something university professor Howard Storm described during his NDE may give insight into the appearance of age in Heaven. Brilliant beings of light he came to think of as saints and angels came to meet him and asked, "Would you like to see us in our human form?" The implication, Storm explained, was that they could take a different appearance if he would feel more comfortable with them in a human form.[11] Storm answered, "No. Please . . . you're more beautiful than anything I've ever seen."[12]

So maybe in Heaven we will be known for our true identity and our outer appearance can adapt to the needs of others. Steve Miller noted this from his studies: "People seem to consist of something more akin to energy than cells. This could explain why, when one NDEr expressed surprise that her deceased relative looked so old, the relative explained that she could appear however she wanted and immediately changed to a younger look."[13] Maybe our appearance of age can change in the intermediate Heaven. I'm not sure what that would imply for our resurrected body's age in the new Heaven and earth (my vote is 29!). One day we will know for sure.

New Family Values

One thing you don't need to worry about in Heaven: family feuds. In Heaven, what Jesus taught us to pray will always be true: "[Our Father in Heaven,] your kingdom come, your will be done, on earth *as it is in heaven*" (Matthew 6:10, italics mine). "Our will be done" has ruined earth, so only those surrendered to letting God be God instead of trying to play God can be allowed in Heaven. Otherwise, we'd ruin it too! Just because people get a peek at Heaven does not mean Heaven is automatically their permanent residence (we'll talk more about why in later chapters). But God will have new family values that will make all the relational challenges of earth fade away.

First, communication will be perfect. Nothing will be hidden in Heaven. Brian was born totally deaf, but at age ten he nearly drowned. He recalls that in his NDE,

> I approached the boundary. No explanation was necessary for me to understand, at the age of ten, that once I cross[ed] the boundary, I could never come back—period. I was more than thrilled to cross. I intended to cross, but my ancestors over

another boundary caught my attention. They were talking in telepathy, which caught my attention. I was born profoundly deaf and had all hearing family members, all of which knew sign language! I could read or communicate with about twenty ancestors of mine and others through telepathic methods. It overwhelmed me. I could not believe how many people I could telepathize with simultaneously.[14]

Although we will be able to talk and sing with our voices in Heaven, most indicate the preferred way of communicating with God, angels, and people will be directly heart to heart. God tells the prophet Isaiah about Heaven's communication, saying, "Before they call, I will answer; while they are still speaking I will hear" (Isaiah 65:24). People describe this in different ways, but it's uncanny how consistently NDErs describe this nonverbal, perfect communication in Heaven.

Crystal likens this perfect communication to having a password that allows instant access to another's innermost thoughts, as well as everything that person has ever said, thought, written, or believed in the past, present, and future. Having such access allows a more complete understanding and connection than could ever be possible on Earth. "There was no room whatsoever for secrets or shame or misunderstanding or anything negative," she remembers. "There was just this wonderful, beautiful, nourishing sense of knowing."[15]

Some seemed to indicate that one of the rules of Heaven is "no invading people's thoughts without their permission." Dean states,

[When] beings wanted to communicate, generally they did so through thought only. Because everything is alive, everything can communicate so that you "experience" the communication—you don't just hear it. There was no miscommunication, no misunderstandings. There was nothing you would hide from one another . . . every thought was pure. There was a rule that you did not go into any other's thoughts without them giving you permission to do so.[16]

It's like Jesus said, "There is nothing concealed that will not be disclosed, or hidden that will not be made known. What I tell you in the dark, speak in the daylight; what is whispered in your ear [implying this direct-to-mind communicating from God], proclaim from the roofs" (Matthew 10:26–27). In this perfect place, all the evils and deceptions of lying, hiding, and covering the truth must be left behind.

But it's not that voices cannot be used. Betty Malz recalls joining in singing wonderful songs harmonized in many languages:

> The voices not only burst forth in more than four parts, but they were in different languages. I was awed by the richness and perfect blending of the words—and I could understand them! I do not know why this was possible except that I was part of a universal experience. Communication between us was through the projection of thoughts. . . . We all seemed to be on some universal wave length. I thought at the time, *I will never forget the melody and these words*. But later I could only recall two: "Jesus" and "redeemed."[17]

May They Be One

With perfect communication and perfect love comes perfect unity. The very thing Jesus prayed that we would learn to experience more and more on earth will happen fully in Heaven's Family: "I pray also for those who will believe in me through their message, that all of them may be one, Father, just as you are in me and I am in you. May they also be in us so that the world may believe that you have sent me. I have given them the glory that you gave me, that they may be one as we are one—I in them and you in me—so that they may be brought to complete unity. Then the world will know that you sent me and have loved them even as you have loved me" (John 17:20–23). In Heaven, Jesus's prayer is tangibly felt by all.

Captain Dale Black describes it: "The best unity I have ever felt on earth did not compare with the exhilarating oneness that I experienced with my spiritual family in heaven. This love . . . God's love, was transforming. To experience something so sacred, so profound as the boundless love of God was the most thrilling part of heaven."[18]

Jeff Olsen reflected on his experience, saying,

> We were all connected pieces in a huge puzzle of oneness. Words Jesus had said rushed to my recollection: "Inasmuch as ye have done it unto the least of these my brethren ye have done it unto me." Was he talking about the awareness I was experiencing? Did he feel the same thing I was feeling? Was this how he walked the earth, in the consciousness of knowing each individual soul at this deep level of love? . . . We are all linked and equal in God's eyes. I was seeing it, feeling it, and experiencing it.[19]

"Instead of just hearing the music and the thousands of voices praising God, I had become part of the choir," Don Piper recalls. "I was one with them, and they had absorbed me into their midst."[20]

Harvard neurosurgeon Eben Alexander describes in his near-death experience remaining distinctly himself—not a Buddhist oneness where you lose your unique personhood, but the unity Jesus described. "Everything was distinct," he remembers, "yet everything was also a part of everything else."[21] He recalls that hearing and seeing were not separate in this other place. He could somehow hear the visual beauty of the beings that flew above his head and see the "surging, joyful perfection" of their songs. Dr. Alexander felt that in the act of listening and seeing, he was actually melding with the sounds and sights, somehow mysteriously uniting or joining together with them.

The only way this perfect family unity, oneness, and communication is made possible: Heaven has no room for sin. Dale Black recalls this epiphany:

> Part of the joy I was experiencing was not only the presence of everything wonderful but the absence of everything terrible. There was no strife, no competition, no sarcasm, no betrayal, no deception, no lies, no murders, no unfaithfulness, no disloyalty, nothing contrary to the light and life and love. . . . The absence of sin was something you could feel. There was no shame, because there was nothing to be ashamed of. There was no sadness, because there was nothing to be sad about. There was no need to hide, because there was nothing to hide from. It was all out in the open.[22]

The Family Restored

Jeff Olsen was back in Heaven. "I danced and ran, feeling so joyful . . . and I marveled at the indescribable beauty around me. It was vast and open and beautiful. I could feel, touch, and taste everything as if I had not five but fifty senses. It was amazing."

Jeff had struggled in months of recovery after the tragic auto accident. He blamed himself and felt intense despair over losing Tamara and baby Griffin. He struggled to let them go, wanting to die and be with them, yet knowing he needed strength to stay and father four-year-old Spencer. At a low point in his recovery, he had another near-death experience of Heaven.

> As I walked, on two healthy strong legs, I entered into a long hallway . . . and at the end of the hallway was a baby crib. I rushed to the crib, and peeking in, saw something beyond joyful. There lying in the crib was my son. It was little Griffin! He was alive and well. He slept so peacefully. I looked at him and took in every detail. How his chubby little hands lay so peacefully beside his perfect face . . . how his hair lay gently across

the tops of his ears. I reached into the crib and swept him up into my arms. I could feel the warmth from his little body. I could feel his breath on my neck and the smell of his delicate hair. He was so familiar and so alive! . . . I held him close and cried tears of joy as I laid my cheek against his soft little head as we had always done. . . . It was Griffin! He was alive, and I was with him, holding him in this wonderful place. . . . I felt something or someone move up behind me. The feeling coming from this being was so powerful and yet so loving that it almost startled me. I felt light and love engulf me. . . . I knew my wife and son were gone. They had died months earlier, but time didn't exist where I was at that moment. Rather than having them ripped away from me, I was being given the opportunity to actually hand them over to God. To let them go in peace, love, and gratitude. Everything suddenly made sense. Everything had divine order. I could give my son to God and not have him taken away from me. . . . I held my baby son as God himself held me. I experienced the oneness of all of it . . . the being behind me inviting me to let it all go and give Griffin to Him. In all that peace and knowledge, I hugged my little boy tightly one last time, kissed him on the cheek, and gently laid him back down in the crib. I willingly gave him up. No one would ever take him away from me again. He was mine. We were one, and I was one with God. . . . Griffin was alive in a place more real than anything here.[23]

That's Heaven. Life, love, together again—everything restored and alive in a place more beautiful than you can imagine. Let's imagine just how beautiful it will be.

8

The Most Beautiful Place Imaginable!

C APTAIN DALE BLACK has logged 17,000 hours flying around the globe as a commercial airline pilot. During that time, he has also volunteered on almost one thousand flights to fifty countries building orphanages, medical clinics, and churches in order to share God's love with people in need. Captain Black says his motivation comes from a horrible airline accident and what he saw that changed his life.

Dale had always dreamed of being a commercial pilot. By nineteen, he already had his pilot's license. Chuck and Gene, commercial pilots who had taken Dale under their wings, kindly let Dale fly with them on delivery runs across California to log more hours. One fateful day, the three of them took off in a twin engine Piper Navajo into a clear Los Angeles sky. Gene throttled to maximum takeoff power, but suddenly they found themselves airborne at an abnormally slow speed. Unable to clear the tops of the trees, Gene veered off directly into a seventy-five-foot-high aviation monument. The plane disintegrated as the three pilots smashed into the stone edifice at 135 miles per hour, then plunged seventy feet to the ground. Only Dale survived, sort of.

The last thing I remembered was the sight of Chuck's hands on the controls, violently wrenching the flight controls fully left and fully back. . . . Suddenly I found myself suspended in midair, hovering over the wreckage of my body. My gray pants and short-sleeve shirt were torn to shreds and soaked in blood. . . . I sped through what appeared to be a narrow pathway. . . . It wasn't a tunnel of light that I was traveling through. It was a path in the darkness that was delineated by the light. Outside of this pathway was total darkness. But in the darkness millions of tiny spheres of light zoomed past as I traveled through what looked like deep space, almost as if a jet were flying through a snowstorm at night. . . . At this time, I became aware that I was not traveling alone. Accompanying me were two angelic escorts dressed in seamless white garments woven with silver threads. They had no discernible gender but appeared masculine and larger than I was. . . . Remarkably, my peripheral vision was enhanced, and I could see both of their glowing faces at the same time. I could even see behind me while hardly moving my head. . . .

I was fast approaching a magnificent city, golden and gleaming among a myriad of resplendent colors. The light I saw was the purest I had ever seen. And the music was the most majestic, enchanting, and glorious I had ever heard. I was still approaching the city, but now I was slowing down. Like a plane making its final approach for landing. I knew instantly that this place was entirely and utterly holy. Don't ask me how I knew, I just knew.

I was overwhelmed by its beauty. It was breathtaking. And a strong sense of belonging filled my heart; I never wanted to leave. Somehow I knew I was made for this place and this place was made for me. . . . The entire city was bathed in light, an opaque whiteness in which the light was intense but diffused. In that dazzling light every color imaginable seemed to exist and—what's the right word?—played. . . . The colors seemed to be alive, dancing in the air. I had never seen so many different colors. . . . It was breathtaking to watch. And I could have spent forever doing just that.

The closer I got to the city, the more distinct the illumination became. The magnificent light I was experiencing emanated from about forty or fifty miles within the city wall . . . [from] a focal point that was brighter than the sun. Oddly, it didn't make me squint to look at it. And all I wanted to do was to look at it. The light was palpable. It had substance to it, weight and thickness, like nothing I had ever seen before or since. The light from a hydrogen bomb is the closest I can come to describing it. . . .

Somehow I knew that light and life and love were connected and interrelated. . . . Remarkably, the light didn't shine on things but through them. Through the grass. Through the trees. Through the wall. And through the people who were gathered there. There was a huge gathering of angels and people, millions, countless millions. They were gathered in a central area that seemed over ten miles in diameter. The expanse of people was closer to an ocean than a concert hall. Waves of people, moving in the light, swaying to the music, worshiping God. . . . Somehow the music in heaven calibrated everything, and I felt that nothing was rushed.

I was outside the city, slowly moving toward its wall, suspended a few hundred feet above the ground. I'm not sure how I knew directions there, but I had a strong, almost magnetic sense, that it was northwest. Which meant I was approaching the city from the southeast. A narrow road led to an entrance in the wall, which led into the city. I moved effortlessly along the road, escorted by my two angelic guides, on what seemed to be a divine schedule.

Below me lay the purest, most perfect grass, precisely the right length and not a blade that was bent or even out of place. It was the most vibrant green I had ever seen. If a color can be said to be alive, the green I saw was alive, slightly transparent and emitting light and life from within each blade. The iridescent grass stretched endlessly over gently rolling hills upon which were sprinkled the most colorful wild flowers, lifting their soft-petaled beauty skyward, almost as if they were a chorus of flowers caught up in their own way of praising God.

The fragrance that permeated heaven was so gentle and sweet, I almost didn't notice it amid all there was to see and hear. But as I looked at the delicate, perfect flowers and grass, I wanted to smell them. Instantly, I was aware of a gentle aroma. As I focused, I could tell the difference between the grass and the flowers, the trees and even the air. It was all so pure and intoxicating and blended together in a sweet and satisfying scent.

In the distance stood a range of mountains, majestic in appearance, as if they reigned over the entire landscape. These were not mountains you wanted to conquer; these were mountains you wanted to revere. . . .

The road was only wide enough for two people and followed the contours of the hills. Then it began sloping upward toward the huge wall that encircled the city. . . . Next I heard the faint sound of water rushing in the distance. I couldn't see the water, but it sounded as if it were rivers cascading over a series of small waterfalls, creating music that was ever changing. . . .

Between the central part of the city and the city walls were groupings of brightly colored picture-perfect homes in small, quaint towns. . . . Each home was customized and unique from the others yet blended harmoniously. Some were three or four stories, some were even higher. There were no two the same. If music could become homes, it would look like these, beautifully built and perfectly balanced. . . . [The city wall] stretched out to my left and right as far as I could see in both directions. . . . A powerful light permeated the wall, and you could see all the colors of the rainbow in it. Strangely, whenever I moved, the colors moved ever so slightly as if sensing my movement and making an adjustment. . . .

My eyes were next drawn to a river that stretched from the gathering area in the middle of the city to the wall. It flowed toward the wall and seemed to end there, at least from my vantage point. The river was perfectly clear with a bluish-white hue. The light didn't shine on the water but mysteriously shone within it somehow. . . .

The flowers in heaven fascinated me. Again, a delightful and delicate balance between diversity and unity. Each was unique. All were one. And they were beautiful to behold. Each petal and leaf illuminated with that glorious light and added just the right splashes of color to the velvety expanse of green grass. As I described previously, the grass, the sky, the walls, the houses, everything was more beautiful than I ever dreamed anything could be. Even the colors. They were richer, deeper, more luminescent than any colors I have ever seen in the farthest reaches of earth or in the most fantastic of dreams. They were so vibrant they pulsated with life.[1]

Earth Is the Shadow

Heaven sounds like a place of imaginative fictional fantasy. But maybe the reason we possess within us such imaginative fictional capacity is because of a longing for eternity that God placed in the human heart. Like a bird's homing instinct, it's pointing us homeward. There's a little bird called the bar-tailed godwit that flies 15,000 miles roundtrip from Alaska to New Zealand each year. That's a long flight to a small island—what if they missed? They would be breeding with the penguins. But they don't miss. Ever! Something wired into them points them to New Zealand.

"[God] has also set eternity in the human heart" (Ecclesiastes 3:11). There is something wired into us that we all long for, something we crave, and yet every human experience leaves us still searching. As U2 sings, "But I still haven't found what I'm looking for." All our longings point toward Heaven. And NDErs say it's more real and far more beautiful than we can imagine.

What would possess a veteran commercial airline pilot to make up such a tale? Or an even more confounding question:

How did hundreds of people—doctors, airline pilots, bank presidents, tenured professors—who didn't need to make up wild stories to make money (and would lose professional credibility doing so), come to describe an amazingly similar place?

The Scriptures have always described just such a place—more beautiful than you can imagine. If you've ever secretly nursed a fear that Heaven might be this ethereal, fuzzy, less-than-real, cloudy place . . . think again! The language of Scripture and the words NDErs use over and over again emphasize the opposite—this temporal (temporary) life is the fuzzy, less-than-real shadow of the brilliant, beautiful-beyond-your-wildest-dreams, solid Life you need to grab onto.

The forty different writers of the Scriptures have revealed a consistent picture of Heaven's super-reality. God even had Israel build an earthly copy of a heavenly reality. "[Earthly priests] serve at a sanctuary that is a *copy and shadow* of what is in Heaven. This is why Moses was warned when he was about to build the tabernacle: 'See to it that you make everything according to the pattern shown you on the mountain'" (Hebrews 8:5, italics mine). Randy Alcorn notes, "The verses in Hebrews suggest that God created Earth in the image of Heaven, just as he created mankind in his image."[2]

Alcorn points out that often our thinking is backward. We think of earth as the real thing, and Heaven as the ethereal, less-than-real shadow. But Scripture tells us, and NDEs attest, that the opposite is true—earthly realities are derived from Heaven's counterparts. We're able to better imagine Heaven when we realize that all we love about this earth is merely a shadow of the greater Reality to come—a beautiful place made for us.

The night before Jesus's crucifixion, he gathered for his last meal with his closest friends to assure them, "Don't let your hearts be troubled. Trust in God, and trust also in me. There is more than enough room in my Father's home. If this were not so, would I have told you that I am going to prepare a place for you? When everything is ready, I will come and get you, so that you will always be with me where I am" (John 14:1–3 NLT).

Imagine this place, full of the beauty God created on earth. Because after all, when God created the earth he declared, "It is good" (Genesis 1), but earth's beauty has been marred by evil and subjected to death and decay, so that we will realize what's missing—God's perfect will and ways. "All creation was subjected to God's curse. But with eager hope, the creation looks forward to the day when it will join God's children in glorious freedom from death and decay" (Romans 8:20–21 NLT). Imagine creation restored, more real, more beautiful, and more alive than ever. God promises that our earth will ultimately be renewed and joined with Heaven, but the present Heaven is already beautiful and glorious.

The Old Testament prophet Isaiah saw Heaven and heard "[angels] calling to one another: 'Holy, holy, holy is the LORD Almighty; the whole earth is full of his glory'" (Isaiah 6:1–3). Imagine . . . all the beauty of earth—the majestic Sierras plunging into the deep-blue California coastline, the purple-and-green aspen-lined mountain valleys of Colorado, the turquoise-encircled white sand beaches of the Virgin Islands, the gorgeous jagged coastlines of Hawaii—all of it reflects the beauty, splendor, and glory of God.

If that's true, then why would we ever think Heaven, where the Creator reigns, would be less glorious and beautiful than earth, where the Creator hides himself behind the knowledge of good and evil? The prophets like Isaiah were told by God that the new Heaven and new earth will have similarities to the beauty of the present earth, but restored and improved:

> "See, I will create
>   new heavens and a new earth. . . .
> . . . I will create Jerusalem [the City of God] to be a
>   delight
>   and its people a joy.

> I will rejoice over Jerusalem
> > and take delight in my people. . . .
> They will build houses and dwell in them;
> > they will plant vineyards and eat their fruit. . . .
> Before they call I will answer;
> > while they are still speaking I will hear.
> The wolf and the lamb will feed together. . . .
> They will neither harm nor destroy
> > on all my holy mountain,"
> > > says the LORD. (Isaiah 65:17–25)

God tells Isaiah his Holy City will be a place of beauty and joy, with plants and trees, vineyards and fruit, mountains and valleys, where all of creation finally will live in harmony. As we intuitively know it *should be.*

Through the Wormhole

And why would we struggle to believe in a place called Heaven when science has been pointing to an unseen fifth dimension, wormholes through space-time, and theorized parallel universes as a possible explanation of the mysterious ways of nature? String theory proposes there are actually hidden dimensions beyond our three spatial dimensions of height, width, and depth. Why then can't we conceive of Heaven existing in a higher dimensional space we can't see?

Science used to think of matter as solid, but we now know the tiny atoms that make up matter are more like invisible waves, more mind-like than particle-like. In fact, atoms are 99.999 percent empty space.[3] Cambridge and Princeton physicist James Jeans wrote, "The stream of knowledge is heading toward a non-mechanical reality; the universe begins to look more like a great thought than like a machine. Mind no longer appears to be an accidental intruder into the realm of matter; we ought rather hail it as the governor of the realm of matter."[4]

When people describe the transition from life to Life, many experience leaving their bodies and observing the medical efforts from a point on the ceiling, but then many pass through a black tunnel or in some cases a colorful tunnel or pathway that leads to this beautiful paradise like Dale Black described. I wonder if this tunnel is like a wormhole, leading out of our space-time dimension into Heaven's expanded dimensions all around us?

Moody talks about how everyone uses a little different language to describe the passageway—some a dark space, some an enclosure, a tunnel, a funnel, a vacuum, a void:[5]

> I went through this dark, black vacuum at super speed. . . .
>
> Suddenly, I was in a very dark, very deep valley. It was as though there was a pathway, almost a road, through the valley, and I was going down the path. . . .

This person recalls thinking that they finally understood the biblical reference to "'the valley of the shadow of death'" in Psalm 23:4, because now he had actually experienced it.[6]

Karen, whom I personally interviewed, caught the swine flu and was dying. She told me she passed out of her body into a dark void that was not scary; it was the most peaceful, joyful experience ever. There she saw her grandmother and she realized she must return to her body—she still had work to do on earth. Perhaps Karen and others in the dark void have not gone "through the wormhole" yet. What's clear for those like Dale Black who pass through: there is a world of exquisite beauty waiting on the other side, a beauty even the blind can see.

Unblinded Beauty

Brad Barrows, like Vicki, had been blind since birth and had an NDE at age eight. He had never seen anything, nor did he have mental concepts or pictorial images of anything. Brad lived at the Boston Center for Blind Children when severe pneumonia caused his heart to stop for four minutes.

"Somewhere in the middle of the night," Brad told Ken Ring, "I began to become very stiff and rigid, and I was gasping for air. . . . I really thought I was about to die. . . . It was as if my being was slowly floating up through the room."

Ring notes that Brad was close to the ceiling and could "see" his apparently lifeless body on the bed. He also "saw" his blind roommate get out of his own bed and walk out of the room to get help (a detail later confirmed by his roommate). Next, Brad discovered that he was able to pass through the second-floor ceiling of his room and, like Vicki, "soon found that he was going straight up toward the roof of the building, actually up and over it." Brad "saw" snow everywhere except for the streets, which had been cleared by plows. He also "saw" a streetcar go by, and he recognized a playground used by his schoolmates and a particular hill he used to climb nearby.

When Ring asked if he "knew or saw" these things, Brad said, "I clearly visualized them. I could suddenly notice them and see them. . . . [I was] able to see quite clearly." Ring and Cooper, who studied twenty-one blind people who had NDEs, postulate a kind of vision they coin "mindsight," a visual perception blind NDErs experience beyond normal vision.

At this point, almost exactly like Vicki, Brad was aware of being pulled at approximately a 45-degree angle upward into a dark tunnel where he noticed the absence of his newfound sight.

> When I actually got into the tunnel, I do remember that one thing that puzzled me was the lack of any color. I began to wonder if this was darkness. . . . There was no color whatsoever. It was as black as I can understand blackness to be. But coming out into [a] large field, the closest I could tell you about color was that the brightness and brilliance of that whole area was absolutely indescribable. I could not distinguish fine shades of

color, for some reason. It's possible that I could have, but I had no vocabulary to describe it. I've been told when I was a very young child of four or five that grass could be brown or green or that the sky could be blue . . . but even then my concept of colors, my perception of colors, still remained absolutely beyond my reach. . . . I felt as if I might be entering another realm altogether, an unexplained dimension that I had very little understanding of.

As Brad approached the end of the tunnel, he was aware of an "immense field" stretching before him for what seemed like a great distance. He also noticed huge palm trees with immense leaves and very tall grass.

Brad's experience of the field reminds me of a doctor and his wife who came to our church because of their twins, one who almost died at three years old. Neither parent had faith in God nor had they ever talked about God or Jesus. Their kids had never been to church. Yet as the son was being tucked into bed one night, he declared, "I want to run through the fields and play with Jesus again." His mother was shocked and kept asking who told him about Jesus (they surely hadn't!). He insisted that Jesus came and got him from the hospital and "they ran and played in beautiful meadows together." Their son's detailed experience led his mom and dad to explore faith and eventually come to believe. Maybe it was the same field Brad walked through.

> When I noticed that I was walking up this field, it seemed as if I was so exhilarated and so unbelievably renewed that I didn't want to leave. I wanted to stay forever where I was. . . . It was so unbelievably peaceful that there [is] no way that I could describe the peace and the tranquility and the calm. . . . [The] weather was absolutely perfect in terms of temperature and humidity. It was so fresh, so unbelievably fresh that mountain air on earth could not even come close [a blind person would notice nonvisual environs most]. . . .

There was tremendous light up there. It seemed to come from every direction. . . . It was all around and everywhere that I happened to be looking. . . . It seemed like everything, even the grass I had been stepping on seemed to soak in that light. It seemed like the light could actually penetrate through everything that was there, even the leaves on the trees. There was no shade, there was no need for shade. The light was actually all-encompassing. Yet I wondered how I could know that because I had never seen before that point.

At first I was taken aback by it [sight]. I did not understand what sensation I was experiencing. While I was moving through this particular field, I seemed to accept it very readily. I felt like I wouldn't understand it had it happened on earth. But where I was, I was able to accept it almost immediately.

Like Vicki, Dale, Marv, and many others, Brad notices light (which felt like love) coming *out of* the grass and leaves. I find it fascinating that they all describe the same intriguing way that God's light comes *out of* nature. But how would blind people get that idea? They would never have heard people talking about light coming *out of* grass and trees. Like Vicki and others, Brad also becomes aware of thousands of voices singing:

I remember thinking that the voices seemed to be singing in a language I had never understood or maybe many, many languages. The music I had heard was nothing like anything I have ever experienced. . . .

By this time, I was getting closer to the music and being absolutely fascinated by it. I wanted to join in with this music. It was absolutely precious. Within a very short amount of time, and I had no idea how much time had actually elapsed, but as I was going up the hill, I came to a large stone structure. I could tell that it was stone without even touching it. . . . They were almost like gem stones. They seemed to literally shine with their own particular light. Yet the light itself was actually penetrating right through the stones.[7]

Jesus's youngest disciple, John, had a vision of Heaven recorded in Revelation. Brad is describing the great wall and the beauty surrounding the City that John wrote about: "And [the angel] carried me away in the Spirit to a mountain great and high, and showed me the Holy City, Jerusalem. . . . It *shone with the glory of God*, and its brilliance was like that of a very precious jewel, like a jasper, clear as crystal. It had a great, high wall with twelve gates. . . . The foundations of the city walls were decorated with every kind of *precious stone*. . . . The city does not need the sun or the moon to shine on it, for the glory of *God gives it light*, and the Lamb is its lamp" (Revelation 21:10–12, 19, 23, italics mine).

I used to think the descriptions in Revelation were purely metaphorical. While I still think much is symbolic, when so many NDErs (even blind ones) describe the same supernatural beauty John described, you have to wonder! If it's true, imagine how awesome, how intriguingly beautiful, how much like earth Heaven will feel, and yet so much more alive, all of it vibrant, colorful, infused with the very light and life of God permeating everything.

Meadows, Grass, and Trees

A color-blind British NDEr suddenly saw beauty in all kinds of colors with a new vision many speak about: "What I saw was too beautiful for words. I was looking at a magnificent landscape full of flowers and plants that I couldn't actually name. It all looked hundreds of miles away. And yet I could see everything in detail. It was both far away and close. It was completely three-dimensional and about a thousand times more beautiful than my favorite holiday destination in spring. I was always surrounded by loving spiritual beings of light."[8]

Because most people have never read Revelation, they don't realize the earthlike beauty John mentions in his vision of Heaven:

After this I saw . . . [people] from every nation and tribe and people and language. . . . They were clothed in white robes and held palm branches in their hands. . . . He will lead them to springs of life-giving water. . . . He took me in the Spirit to a great, high mountain, and he showed me the holy city, Jerusalem. . . . It shone with the glory of God. . . . Then the angel showed me a river with the water of life, clear as crystal, flowing from the throne of God and of the Lamb. It flowed down the center of the main street. On each side of the river grew a tree of life, bearing twelve crops of fruit. (Revelation 7:9, 17; 21:10; 22:1–2 NLT)

Brad and others claim to see exactly what Scripture says—a beautiful place of mountains, streams, trees, and apparently amazing grass!

Marv Besteman, as a retired bank president, loved to golf. So naturally, what he noticed in Heaven was the grass. "I saw babies and children and grown-ups of all ages playing and talking and laughing on grass that was the greenest green I've ever seen. . . . Picture the verdant, luscious grass at the Masters [golf tournament] and then try to imagine grass far greener and more deluxe. That's how green the grass is in heaven."[9]

Flowers and Forests Forever

At age five, Margret was misdiagnosed with scarlet fever. In reality, her appendix had ruptured and the infection took her to the edge of death. One night, says Margret,

this marvelous feeling of peace came over me. I was basking in that because it was so beautiful, when suddenly I became aware that someone was holding my right hand. I looked up and my eyes were traveling over a white gown. I came to the head of this beautiful woman. . . .

She walked along with me holding my hand. . . . I became aware of a fragrance in the air that was becoming stronger and stronger. It was of flowers, and they just seemed to permeate my whole body. And when I took notice of what was around me besides her, I realized that the path was banked with flowers way over our heads. These flowers were close together the way a Colonial bouquet would be, and they were massive. I was just so overwhelmed by this fragrance that I said to her like a little kid, which I was, "Are these flowers real?"

She smiled and looked down at me and said, "yes they are." I could see her chuckling, trying to hold back a laugh.

After this beautiful woman told her she must go back, it took Margret a year to recover. Years later, in her sixties, she decided to paint the beautiful arbor pathway of Heaven. While painting it, Margret had to see her doctor. Her doctor mentioned near-death experiences, and she told him she was painting hers. He asked for a reproduction of it, and the doctor ended up hanging Margret's painting among ten other pictures in his office.

Several weeks later, a new patient named Mary Olivia came into the doctor's office. As a single mom facing a terminal illness with three children, she needed a second opinion. When Mary saw the painting in the doctor's office, she just stood and stared for several minutes before exclaiming to the doctor,

"I know where this is."

He said, "You know what that's a picture of?"

"Of course I do. I walked along that path when I was five years old and almost died."

Mary relayed how THE MAN (capitalized at her request) said he would always be with her as they walked beneath the arbor's beautiful flowers. Did two five-year-olds really walk through the same flower-lined arbor in Heaven? Margret feels God led her to paint that picture because Mary Olivia needed to be reminded "I'm always with you" (Matthew 28:20).[10]

Scripture tells us of a beauty in Heaven, not unlike the flowers and forests of earth, yet so much greater. Dr. Richard Eby considered himself an amateur botanist, and he couldn't even name all the varieties of trees and flowers he saw during his NDE. He also noticed a new type of life in the flora:

> My gaze riveted the exquisite valley in which I found myself. Forests of symmetrical trees unlike anything on earth covered the foothills on each side. I could see each branch and "leaf"— not a brown spot or dead leaf in the forest. ("No death there" includes the vegetation!). . . . They resembled somewhat the tall arbor vitae cedars of North America, but I could not identify them. The valley floor was gorgeous. Stately grasses, each blade perfect and erect, were interspersed with ultra-white, four-petalled flowers on stems two feet tall, with a touch of gold at the centers. . . .
> Then I sensed a strange new feel to the stems—no moisture! I felt them carefully. Delicately smooth, yet nothing like earthly stems with their cellular watery content. Before I could ask, again I had the answer: earthly water is hydrogen and oxygen for temporary life support; here Jesus is the Living Water. In His presence nothing dies. . . .
> I instinctively looked behind me where I had been standing on dozens of blooms. Not one was bent or bruised. Then I watched my feet as I walked a few more steps upon the grass and flowers; they stood upright inside my feet and legs! We simply passed through one another.[11]

Richard Sigmund, a messianic Jew, died in a horrible car accident, leaving him with a broken back, neck, and both arms, and two ribs puncturing his heart. The medics said he had been dead for about eight hours when they found him. But Richard revived to describe the beauty of Heaven and the new life found within. He also mentioned not only how green the grass was, but how alive the grass and flowers seemed with a new kind of life:

I was walking through a garden that stretched for as far as I could see in either direction. And I saw great groups of people. On either side of the pathway was the richest turf-green grass I had ever seen. And it was moving with life and energy. . . . There were flowers of every imaginable size and color along the path. . . . The air was filled with their aroma, and they were all humming. I asked if I could pick one to smell, and I was told that I could. It was wonderful. When I put the flower down, it was immediately replanted and growing again. Again, there's no death in heaven. . . . The beautifully manicured park was filled with huge, striking trees. They had to be at least two thousand feet tall. And there were many different varieties. Some I knew; others, I had no idea what species they were. . . . There was a continual sound of chimes coming from the leaves [of one tree] as they brushed against one another. . . . The fruit was pear shaped and copper colored. When I picked it, another fruit instantly grew in its place. When I touched the fruit to my lips, it evaporated and melted into the most delicious thing I had ever tasted.[12]

Living Water

I love water! I love the ocean. Sailing, surfing, scuba diving—I love it all. So one of John's statements about Heaven's nature has always bugged me: "Then I saw 'a new heaven and a new earth,' for the first heaven and the first earth had passed away, and there was no longer any sea" (Revelation 21:1–2). No longer any sea!? I was bummed. But the longer I've thought about this, John might not have been making a statement on the eternal state, but just what he noticed *not there* in his vision. After all, John had been imprisoned on the island of Patmos for years— the sea was his prison cell.

What we do know is that there is water in Heaven—living water! Ian McCormack, a New Zealand surfer who "died" while night diving, saw water in this place of exquisite beauty during his NDE:

> Through the centre of the meadows I could see a crystal clear stream winding its way across the landscape with trees on either bank. To my right were mountains in the distance and the sky above was blue and clear. To my left were rolling green hills and flowers, which were radiating beautiful colours. Paradise! I knew I belonged here. I felt as though I had just been born for the first time. Every part of me knew I was home.[13]

John also notes in Revelation: "Then the angel showed me the river of the water of life, as clear as crystal, flowing from the throne of God and of the Lamb down the middle of the great street of the city" (Revelation 22:1). Many NDErs have mentioned rivers, waterfalls, a sea, but only Marv Besteman and a few others have mentioned boats. That may be an outlier from the common NDE, but as one who loves to sail, I'm banking on it:

> About sixty yards away, in the middle left of the panorama before me, were some old fishing boats pulled up on the shore of a huge, rippling lake. The boats looked worn and aged, not sleek and razzy dazzy like the boats we see zooming around on Lake Michigan. . . . They lay on a sandy, rocky seashore. The blue of the lake was a darker, less brilliant blue than the shade of heaven's sky, and the surface had a few gentle waves. Like an ocean or one of the Great Lakes, I couldn't see the other side.[14]

Imagine if aliens landed in New York State, made observations for one hour, then returned home to tell what they saw. Some would say earth was full of tall buildings everywhere, another might land in the subway and walk out into the light to say earth is a dark tunnel leading to brightly lit buildings. Others might land in Central Park and speak of beautiful grass, trees, and gardens, while others landing in upstate New York would describe yellow and orange autumn leaves on tree-covered hillsides. Each has but a small perspective, but together you'd get a composite picture. That's what I believe NDEs are giving us, and what's amazing is how much they're describing what Jesus and the prophets already told us in Scripture.

As I write these words, I'm in the mountains above Los Angeles at an arts conference called Terra Nova (New Earth). The sheer beauty of this rugged mountain valley tantalizes the senses. I wish my son were here, because we would explore it together. How great it will be when my son and I can explore the wonders of a creation that makes earth's beauty pale in comparison. When my wife, daughter, and son can travel with me to faraway places for the most panoramic picnic imaginable. Maybe that's why the universe is so vast! When thought can take us anywhere, maybe we will find endless adventure exploring God's wondrous universe in a new time and space. What might that be like? Let's imagine!

9

Alive in New Dimensions

ON NOVEMBER 10, 2008, Harvard neurosurgeon Eben Alexander was struck by a rare illness causing his entire neocortex—the part of the brain that makes us human—to shut down. What he experienced reversed the conclusions he had formed through medical school—he found himself alive like never before, experiencing a world where time and space become far more expansive than we could ever conceive.

As a neurosurgeon, Dr. Alexander had heard many stories from his patients over the years, usually from those who had experienced cardiac arrest—stories about travels to mysterious, beautiful landscapes, of reuniting with dead relatives, even of meeting and speaking with God himself. "But all of it, in my opinion, was pure fantasy," Eben says. "If you don't have a working brain, you can't be conscious." He reasoned that the brain is the machine that produces consciousness, so when the machine stops, consciousness stops. Pull the plug and the computer goes dead. Or so he thought, until his own brain crashed.

Dr. Alexander's experience proved to him that the death of the body and the brain are not the end of consciousness. He concludes that "human experience continues beyond the grave. More important, it continues under the gaze of a God who loves and cares about each one of us."

When his brain ceased to function, Dr. Alexander found himself in a strange, new, beautiful world. Words cannot begin to convey the beauty of this world, he explains. "Brilliant, vibrant, ecstatic, stunning. . . . I could heap on one adjective after another to describe what this world looked and felt like, but they'd all fall short," he says.[1]

Dr. Alexander found himself flying over a green, gorgeous, idyllic landscape that seemed very much like earth, yet at the same time was very different. He talks candidly about his experience in a live interview:

> I remember ascending up into this brilliant, ultra-real valley . . . this brilliant greenery lush with life. . . . I remember how we would dip down and go through that lush greenery, and there would be flowers and blossoms and buds on trees that would open up even as we flew by. I remember the rich textures and colors beyond the rainbow. In that beautiful valley as we would come up and ascend above all that greenery, I could see that there were hundreds of souls dancing. I describe them as being dressed in peasant garb—very simple clothing, yet beautiful colors, and tremendous joy and merriment, and there were lots of children playing and dogs jumping. It was just a wonderful festival! And it was all being fueled because up above—in the velvety skies above—were pure spiritual beings [angels, he later thought], orbs of golden light, swooping and swirling in formation leaving sparkling golden trails, emanating these hymns, chants, anthems—powerful like a tsunami wave, crescendo after crescendo of the most beautiful music. Waves washing through me—and that's what was fueling this incredible joy and mirth going on in this gateway valley.[2]

Reflecting on his experience later, it occurred to him that the joy of these creatures was so great, they were compelled to burst forth this anthem. He was certain that if the joy didn't come out in song, they would not be able to contain it.

He has no idea how long he resided in this world. Time and space operated on another dimension. Yet he insists, "The important thing to understand is this gateway valley was *much more real* than this world—far sharper, crisper, more real than this—this [world] is very dream-like by comparison. That was a deep, deep mystery to me for a long time, trying to understand that ultra-reality."[3] Eben grapples for words to explain it:

> When you go to a place where there's no sense of time as we experience it in the ordinary world, accurately describing the way it feels is next to impossible. . . . I saw that there are countless higher dimensions, but that the only way to know these dimensions is to enter and experience them directly. . . . Cause and effect exist in these higher realms, but outside of our earthly conception of them. The world of time and space in which we move in this [earthly] terrestrial realm is tightly and intricately meshed within these higher worlds. . . . From those higher worlds one could access any time or place in our world.[4]

Given his experience, Dr. Alexander acknowledges now why so much writing about this mysterious spiritual dimension can seem confusing or even nonsensical from our earthly perspective. In the spiritual world, time is nonlinear; it doesn't behave as it does on earth. There, he says, "a moment can seem like a lifetime, and one or several lifetimes can seem like a moment."[5]

Exploring New Dimensions of Reality

Imagine what an adventure it will be exploring Heaven's beauty and experiencing the wonders of God's creation—which will not be unlike earth's beauty or our experiences of earth, but so much more expansive! Like seeing a two-dimensional painting of the beautiful southern coast of France does not even come close to living there, so the beauty, wonders, and good gifts of earth are only a flat, two-dimensional painting of the multi-dimensional world God has for us to experience.

Jesus's half-brother James reminds us of this: "Do not be deceived, my beloved [brothers and sisters]. Every good thing given and every perfect gift is from above, coming down from the Father of lights, with whom there is no variation or shifting shadow" (James 1:16–17 NASB). Imagine some of the good gifts of Heaven to come!

Don Piper helps us imagine how it will feel to experience Heaven's gifts from his *90 Minutes in Heaven*:

> As I looked around, I could hardly grasp the vivid, dazzling colors. Every hue and tone surpassed anything I had ever seen. With all the heightened awareness of my senses, I felt as if I had never seen, heard, or felt anything so real before. I don't recall that I tasted anything, yet I knew that if I had, that too would have been more glorious than anything I had eaten or drunk on earth. The best way I can explain it is to say that I felt as if I were in another dimension. Never, even in my happiest moments, had I ever felt so fully alive.[6]

Time and Eternity

Dallas Willard, former USC professor of philosophy, once noted, "Time is within eternity, not outside of it. The created universe is within the kingdom of God, not outside it. . . . When we pass through what we call death, we do not lose the world. Indeed, we see it for the first time as it really is."[7] Do you know the Genesis account of creation is the only creation story among the world's religions where God creates time (creates *ex nihilo*, from outside of our time "*out of nothing*")? But God also created Heaven "out of nothing," and our space-time dimensionality seems to exist within it somehow. So we don't lose the experience of our three-dimensional earth, we expand it.

Imagine if earth is a two-dimensional, black-and-white painting in God's three-dimensional house. When you die, you are separated (death means separation) from the flat canvas of life and liberated into the new dimensions and colors of God's house all around you. Now you can see the flat, black-and-white world on the walls of this new place for what it is. Imagine returning to the painting to try to describe a three-dimensional world of color to a flat, black-and-white world. By analogy, that's why NDEs struggle for words.

Maybe that's what the prophet Elisha showed his servant who was afraid of the armies surrounding them—Elisha prayed the veil might be lifted, and suddenly his servant saw that Heaven's angels were all around to protect them (2 Kings 6:16–17). Revelation 21 foretells a day when Heaven and earth unite—seeming to imply that our space-time fabric is simply contained within a more expanded space and time that will one day reunite. What might the higher dimensional Reality of Heaven afford? Let's stretch our imaginations.

Imagine a world where time is no longer an enemy, where travel no longer feels bothersome, where sights and sounds, light and color, music and singing all come alive in a way that brings euphoric ecstasy to the residents of Heaven. Let's imagine the possibilities that new dimensions of time and space might bring on the other side.

Enhanced Vision

"The eyes of the LORD search the whole earth in order to strengthen those whose hearts are fully committed to him" (2 Chronicles 16:9 NLT). Obviously, God's sight is not limited like ours. Not that we will have God's omniscient ability to see all and be ever present, but the apostle John in seeing Heaven's visions describes a lot of fine detail he couldn't possibly have seen clearly from up on a high mountain without enhanced vision (Revelation 21:10–22). Dr. Long notes that 66 percent of NDErs he surveyed describe vision as a heightened, unworldly brightness, clarity, and vividness. Some described a 360-degree vision, others the ability to "telescope" to long distances and see things far away up close.[8]

Moody interviewed a woman who had observed her car accident from above her body. She described taking notice of the people scurrying about the scene of the accident, including the ambulance that had arrived. Each time she looked at a person and wondered what that person was thinking, "it was like a zoom-up, exactly like through a zoom lens, and I was there," she explained.[9] From this vantage point, she recalled feeling able to witness anything happening in any part of the world if she had desired to do so.

Others speak of a 360-degree vision, like Dale Black mentions in the last chapter, but not just 360 degrees in a circle: a spherical vision up, down, and all around simultaneously. Ray, a kid doing judo moves with a friend on the playground, got thrown down, hit his head hard against the ground, and left his body: "I still had a 'body,' but it was entirely different. I could see in three dimensions as if I had no body at all. . . . I could see all directions at once, yet there were no directions or dimensions as we think of them."[10] Imagine both the ability to see all around us, or to focus in on any one thing like we experience now.

Leonard had a heart attack. He described his vision as he watched the frantic efforts to resuscitate him: "First, I had 360 degree vision, I could see above, below, on my right, on my left, behind, I could see EVERYWHERE at the same time! Secondly, I could zoom on a particular point. Also I travelled at the speed of thought, I just needed to think about a place or somebody and I was instantly there! I could go through walls, I went through matter, and it was VERY EXCITING!"[11] Leonard also got a special color-commentary on his surgery by God himself: "On the other side communication is done via telepathy (thought transfer). I must tell you that God has a fantastic sense of humor; I never laughed so much in all my life!"[12]

Most NDErs talk of a clarity and visual acuity, a light and brightness, that they somehow knew would not be possible on earth. Dr. Richard Eby noticed, "The light in Heaven would blind our natural eyes immediately. He is the Sun of Heaven. With spiritual eyes I could see anywhere and through anything."[13]

"It seemed that my vision had been extremely enhanced," Dale Black recalls. "How otherwise could I see the colors I was seeing or the light that was in everything? It was something like being in a 3-D movie and then putting on the 3-D glasses. . . . Suddenly everything has more dimensions, more richness. But that is an understatement. Multiply that by ten thousand and it would be like what I was experiencing."[14] With this new, expanded vision, some NDErs say God has a treat for the eyes in store for us. "THINGS WHICH EYE HAS NOT SEEN AND EAR HAS NOT HEARD . . . ALL THAT GOD HAS PREPARED FOR THOSE WHO LOVE HIM" (1 Corinthians 2:9 NASB).

Heaven's Light Show

Colton Burpo had told his dad he stayed with Pop, Todd's deceased grandfather, in Heaven. Todd decided to test his four-year-old son. After all, a four-year-old claiming he visited Heaven has never read the book of Revelation. So Todd asked him what he and Pop did when it got dark and he went home with Pop.

Colton frowned at him. "It doesn't get dark in heaven, Dad! Who told you that?"

"What do you mean it doesn't get dark?"

"God and Jesus light up heaven. It never gets dark. It's always bright."

Todd was shocked. Colton passed the test.[15]

The book of Revelation tells us, "The city does not need the sun or the moon to shine on it, for the glory of God gives it light, and the Lamb [Jesus] is its lamp. The nations will walk by its light. . . . There will be no more night. They will not need the light of a lamp or the light of the sun, for the Lord God will give them light" (21:23–24; 22:5). Most all who see Heaven's beauty mention this new light, which far exceeds anything we can comprehend. Our sun is but a dim, very limited spectrum of the colors of light visible in Heaven. And combined with a new, expanded sense of sight, the Light brings everything alive in a whole new dimension.

Dean Braxton recalls, "The most gorgeous sky ever seen here on earth cannot even come close to the atmosphere in Heaven. It is bright because of the glory of our God. . . . The atmosphere is something you experience, not just see. It is golden, yellow, white, and had more colors moving throughout it . . . like the Aurora Borealis Lights."[16] I have a picture on my phone of the most gorgeous tropical sunset I could ever imagine, yet compared to the extravagant brilliance of Heaven's sky, I imagine it would feel bland. And unlike earth, Heaven's colors appear to be alive, enchanting, even adjusting to the viewer's sight.

Dale Black mentioned experiencing the atmosphere of Heaven: "The colors seemed to be alive, dancing in the air. I had never seen so many different colors. . . . It was breathtaking to watch. And I could have spent forever doing just that."[17] Our earthly eyes cannot see ultraviolet or infrared colors that make up our sun's spectrum. Apparently, God's Light contains an exquisite pallet of thousands more colors, internally lighting everything. And the light is palpable—infused with the love and joy of God.

"I saw the most dazzling colors, which was all the more surprising because I'm color-blind," a Dutch patient in Dr. Pim van Lommel's study recalls. "I can distinguish the primary colors, but pastels all look the same to me. But suddenly I could see them, all kinds of different shades. Don't ask me to name them because I lack the necessary experience for that."[18]

Marv found himself captivated as the atmosphere projected a heavenly light show, displayed on the most brilliant shades of deep blue sky as the backdrop:

> The sky in which I flew to heaven, and the firmament surrounding the heavens, were a wilder and bluer yonder than you would ever believe. . . . The closest shade I can associate this otherworldly blue with is the surreal tones of the water in the Caribbean or off the coast of Hawaii at sunset. . . . That color is waiting for you and me on the other side. . . .
>
> The colors and lights in heaven were simply sublime. . . . They were the deepest, richest, most gloriously lush colors I had ever seen, and some I had never seen before. Heaven is a dream-come-true for those who love all things colorful, and our home there is lit by the Father of Lights. . . . [There were] robust and bold and vigorous beams that were somehow gentle to my eyes. I simply don't think those colors and lights exist on earth. . . .
>
> The white in heaven was—forgive me!—like none other I can compare. From a brilliant white to an opal stone to a milk glass moon color, the white shades clustered in the sky like a huge bridal bouquet. . . . The colors in heaven would meld from whites into blues and reds and purples and greens. The multiple colors would change and shift and move constantly, twirling and twisting and floating . . . shape-shifting in a way that fixated and enthralled me. The closest I can come to describing what that light show was like is probably the aurora borealis, or the northern lights. . . . Then again, if I compare the light show in Alaska to the light show in heaven . . . it's not even close. . . . Even just the light show was utterly transfixing.[19]

What about Sleep?

This morning, I had the privilege of hitting snooze five times— it's Labor Day, the day when we rest from and celebrate our labors in America. As I enjoyed sleeping, in my twilight of consciousness, I thanked God for the gift of sleep. Then I thought, *But we won't sleep in Heaven, will we? How can we sleep if it's never dark?* Then I started considering why we need sleep. In our finite world, our energy gets depleted, and rest restores us. Under the curse of the knowledge of evil (a world going against God's ways), sleep is God's gift to give us a respite from the trials, the strivings, and the sufferings.

In Heaven, we enter God's rest, so we no longer need sleep, because we enter a rest that's alive and full of endless energy flowing from connection to the Source. "So God's rest is there for people to enter, but those who first heard this good news failed to enter because they disobeyed God. So God set another time for entering his rest, and that time is today. God announced this through David much later . . . : 'Today when you hear his voice, don't harden your hearts.' . . . So there is a special rest still waiting for the people of God. For all who have entered into God's rest have rested from their labors" (Hebrews 4:6–10 NLT).

As we will see, this rest comes from an eternal peace through connection with God. Imagine that in Heaven we will forever be at rest in our being, so we will not need to sleep. But don't worry; you won't miss it. I imagine it will feel like when you were young and fought sleep because life was too exciting. It will be a restfulness that's full of energy, excitement, adventure, projects that aren't laborious, and a peace that changes everything. All the strife, struggle, and conflict we escaped through sleep will be gone for good.

In the seventh century BCE, the prophet Isaiah was given a vision of the life to come, when the old Jerusalem and all the endless conflict of the Middle East will finally come to an end under the peaceful rule of God:

> No longer will violence be heard in your land,
>   nor ruin or destruction within your borders,

> but you will call your walls Salvation
> and your gates Praise.
> The sun will no more be your light by day,
> nor will the brightness of the moon shine on you,
> for the LORD will be your everlasting light,
> and your God will be your glory. . . .
> And your days of sorrow will end. (Isaiah 60:18–20)

Imagine that day, when time no longer stands as the enemy, neither magnifying our suffering nor delaying our satisfaction, but peace becomes a constant companion, and time becomes a friend.

When Time Is a Friend

What will time be like in Heaven? Scripture tells us that God's time is exactly what Eben Alexander claimed to experience: "But do not forget this one thing, dear friends: With the Lord a day is like a thousand years, and a thousand years are like a day" (2 Peter 3:8). Other NDErs experienced what felt like timelessness, and to others it felt like time but in another dimension.

Those on the NDERF website described time in various terms:

> It seemed as though I experienced so much in such a small length of earthly time. . . .
> Both time and space in earth stopped completely. Simultaneously, "the time and the space" on the other side was completely alive, evident[ial], and real.[20]

> Yes, while I was in the light, I had . . . [no] sense of time as I know it here on Earth. In other words, no sense of the serial nature of time . . . past, present, or future. All times (past, present, and future) were experienced at every moment in time while I was in the light.[21]

Some describe it as timelessness, others note that there is a sense of time, but not in the same one-dimensional way we experience it on earth. And we see this indicated in Scripture as well, that time in Heaven does not equate with our linear time, yet time can be experienced in Heaven. John noticed time in Heaven. "When he opened the seventh seal, there was silence in heaven for *about half an hour.* . . . On each side of the river stood the tree of life, bearing twelve crops of fruit, yielding its fruit *every month*" (Revelation 8:1; 22:2, italics mine). So even though a day in Heaven may be like one thousand earthly years, there still seems to be the ability to experience some measure of time.

Three people even spoke of a different kind of day and "night" they observed, though I would call this an outlier (I did not hear many others say this). But I mention it because it seems to accord with Scripture:

> Heaven is a very interesting place, there's nothing monotonous including the passage of time. . . . [On earth] the clock ticks, you know, the sun goes over the horizon and you sense the passing of time, you don't sense the passing of time [in Heaven] but there are different periods of time. There's a time when the sky is bright and this [they] call day and then there's a time when the sky is not so bright. . . . It's a time when activity seems to slow down. And this day and "night" so they call it, no night in heaven but light and less light   would go in seven-day lengths so then you have the week.[22]

Bill observed something similar: "Then the light faded somewhat. It wasn't dark, just not as light as it had been. The area where I was standing became quiet and still."[23] If this is true that Heaven has its own kind of days, I guess it gives context to how Heaven's trees could bear fruit *each month* (Revelation 22:2, italics mine).

Two-Dimensional Time

Imagine if in Heaven, we experience time in a new second dimension. On earth, we experience three dimensions of space

131

(height, width, depth), but only one dimension of time—time is linear in one direction. Picture a line (see diagram 1). We experience one event (A), then another event (B), then another (C). And if something wonderful happens in moment A, time won't wait for you to fully enjoy it. Before you know it, the moment's gone. That's why time's an enemy—there's never enough for the wonderful moments.

Diagram 1

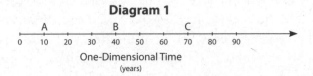

One-Dimensional Time
(years)

But if in Heaven we experienced a second dimension of time, at each point along earth's timeline there would be another "timeline" perpendicular to each point in time, so you could spend all kinds of time enjoying moment A—nothing would ever be rushed.[24] (See diagram 2.)

Diagram 2

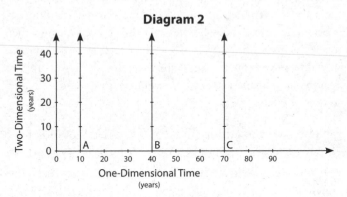

Crystal noted this feeling of unrushed time, contrasting the linear, sequential time on Earth with the feeling of timelessness she experienced in Heaven. "Everything happened at once—yet with no sense of rush or urgency," she explained. "In heaven, there are no minutes or hours or days . . . no such thing as 'time.'" She still struggles to understand whether events actually unfold differently in Heaven, or whether we simply perceive them differently.[25] Clearly, NDErs differ in trying to describe something difficult to put into our time-space-bound words, but multiple dimensions of time would have this effect.

Astrophysicist Hugh Ross points out that if Heaven affords three dimensions of time, all those two-dimensional vertical timelines extending out from each point (A, B, C, etc.) would all meet in a singular point of time.[26] Picture a globe—for each linear point of earthly one-dimensional "horizontal" time (A, B, C), there is plenty of second-dimensional "vertical" time, all traveling along longitudinal lines that meet at one third-dimensional point (a globe's North Pole!). That means one could experience the past, present, and future of earth's time at a single (North Pole) point of third-dimensional time (diagram 3).

Diagram 3

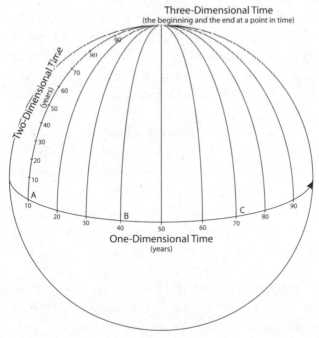

Three-Dimensional Time
(the beginning and the end at a point in time)

One-Dimensional Time
(years)

I'm not sure if that's what we experience in Heaven, but God declared, "I am the Alpha and the Omega, the Beginning and the End. To the thirsty I will give water without cost from the spring of the water of life" (Revelation 21:6). God is infinite, unbound by any dimensions of time (since he created time), but that does not mean he can't act in lower dimensions of time. Maybe we will experience additional dimensions of time too.

News from Earth

But will we know what's happening in earth's time from Heaven? I think we will to some degree. Those killed for their faith ask God, "How long, Sovereign Lord, holy and true, until you judge the inhabitants of the earth and avenge our blood?" (Revelation 6:10). They are told to *wait* a little longer. Waiting requires the passing of time, but as mentioned, time may pass very differently. This also shows a continuity with what happened on earth. We will be the same people, with our memories of earth, and with the ability to know what's happening on earth to some degree, but from Heaven's eternal viewpoint.

Four-year-old Colton Burpo asked his father if he knew that God is three persons. His dad is a pastor! Colton said, "I was sitting by God the Holy Spirit because I was praying for you. You needed the Holy Spirit, so I prayed for you."[27] That took Todd's breath away, because he remembered his shouting match with God when Colton was dying. How did Colton know? Perhaps we will know all or some of earth's news, but in time with Heaven's perspective.

Just imagine how wonderful it will feel—never rushed, never hurried, never late, plenty of time to laugh, plenty of time to create, plenty of time to explore God's universe.

134

Heavenly Travel

"Instantly the sense of timelessness made all hurry foolish," Dr. Eby recalls.

> I had instantly noted that my eyes were unlimited in range of vision; ten inches or ten miles—the focus was sharp and clear. . . . The illumination fascinated me—not a shadow anywhere. There was no single light source as on earth. I realized that everything seemed to produce its own light. . . . There is nothing in the physics of Heaven that's similar to the physics on earth. He was speaking inside my mind and I was answering with a rapidity that can only be imagined. . . . If I asked a question, He had the answer ready before I even asked it. Jesus and I walked in Heaven together, but it was more like flying than walking. We were talking while suspended in midair. There is no weight or gravity in Heaven, so there's no need to touch the ground. . . . Space is also limitless.[28]

Imagine the possibilities of travel in Heaven. As many NDErs have already noted, various types of flying seem natural in Heaven. As science-fictional as this sounds, when Jesus appeared to his followers after the resurrection, he had the ability to pass through walls and appear in a locked room (John 20:19). In front of 120 people, "[Jesus] was taken up before their very eyes, and a cloud hid him from their sight. They were looking intently up into the sky as he was going" (Acts 1:9–10). Apparently the laws of Heaven supersede the laws of earth.

Imagine how awesome it would be not only to fly, but to be able to travel great distances literally in the blink of an eye. Imagine where we could go! One person differentiated several different modes of travel:

> It is possible to move by the speed of thought. You have to go somewhere and just like that you're there. But there is a mode to move slowly. You have the sensation of moving which in itself is

delightful. When you ride down a scenic road, you can look out and see the scenery whereas travelling by thought you wouldn't see that because right away you're there. But to travel, you see, you learn as you travel, oh it's delightful to learn. . . . And then you just appear to be floating through space. . . . While we don't have any wings we just float through space.[29]

Dale Black, Dr. Alexander, and other NDErs described this slower travel, a kind of floating through space. But others also described what seemed like an ability to travel by thought. Imagine how much fun you and your friends and family would have, exploring Heaven's miles of scenic beauty together. "Heaven is huge and expanding," Dean claims to have discovered. "There is no distance, as we know it here on earth. I seemed to be far from things and yet near. If I wanted to be somewhere else in Heaven I just had to think it, and I was there."[30]

Have you ever looked up at the billions of stars in a clear night sky and wondered—why would God create such a vast universe so beyond our reach? Maybe it's so that we can explore it forever. "The heavens declare the glory of God; the skies proclaim the work of his hands" (Psalm 19:1). I can imagine friends and family members, maybe special exploration teams, sent to explore and study up close the wonders of the universe because all of it declares how majestic and awesome is the Mind who made it.

What glory God will get from basking in his children's discovery of more and more of his wonders. I can imagine searching out the wonders of God's creative beauty for all eternity as an endless act of worship. But nothing can compare, and nothing appears to be of more interest to NDErs, than just being with God himself. Imagine seeing God!

10

A Love You'll Never Want to Leave

TWENTY-YEAR-OLD IAN MCCORMACK set out from his native New Zealand to find the perfect wave, the perfect high, the perfect girl, and the surfer's life while traveling throughout Australia, Africa, and Indonesia—two years of doing whatever he pleased. But death never sends a meeting request, and one night while scuba diving with friends on the reefs off Mauritius, an island in the Indian Ocean, a school of box jellyfish stung Ian four times—and one sting is deadly!

In the ambulance on the way to the hospital, Ian's life began to vividly replay before his eyes. "People say just before they die their life flashes before them." Ian recalls,

> My thoughts were racing. "I'm too young to die, why did I go diving?" . . . I lay there wondering what would happen if I died? Is there anything after I die? Where would I go if I died?
>
> Then I saw a clear vision of my mother. It was as though she was speaking out those words she had spoken so long ago; "Ian, no matter how far from God you are, no matter what you've done wrong, if you cry out to God from your heart, he will hear you and he will forgive you."

In my heart I was thinking, "Do I believe there is a God? Am I going to pray?" I'd almost become a devout atheist. I didn't believe anybody. Yet, I was confronted by this vision of my mother.[1]

Ian found out later that his mother had been roused awake from a dream showing her that Ian was dying at that very same moment, and there in New Zealand she prayed for her son with all her might. Ian recalls, "I didn't know what to pray or whom to pray to. Which god should I pray to? Buddha? Kali? Shiva? There are thousands of them. Yet I didn't see Buddha or Krishna or some other god or man standing there, I saw my mother—and my mother followed Jesus Christ. I wondered what I should pray."

The Lord's Prayer his mom had taught him came to mind, but then he couldn't remember it. As his elevated legs pressed the poison deeper into his brain, Ian desperately pleaded with God to help him remember. "Forgive us our sins" came up in his mind. "God, I ask you to forgive my sins, but I've done so many wrong things," Ian said. "I don't know how you can, but please forgive me of my sins." The next line came up: "Forgive those who have sinned against you." Ian thought, "Well, I don't hold grudges." Then came the question, "Will you forgive the Indian that pushed you out of the car and the Chinese men that wouldn't take you to the hospital?" I thought, "You must be joking!" But Ian says that no more lines would come. He realized that if God could forgive him, he must also forgive others. Line by line he prayed for God's will to be done in his life. Then he slipped away.[2]

At first, Ian found himself fully alive, but in utter darkness that terrified him. We will explore this often-overlooked part of his story in coming chapters. Ian describes what happened next:

I was weeping by now and I cried out to God, "Why am I here, I've asked you for forgiveness, why am I here? I've turned my heart to you, why am I here?" Then a brilliant light shone upon me and literally drew me out of the darkness. . . . I could see that the source of the light was emanating from the very end of the tunnel. It looked unspeakably bright, as if it was the centre of the universe, the source of all light and power. It was more brilliant than the sun, more radiant than any diamond, brighter than a laser beam. Yet you could look right into it. . . .

As I was being translated through the air I could see successive waves of thicker intensity light break off the source and start traveling up the tunnel towards me. The first wave of light gave off an amazing warmth and comfort. It was as though the light wasn't just material in nature but was a "living light" that transmitted an emotion. The light passed into me and filled me with a sense of love and acceptance.

Halfway down another wave of light passed into me. This light gave off total and complete peace. . . . I tried everything I could think of to find peace and contentment in my life, and I'd never found it. Now from the top of my head to the base of my feet I found myself totally at peace.

In the darkness I hadn't been able to see my hands in front of my face but now as I looked to my right to my amazement there was my arm and hand—and I could see straight through them. I was transparent like a spirit, only my body was full of the same light that was shining on me from the end of the tunnel. . . . I came out of the end of the tunnel and seemed to be standing upright before the source of all the light and power. My whole vision was taken up with this incredible light. It looked like a white fire or a mountain of cut diamonds sparkling with the most indescribable brilliance. . . .

As I stood there, questions began racing through my heart; "Is this just a force, as the Buddhists say, or karma or Yin and Yang? Is this just some innate power or energy source or could there actually be someone standing in there?" I was still questioning it all.

As I thought these thoughts, a voice spoke to me from the centre of the light. It was the same voice that I had heard earlier in the evening [guiding his prayer]. The voice said, "Ian, do you wish to return? . . ." I replied, "If I am out of my body I don't know where I am, I wish to return." The response from this person was, "If you wish to return Ian you must see in a new light."

The moment I heard the words "see in a new light," something clicked. I remembered being given a Christmas card, which said, "Jesus is the light of the world," and "God is light and there is no darkness in him." . . . So this was God! He is light. He knew my name and he knew the secret thoughts of my heart and mind. I thought, *If this is God then he must also be able to see everything I've ever done in my life.*

I felt totally exposed and transparent before God. You can wear masks before other people but you can't wear a mask before God. I felt ashamed and undone. . . . My first thought was that this light was going to cast me back into the pit, but to my amazement a wave of pure unconditional love flowed over me. It was the last thing I expected. Instead of judgment I was being washed with pure love. Pure, unadulterated, clean, uninhibited, undeserved, love. It began to fill me up from the inside out. . . .

I proceeded to tell him about all the disgusting things I'd done under the cover of darkness. But it was as though he'd already forgiven me and the intensity of his love only increased. In fact, later God showed me that when I'd asked for forgiveness in the ambulance, it was then that he forgave me and washed my spirit clean from evil.

I found myself beginning to weep uncontrollably as the love became stronger and stronger. It was so clean and pure, no strings attached. . . . This love was healing my heart and I began to understand that there is incredible hope for humankind in this love.

I was so close I wondered if I could just step into the light that surrounded God and see him face to face. . . . As I stepped into the light it was as if I'd come inside veils of suspended shimmering lights, like suspended stars or diamonds giving off the most amazing radiance. And as I walked through the light it continued to heal the deepest part of me. . . . Standing in the centre of the light stood a man with dazzling white robes reaching down to his ankles. I could see his bare feet. The garments were not man-made fabrics but were like garments of light. As I lifted my eyes up I could see the chest of a man with his arms outstretched as if to welcome me.

I looked towards his face. It was so bright; it seemed to be about ten times brighter than the light I'd already seen. It made the sun look yellow and pale in comparison. It was so bright that I couldn't make out the features of his face. . . . I knew that I was standing in the presence of Almighty God—no one but God could look like this.[3]

The Mystical Being of Light

The highlight of many NDEs, for all who claim to have come near, is this mystical Being of Light who fills them with a love beyond imagination. Dr. Long's study asked if participants had seemed to encounter a mystical being or presence. NDErs responded with 49.9 percent selecting "Definite being, or voice clearly of mystical or otherworldly origin."[4] But just who is this Being of Light? Not surprisingly, this question is where researchers' opinions diverge most.

Osis and Haraldsson, two researchers, studied five hundred Americans and five hundred Indians to determine how much religious or cultural conditioning shaped one's near-death experience. They noted, "If the patient sees a radiant man clad in white who induces in him an inexplicable experience of harmony and peace, he might interpret the apparition in various ways: as an angel, Jesus, or God; or if he is a Hindu, Krishna, Siva, or Deva."[5]

Though I have heard researchers state conclusions like this, I have never read of NDErs describing anything like Krishna (who has blue skin), Siva (who has three eyes), or the descriptions of

141

dissolution of the individual self in the impersonal Supreme Brahma (the ultimate Hindu reality). Though they may make different interpretations, what they do describe is similar across cultures.

After reading or listening to nearly a thousand NDE accounts, the characteristics of the Being of Light they report seem amazingly consistent with what the Old Testament prophets and Jesus revealed. In the next few chapters, I'm going to not only help you imagine how loving and personal God is, I want to show you why I've come to this conclusion. You may differ with my interpretation of this Being of Light, but at least consider how clearly NDE testimonies correlate with Scripture. After all, if this Being of Light is truly as wonderful as NDErs say, don't we want to know who he is and how we can know him personally?

Simran nearly died in a bus crash in Mumbai. She recalls, "A bright light appeared, having a soft man's voice that told me, 'You will leave everything behind—your loved ones, the hard-earned award, money, even your clothes. You'll come to me empty-handed.' The light also gave me an important message to follow it. . . . How can I put it in words? The feeling is way too beautiful and miraculous for someone to believe. But so true, so loving, so peaceful."[6]

An Indian woman reported to her doctor before dying, "Look, I am seeing heaven. There are beautiful gardens and flowers . . . children are playing and singing there. Many people, high houses. There I also saw God. It looks very beautiful."[7]

Osis and Haraldsson make the case that "the phenomenon within each culture often do not conform with religious afterlife beliefs. . . . Christian ideas of 'judgment,' 'salvation,' and 'redemption' were not mirrored in the visions of our American patients." We will examine why this might be and what this means in a later chapter, but Osis and Haraldsson also note:

Several basic Hindu ideas of the afterlife were never portrayed in the visions of the Indian patients. The various Vedic "loci" of an afterlife—Hindu Heaven—were never mentioned. Nor were reincarnation and dissolution in Brahma, the formless aspect of God which is the goal of Indian spiritual striving. The concept of Karma—accumulation of merits and demerits—may have been vaguely suggested by reports of a "white robed man with a book of accounts."[8]

The researchers note that none of the Indians mention the ultimate Hindu goal of *moksha*, the self finally absorbed into the impersonal ultimate form of God, yet Indians did sometimes describe this very loving, personal, white-robed Being of Light with a beard and a book of accounts. "The [Indian] patient seemed to die. After some time, he regained consciousness. He then told us that he was taken away by messengers in white clothing, and brought up to a beautiful place. There he saw a man in white, with an account book."[9] Another Indian "saw a 'bearded man' standing at the opening to a long, golden corridor."[10] An Indian doctor reported that his patient "saw a beautiful scene, lovely flowers. In there he saw a man dressed in white sitting with an open book."[11]

Osis and Haraldsson mention, "[In Indian NDEs] the man with the 'book of accounts' is always pictured as a benign ruler. An aura of sacredness rests upon him regardless of whether he is called 'the man in a white robe' or 'God.'"[12] Steve Miller studied Western versus non-Western NDE accounts and discovered the same: "An Indian reported a person with a beard, looking through books to see if the NDEr was to remain or to be sent back. . . ." Miller says, "I found all the common western elements in the nonwestern experience."[13]

Dr. Bruce Greyson, studying cross-cultural NDEs, concludes, "Even the cross-cultural differences observed suggest that it is not the core experience that differs but the ways in which people interpret what they have experienced."[14] What these researchers do not seem to realize is their subjects might *not* be describing their own cultural ideas of Heaven, but they *are* describing the Heaven of the biblical prophets. The Old Testament prophet Daniel, living in Babylon in the sixth century BCE, saw this vision of Heaven:

> As I kept looking, thrones were set up and the One Who has lived forever took His seat. His clothing was as white as snow and the hair of His head was like pure wool. His throne and its wheels were a burning fire [describing brilliant light]. . . . The Judge was seated, and The Books were opened . . . [and I] saw One like a Son of Man coming with the clouds of heaven. He came to the One Who has lived forever, and was brought before Him. And He was given power and shining-greatness, and was made King, so that all the people of every nation and language would serve Him. His rule lasts forever. It will never pass away. (Daniel 7:9–10, 13–14 NLV)

Daniel sees God surrounded by brilliant light, books are opened, and one like a Son of Man, the Jewish Messiah, is given supreme authority and rule over all nations. (The Dead Sea Scrolls attest that Daniel was written before Jesus's birth.)

David also mentions the books of Heaven, saying, "Your eyes saw my unformed body; all the days ordained for me were *written in your book* before one of them came to be" (Psalm 139:16, italics mine). When you look at the characteristics of the God described by the ancient Jewish prophets, it's amazing how NDErs seem to be experiencing either the same wonderful God, or an amazingly good counterfeit. Let's imagine for a moment what it will be like to be with the One who created you for himself.

God *Is* Love

Have you ever wondered how there could be so many love songs? I've come to believe that every form of love we experience on earth, no matter how intense, is merely a drop in the ocean of love God created you and me to experience. We can't get enough of love because ours always falls short of what we crave. The Old Testament prophets tell us that God created all people for a unique, loving relationship with him, and even though humanity turns away from God to taste the bitter fruit of the knowledge of evil, God's love has pursued us relentlessly.

Around 4,000 years ago, 1,500 years before most of today's world religions originated, God chose Abraham and Sarah to create a special nation to preserve his promises and foretell his coming as Messiah for all nations. God's love has always extended to all the nations—in contrast, most deities are local, or for a few special people. Yahweh (God) told Abraham, "I will make you into a great nation, and I will bless you. . . . And *all peoples on earth* will be blessed through you" (Genesis 12:2–3, italics mine). Over five hundred times in the Old Testament, God speaks of the nations. Yahweh has always acted out of love for all people of all nations.

Khalida wandered the streets of Bethlehem as a child, orphaned by a missile that took the lives of her whole family. Sold into slavery as a child, she traveled the Arab world with a Bedouin tribe and was married off to a very abusive Muslim man. Her husband eventually beat her and left her for dead, taking her only daughter with him. She then married a man who took her to the United States. When her life was threatened by her second husband's beatings, she managed to flee with her two children. She was homeless and penniless. A woman saw Khalida's plight and offered her a job and a home for her and her children, and she told Khalida of the love of God found through Jesus.

Khalida wanted the love this woman had and asked Jesus to show her if he was God. Khalida claims she had a vision of Heaven much like the prophet Isaiah or Daniel. Now, I don't believe everyone who claims to have visions (I've never had one), but I've heard multiple accounts like Khalida's among

Muslims. Reporting such a vision can bring severe persecution. She claimed to experience this vision of Heaven, which shows God's persistent love for all people, and is consistent with the Bible and NDE descriptions:

A person was standing in front of me, but different from any person I'd ever known. I heard His voice—it was the same voice I heard years before. Though I didn't know who it was then [while still in Palestine], He said over and over to me when my Muslim husband was beating me and threatening my life, "Leave the darkness for the light."

[Now] He said in Arabic, "I am the truth, the life, and the way, and no one comes to the Father except by Me." His voice was like rushing waters, powerful and soothing at the same time. The minute He said, "I am the truth," I knew immediately it was Jesus. He didn't say, "I am Jesus," but every fiber of my being knew who He was. I had never read the Bible before, but somehow I knew what Jesus was saying to me was in the Bible. I was so consumed by His presence that I dropped to my knees and looked up at Him. He is so glorious, so beautiful. All light inside of Light.

I said, "Lord! You are Lord!" He said, "Yes, I am Jesus, the One you denied. The One you said is not the Son of God. I came to save you, to make you a happy person. You don't have to do anything, just know that I love you."

I said, "That's it?"

He said, "Yes, believe in Me."

It was like I went to school and studied everything in one day. All of a sudden Jesus made sense to me. . . . He got so close that there was too much light to even see the color of His eyes. It was not like looking at any human being. Somehow with His being and His voice came light. A huge light. An overwhelming light. He was talking to me, but at the same time I was seeing Heaven right before my eyes. . . . He didn't preach to me; He was just talking to me like another person, but with a beautiful and strong voice. It was loving, and sweet like honey.[15]

Around 1,500 years before Jesus was born, God appeared to Moses in the form of a brilliant light, a burning bush that didn't consume it, and a voice spoke to Moses from the flaming light to tell him to go rescue the Jewish people from Egyptian slavery. When Moses led them out, God told them what matters most to him. It became the central tenet of the Jewish faith: "Hear, O Israel: The LORD our God, the LORD is one. Love the LORD your God with all your heart and with all your soul and with all your strength" (Deuteronomy 6:4–5).

Love matters most to God because he is love at the core of his being. "He passed in front of Moses, proclaiming, 'The LORD, the LORD, the compassionate and gracious God, slow to anger, abounding in love and faithfulness, maintaining love to thousands, and forgiving wickedness, rebellion and sin. Yet he does not leave the guilty unpunished'" (Exodus 34:6–7). After being in God's glorious light for forty days, "When Moses came down from Mount Sinai with the [Ten Commandments] . . . his face was radiant because he had spoken with the LORD" (Exodus 34:29). God is light and love. God is also just, but his justice is his loving response to evil when it hurts the people he loves.

God is love. It's what the prophets revealed. It's what NDErs experience. Just think: love is intrinsic to God, so everything in the created universe exists because of perfect love, including us. As my friend Michael Warden explains, "Like an eagle is made to soar the heights, we were made for God's love. Love is our native atmosphere. Yet in a fallen world, we have been separated from love. What we experience as 'normal life' is anything but. We are eagles chained to the earth, longing to soar." That's why NDErs never want to leave the love of God once they experience it.

One man from Moody's study made it emphatically clear in no uncertain terms that he *never* wanted to leave the Being's presence. Even a mother of young children whom she loved more than anything expressed, with difficulty, that being in the presence of this light was so wonderful, "I really didn't want to come back. But . . . I knew that I had a duty to my family. So I decided to try to come back."[16]

God must be our first love because only then can he teach us how to love others as he loves us. God tells Moses and the Israelites twenty times that loving God must be top priority. Then he can lead them to truly love others. "Do not seek revenge or bear a grudge . . . but love your neighbor as yourself. I am the LORD" (Leviticus 19:18 NLT). The first four of the Ten Commandments were about loving God. He wants to be our first priority, and he's jealous for our love, not for his sake, but for ours—all other things we put first in our lives make bad gods that will let us down. We were made for God's love first. His love rightly orders all other loves.

Eben Alexander says the central message he received could be summed up, *"You are loved."* Or, to simplify even further: love. Dr. Alexander's experience taught him "none of us are ever unloved. Each and every one of us is deeply known and cared for by a Creator who cherishes us beyond any ability we have to comprehend. That knowledge must no longer remain a secret."[17]

It's the message God made central throughout the ages for all who read the Scriptures. It hasn't been a secret, but it has been largely ignored. Imagine a love so great, no earthly love even compares—and better still, all earthly loves find new depth. Even though NDErs may call God by other names, the God they're describing matches the God of the Bible. He wants us to know how much he loves us, and he wants to know, "Do you love me?"

Moody interviewed a patient who was asked that very question. The person described floating through a screen door, as if it didn't even exist, and then up into an illuminating, crystal clear light that radiated an intense brightness, yet was not painful or harmful. "I didn't actually see a person in this light," the patient explained, "and yet it has a special identity, it definitely does. It is a light of perfect understanding and perfect love. The thought came to my mind, 'Lovest thou me?'" The patient interpreted the words from the light not necessarily as a question, but as a gentle directive to let his love for God motivate him to return to earthly life and complete what had been begun there.[18]

God Is Personal

By Moody's accounts, every single person who saw this light expressed seemingly identical sentiments: it was a definite being, and one that radiated a light indescribable. They each described the being as personal, possessing a unique personality. Dr. Moody summarizes how "the love and the warmth which emanate from this being to the dying person are utterly beyond words, and he feels completely surrounded by it and taken up in it, completely at ease and accepted in the presence of this being."[19]

Researcher Steve Miller also reports NDErs who confirm the personal, loving, all-knowing nature of this Being:

> I went through this dark, black vacuum at super speed. You could compare it to a tunnel. . . . I saw a bright light, and on my way there I heard beautiful music and I saw colors I'd never seen before. [The light] was of a kind that I'd never seen before and that differs from any other kind such as sunlight. It was white and extremely bright, and yet you could easily look at it. It's the pinnacle of everything there is. Of energy, of love especially, of warmth, of beauty. I was immersed in a feeling of total love.
> . . . From the moment the light spoke to me, I felt really good—secure and loved. The love which came from it is just unimaginable, indescribable. It was a fun person to be with! And it had a sense of humor, too—definitely! I never wanted to leave the presence of this being.
> My whole life so far appeared to be placed before me in a kind of panoramic, three-dimensional review, and each event

seemed to be accompanied by an awareness of good and evil or by an insight into its cause and effect. Throughout, I not only saw everything from my own point of view, but also I knew the thoughts of everybody who'd been involved in these events. . . . And throughout, the review stressed the importance of love.[20]

The prophets write, "The LORD searches every heart and understands every desire and every thought. If you seek him, he will be found by you" (1 Chronicles 28:9). Every single person who encounters this Being of Light, no matter what they call him, knows that he's a person who knows every secret about them and yet loves them more than they ever imagined.

They describe the mystery of the Jewish God, Yahweh, who as Moses said is only one God—yet as Daniel and Isaiah allude, exists in loving relationship as Almighty Father, one like a Son of Man (or Messiah), and his Holy Spirit. The Jewish prophet Isaiah tells how personal and intimate this triune God claims to be with us: "[Yahweh] said, 'Surely they are my people, children who will be true to me'; and so he became their Savior. In all their distress he too was distressed, and *the angel of his presence* saved them. In his love and mercy he redeemed them; he lifted them up and carried them all the days of old. Yet they rebelled and grieved *his Holy Spirit*" (Isaiah 63:8–10, italics mine).

Yahweh reveals himself as a Father who longs for loving children, the Angel of his Presence who is their Savior, and the Holy Spirit who can feel grief. God is emotionally involved with us because we were created in his image—and he is personal. Though God is infinite, omniscient, and powerful beyond our comprehension, he's also personally involved with every person he created.

Eben Alexander speaks of the presence of God during his NDE as vast, infinite, completely other and yet extremely personal, and mediated through an orb of brilliant light. Though I don't agree with all he says, he still seems to describe what others recognize as the Father, which he calls "Om," and Jesus, the "Orb," or mediator. Dr. Alexander recalls seeing "a light that seemed to come from a brilliant orb that I now sensed near me. The orb was a kind of 'interpreter' between me and this vast presence [of God] surrounding me."[21]

Dr. Alexander remembers the voice of the Being as warm and oddly personal, although not speaking in the form of earthly language as we know it. The Being possessed human qualities, though in infinitely greater measure. "It knew me deeply and overflowed with qualities that . . . I've always associated with human beings, and human beings alone: warmth, compassion, pathos . . . even irony and humor."[22]

Dr. Alexander seems to describe the God who revealed himself as Eternal Father and the Son (Orb/man of light) who "interprets" God by becoming human. "There is one God and one mediator between God and mankind, the man Christ Jesus" (1 Timothy 2:5). The Old Testament prophets revealed this mystery of one God who is love—but whom did God love before his creation? The person of the Father loves the Son loves the Spirit loves the Father. God is love because God is personal.

With a Voice like Many Waters

As a person, God has a voice unlike any other. Khalida recognized it as a voice inside her telling her to "leave the darkness for the light," but then in God's presence she heard a "voice like *mighty rushing waters*, powerful and soothing at the same time."[23] It's amazing how many people describe the voice of God with the same words as the prophets, even though they didn't know the Scriptures. At times his voice is soft and loving yet authoritative; other times it's unmistakably powerful.

The prophet Ezekiel said, "I saw the glory of the God of Israel coming from the east. His *voice was like the roar of rushing waters*, and the land was radiant with his glory" (Ezekiel 43:2, italics mine). The Jewish prophet Daniel saw the Angel of God's Presence and described a man of brilliant light with a similar voice: "I looked up and there before me was a man. . . . His face like lightning, his eyes like flaming torches, his arms and legs like the gleam of burnished bronze, and his *voice like the sound of a multitude*" (Daniel 10:5–6, italics mine). These Old Testament prophets describe this same Being of Light as a man with an unmistakable voice, just as NDErs do.

One NDEr recalls, "When he spoke, it was like somebody had put it on a *tremendous loudspeaker* and it just bounced off the clouds: 'Take her back.' . . . The light was so beautiful! It was so bright all around the Lord, and his voice was so *commanding and yet gentle*."[24]

"I heard a commanding voice that came from everywhere all at once. I even heard it inside of me. It sounded like a thunderous clap of lightening [*sic*], a *great wind and white water rapids* all rolled together, saying, 'It's not your time!'"[25]

Steve Sjogren described how "the voice of God . . . was like the *voice of a hundred friends* talking in harmonious unison. . . . I was alarmed—until I listened to what he had to say. 'Don't be afraid,' God assured me. 'You have nothing to fear. It's all going to be okay.'"[26]

All over the globe, those who experience God hear the same voice. Samaa from the Middle East heard this: "'Welcome home, Samaa,' He said in a voice sweet and gentle, yet also powerful, *like the sound of many waters*. He opened His arms to me. His beautiful eyes were like blazing fires of consuming love that overwhelmed me."[27]

Imagine one day . . . seeing this Being of Light with arms open wide speaking in the same voice of loving power, "Welcome home," and it's *your* name he says, and in that moment you realize, *This is the one relationship I've craved all my life!* Let's imagine what relating to God might be like in Heaven.

11

God Is Relational

JACK WOKE UP TUESDAY MORNING in severe pain. After three long weeks in the hospital doing strenuous lung exercises, the lung specialist had cleared him for a delicate spinal surgery. Jack's lung disease complicated matters for the anesthesiologist, but the surgery would now happen the following Friday. As Jack rolled over in bed to ease the pain, a brilliant light appeared in the room and a serene peace came over him. A hand reached out of the light and a voice said, "Come with me. I want to show you something."

Jack reached out and took hold of the hand. Immediately, he experienced the feeling of being pulled away from his body and moving up toward the ceiling above. As he looked back, he could see his body still lying there on the bed. "We started moving through the ceiling and the wall of the hospital room . . . down to a lower floor in the hospital. We had no difficulty in passing through doors or walls," Jack recalled.

Jack then discovered they had journeyed to the hospital recovery room, the location of which he had not known before.

They were hovering above everything up near the ceiling corner. He recalled seeing medical personnel in green uniforms. He also took note of the placement of the hospital beds in the room, and explained how this loving being told him which bed he was going to occupy in the recovery room.

Jack reports he was also told he would know nothing after the operation, and that he would never awaken again or be aware of anything until God would come back to get him after some time. Jack described hearing the voice as unspoken yet completely understandable. It was clear to Jack that God was showing him all this so he would not be afraid, especially since Jack had to go through several other things before his death. Jack shared he had a strong sense that God would be overseeing the whole process and would definitely be there with him at the end.

"We were in such close communion that nothing whatsoever could've bothered me. Again, it was just a peacefulness, calmness, and a serenity that have never been found anywhere else." After their brief journey together through the hospital, the being took him back to his room and in an instant, Jack was back in his body.

When Jack got up the next morning, knowing he would not survive the surgery, he was not at all afraid. Even though he knew he was going to die, "there was no regret, no fear. There was no thought, 'what can I do to keep this from happening?' I was ready."

The night before the surgery, Jack decided to write two letters and hide them—one for his wife and one for his nephew, whom he had legally adopted as his own son. He and his wife had been having trouble with their son, and he wanted to express his feelings to them both. About two pages into his letter to his wife, the floodgates opened, and he began to sob. As he cried uncontrollably, Jack again felt God's presence enter the room.

At first, he wondered if he had cried so loudly that perhaps one of the nurses had come into the room to check on him, but he had not heard the door open or close. The familiar presence was unmistakable to him, even though he did not see a light. Even so, communication with this divine presence just came to him in his thoughts saying, "Jack, why are you crying? I thought you would be pleased to be with me." Jack thought, "Yes, I am. I want to go very much."

Jack told God that he was worried about his nephew and the difficulty his wife would face raising him alone. Jack tried to put his feelings into words, explaining that if he might have been around to assist his wife, he could have helped his nephew get through his setbacks and struggles. God's voice responded, "Since you're asking for someone else, and thinking of others, not Jack, I will grant you what you want. You will live until you see your nephew become a man."

Jack miraculously survived the operation and when he came to, he told Dr. Coleman exactly where he was, including the specific location of his bed as being the first one on the right, just inside the door from the hall. Though the doctor called his recovery miraculous, he thought Jack's excitement of knowing which bed he was in was the anesthesia talking. Because of this, Jack did not share his story with anyone other than his wife, his brother, and his minister. Years later, he told Dr. Moody.[1]

God's Relational Heart

One reason some NDE researchers claim the Being of Light cannot be the God of the Old Testament has to do with a misunderstanding: they believe the Old Testament God is a judging, condemning, and punishing God while the God of the New Testament is loving, forgiving, and compassionate. Neither generalization fits. Let me show you how the relational God NDErs encounter matches the God of the Bible.

The central theme of the Bible is that God wants a relationship of love with you and every person created. Loving relationship motivates God. But love requires several things—freedom, risk, and choice. That means God chose to subject himself to the same emotional relational roller-coaster ride love subjects every person to—the possibility of rejection and heartbreak.

If you listen to the heart of God conveyed through the Old Testament prophets, God uses every relational metaphor we can imagine so that we might understand how God feels about us. God pours out his heart to Jeremiah the prophet when the people he loves keep rejecting him to love and worship other things.

> "I have loved you with an everlasting love.
>   I have drawn you with unfailing kindness. . . .
> Is not Ephraim my dear son,
>   the child in whom I delight?
> Though I often speak against him,
>   I still remember him.
> Therefore my heart yearns for him;
>   I have great compassion for him,"
>   declares the LORD. (Jeremiah 31:3, 20)

> I thought to myself,
>   "I would love to treat you as my own children!"
> I wanted nothing more than to give you this beautiful
>   land—
>   the finest possession in the world.
> I looked forward to your calling me "Father,"
>   and I wanted you never to turn from me.
> But you have been unfaithful to me. (Jeremiah 3:19–20
>   NLT)

God loves us like a father loves a wayward child. Even though we rebel and run away, or break his heart, his Father's heart yearns to show compassion, forgive, and take us back. But God uses even stronger relational imagery. "As a young man marries a young woman, so will your Builder marry you; as a bridegroom rejoices over his bride, so will your God rejoice over you" (Isaiah 62:5).

God chooses our most intimate relationship to liken what he wants with us. As hard as it is for us to fathom, God likens himself to a love-struck groom who sings over his bride. "The LORD your God is with you, the Mighty Warrior who saves. He will take great delight in you; in his love he will no longer rebuke you, but will rejoice over you with singing" (Zephaniah 3:17).

Though only a few NDErs mentioned it, in Heaven Dean heard "God the Father singing back to each and every being giving Him praise before the Throne. He was singing an individual love song to each of His creations. The song was alive and seemed to go inside of the beings it was meant for. . . . That is what was going on in Heaven. Father God was expressing His love for each being and they were expressing their love for Him."[2]

William Smith experienced something similar: "There is a difference in the two identifiable characters who are one and the same God, one comes out of the other. The spiritual person who unites each one, God's Spirit, moves from the Son to the Father. There is no separation between them. . . . There's God Himself—single, only one. He reveals himself in time through the incarnation [Jesus]. Jesus is all that comes from the Father. . . . I became part of his love. He serenaded me and sang me to his throne."[3]

Imagine if that's how God feels about you! All the love songs on earth are a reflection of the image of the One who loves you more. When you're with him, his love overwhelms all loves—it's so amazing, you don't want to be anywhere else. That's the overwhelmingly consistent response of NDErs. That puts in perspective the next relational image God gives through the prophets. "Imagine," God says, "how you would feel if the one you loved most, your own spouse, committed adultery—that's how I feel when those I love are unfaithful to me."

Spiritual Adultery

Listen to the emotion in this passage that emanates from the heart of God—a wounded lover who just found out all he hoped for has been dashed to pieces on the shoals of adultery:

> My faithless people,
>   come home to me again,
> for I am merciful.
>   I will not be angry with you forever.
> Only acknowledge your guilt.
>   Admit that you rebelled against the LORD your God
> and committed adultery against him
>   by worshiping idols under every green tree.
> Confess that you refused to listen to my voice. . . .
> You have been unfaithful to me, you people of Israel!
>   You have been like a faithless wife who leaves her
>   husband. (Jeremiah 3:12–13, 20 NLT)

Can you hear the emotion in the heart of God? As God reveals to the Old Testament prophets, when we forsake our Creator to go our own way against his will, and when we love other things more than God, it breaks his heart (an idol is anything we put first before God). All the warnings of punishment and judgment for sin and rebellion in the Old Testament remind us that our actions have cause-and-effect consequences. When we turn from our Creator, we hurt God, and we hurt each other— always—even if we don't see it yet.

Lisa said, "The being of light knew everything about me. It knew all I had ever thought, said, or done, and it showed me my whole life in a flash . . . all the cause-and-effect relations in my life, all that was good or negative, all of the effects my life on earth had had on others."[4]

Some Christians will probably wonder, *How could God possibly reveal himself to those who don't believe in him?* But they forget God's heart longs for *every person* to come home, from every nation, every language; they were all created by him and for him. And don't forget, there's no measure that he won't take to get them back. He took extreme measures to rescue evil Nineveh. He revealed himself in a blinding light to Saul who was headed to arrest and murder God's people. And the Old Testament prophets foretold the ultimate extreme measure God would take to get us back: he would enter our suffering to restore us relationally.

The Moral Law

NDErs commonly experience two things in the presence of this Being of Light: an overwhelming love and compassion, and a life review where this God of light emphasizes the impact of their actions on others. Steve Miller studied non-Western, non-Christian NDEs and said, "In my nonwestern sample, I saw no significant difference in life reviews compared to western life reviews."[5] Suresh from India recalls the relational nature of her NDE: "I realized that god was love, light and motion and to be able to receive him in the heart one had to cleanse it and mind by apologizing to all people I was associated with and with whom I had differences, arguments or quarrels or all those whom I might have knowingly or unknowingly caused pain. The kind of love that I experienced there cannot be expressed in words."[6]

People commonly say, "All religions basically teach the same things." There's some truth to this. It's actually uncanny how similar the moral laws are across cultures—in ancient China, Babylon, Egypt, Greece, and Rome; across Anglo-Saxon and

American Indian culture; through Buddhist, Hindu, Christian, and Muslim sacred writings—all basically agree in this area. Former Oxford scholar C. S. Lewis gives evidence of this common moral law summarized below:

1. Don't do harm to another human by what you do or say (the Golden Rule).
2. Honor your father and mother.
3. Be kind toward brothers and sisters, children, and the elderly.
4. Do not have sex with another person's spouse.
5. Be honest in all your dealings (don't steal).
6. Do not lie.
7. Care for those weaker or less fortunate.
8. Dying to self is the path to life.[7]

In just about every culture and world religion since the beginning of recorded history, we see this common moral law. "They demonstrate that God's law is written in their hearts" (Romans 2:15 NLT). So we've always known basic right and wrong in every culture for all time, but what does that teach us? How well have we *kept* the moral law? The history of humanity is a pretty peaceful, loving one—right? We don't fight, divide, divorce, kill, destroy, or talk badly about others; we don't harm one another, cheat one another, deceive one another—do we? Watch the news!

No, the history of humanity indicates we don't honor parents, we fail to be kind to siblings or the elderly, we're sexually unfaithful, dishonest, untruthful, greedy, and few of us involve ourselves with those less fortunate because we get self-consumed with our own will and ways. Instead of seeking God's will and ways, we seek first that "my will be done, on earth, and in Heaven." And when God doesn't do as we expect, we get angry and turn from him.

So what do these common truths of the world's religions teach us? We're all royal screw-ups! The world's a mess. We have a real serious problem, humanly speaking. We all know the right things to do; we always have in every culture for all times. And yet, the history of humanity is that we fall short no matter how hard we try! People have a problem—Christians, Jews, Buddhists, Muslims, atheists, you, me—and it's affecting all of us. We all desperately need God's help. The question is, what will God do with our moral failures? Condemn us? Punish us?

Forgive Us

One of the greatest indications that the God NDErs describe is the God of the Jewish/Christian Scriptures is how they depict their life review in his presence. Despite vividly seeing all their deeds, good and evil, and all the relational ripple effects of both, they do not experience a Being who desires to condemn. They experience a compassion coming from this Being of Light. Yet if you search the gods of the world's religions, how many claim to uphold both justice and righteousness, and record our every thought and deed, and still hold out forgiveness and compassion because of a desire for loving relationship?

A woman in Dr. Long's study experienced all this:

Everything I ever thought, did, said, hated, helped, did not help, should have helped was shown in front of me, the crowd of hundreds, and everyone like [in] a movie. How mean I'd been to people, how I could have helped them, how mean I was (unintentionally also) to animals! Yes! Even the animals had had feelings. It was horrible. I fell on my face in shame. I saw how my acting, or not acting, rippled in effect towards other people and their lives. It wasn't until then that I understood how each little decision or choice affects the world. The sense of letting my Savior down was too real. Strangely, even during this horror,

161

I felt a compassion, an acceptance of my limitations by Jesus and the crowd of others.[8]

The fact that people experience compassion instead of judgment makes some NDE researchers conclude this can't be the God of the Bible, yet maybe they do not really understand what the Bible teaches. When a woman caught in adultery was brought to Jesus by the religious leaders who wanted to condemn her and stone her to death, Jesus said to them, "Let any one of you who is without sin be the first to throw a stone at her." They all dropped their rocks and left. "Has no one condemned you?" Jesus asked her. "No one, sir," she said. "Then neither do I condemn you," Jesus declared. "Go now and leave your life of sin" (John 8:2–11).

God loves us and wants to forgive and take back all humanity, but in order to set us free from all condemnation and forgive us all our debts, someone has to pay to make things right. Jesus told Nicodemus, a Pharisee, that's what he came to do: "For God so loved the world that he gave his one and only Son, that whoever believes in him shall not perish but have eternal life. For God did not send his Son into the world to condemn the world, but to save the world through him" (John 3:16–17). That would explain why NDErs experience compassion rather than condemnation. But why was Jesus's death necessary? If God wants to forgive us and restore relationship, why doesn't he just forgive? It's a reasonable question.

Just Forgive?

Imagine if you let me borrow your brand-new $85,000 sports car and asked me not to drive fast on winding roads. I knew I could handle it, so I disobeyed your will and ended up crashing and destroying your car. I'd owe you $85,000 to make things right. But what if I said to you, "Hey, why don't you *just forgive* me?"

If you *just* forgive me the $85,000 I owe to replace your car, *you are going to have to pay* for righteousness to be done—you'll have to pay for a new car to set things right—as they were before I sinned against you.

God told his people through Isaiah, "Surely the arm of the LORD is not too short to save, nor his ear too dull to hear. But your iniquities [wrongs] have separated you from your God" (Isaiah 59:1–2). For justice to be done, someone has to pay to set things right. Either we pay the consequences of rebellion against our Creator—which is separation from the Source of all light, life, and love—or we recognize our need, ask his forgiveness, and he pays it for us through Christ.

Old Testament prophets foretold that God would reveal "his Arm," his own Son, to show us what he's like in a human form we could relate to. And this Messiah would pay our debts for us, so that all willing people could come home to God (Isaiah 53). God removed every barrier between you and himself. You don't have to prove you can be good enough—you can't. You can't perfectly follow the eightfold path of Buddhism, the five pillars of Islam, the Ten Commandments, or even your own moral conscience. Ever say, "I'll never . . . ," but you did? We can't be who God intended without relationship with God—so God paid the ultimate human price to forgive us and restore relationship with every willing person.

God will not force us to seek him, admit we need his forgiveness, or turn back to him. He doesn't want forced slaves; he wants free-willed, loving children who choose to love God. When the cold steel of a terrorist's bomb ripped through Samaa during a church service in a Middle-Eastern country, she only recalls the relational warmth of this God who gives us freedom to choose how we will love him back:

> Thrown ten feet into the air and smashed against the opposite wall, I called out to Jesus silently in my agony: "Jesus, help me!"

And then, in that instant, my spirit left my body and I died. . . . When I opened my eyes I saw brilliant white light illuminating Jesus, the Son of Man, the Son of God. His face was brighter than the sun, and He was so glorious. . . . It was as if Jesus could see through me, reading all the thoughts of my heart. My whole body was shaking. I felt so unworthy to be in His presence. . . . He radiated an amazing love that contained deep acceptance. I felt neither condemnation nor shame. . . .

"Welcome home, Samaa," He said in a voice sweet and gentle, yet also powerful, like the sound of many waters. He opened His arms to me. His beautiful eyes were like blazing fires of consuming love that overwhelmed me. Like a magnet, His love drew me in. . . .

"Do you want to go back or stay here in heaven?" Jesus asked. Then He showed me my life. As if seeing snapshots of a movie, I watched myself growing up. The nineteen years I'd lived passed in front of my eyes. After seeing the choices I had made, I realized I had been living for my own agenda and repented.

Oh, Lord Jesus, I'm so sorry. Please forgive me. All my life I've been living for myself—my ways, my dreams, my desires, my plans. But it's not about me. It's all about You. . . . He wanted me to go back for my family for their salvation, but also for the salvation of His family, which is multitudes! God is all about family, from Genesis to Revelation. As Revelation 5:9 (NIV) says: "You are worthy to take the scroll and to open its seals, because you were slain, and with your blood you purchased for God persons from every tribe and language and people and nation." . . . He is also a Gentleman. He never forced me but gave me the freedom to choose. As I told Him my choice—that I wanted to go back to earth and be a witness for Him—I was motivated by love, not a sense of duty. . . .

"All right, see you soon," He said.

Immediately a fresh wave of love washed over me. It felt so easy to talk to Him, to communicate, like a child speaking to her Father.[9]

The God of Light in India

God wants all people to know him, but he doesn't force us. He tells us if we seek him with all our hearts, we will find him. NDErs concur that this Being of Light indeed knows every thought of the heart. "The LORD searches every heart and understands every desire and every thought. If you seek him, he will be found by you; but if you forsake him, he will reject you forever" (1 Chronicles 28:9).

As I write this, my friend Jaya is visiting me from southeast India. Jaya's grandfather was the Hindu guru for his village. Every year during a special festival, they would set out food in their house for the gods and then leave. When they came back, if the gods had eaten the food, it meant a very special blessing on the house.

At the age of twelve, Jaya decided to hide in the house to see what the gods looked like. To his surprise, rats came and ate the food. When Jaya told his celebrating grandfather that it wasn't gods who ate the food, but rats, his grandfather angrily explained that the gods came as rats to protect young Jaya. If Jaya had seen the gods, he would have died, so the gods mercifully disguised themselves as rats to protect him!

But that didn't appease Jaya's mounting skepticism. He wanted to know if the gods were real, so he broke into his grandfather's locked chest containing the ancient Vedic scriptures written on palm leaves. In the Rigveda (the oldest of the Hindu scriptures), he read about the god of light, the Creator of all, who came as the Purush Prajapati, "the Lord of all creation who became Man," and sacrificed himself to pay so that we could be emancipated from the effects of karma (payback for good and bad deeds).[10] Something inside made Jaya determined to find out about this god of light.

Jaya asked the Hindu priest, who told young Jaya that if he wanted to see the god of light, he must immerse himself in the

Krishna River every night for 100 nights and chant a special mantra 100,000 times. If he did this perfectly, the god of light would appear. The Hindu priest never thought a fourteen-year-old would do this extreme meditation course.

Undaunted by the burdensome task, Jaya spent the next three months chest-deep in the filth and human sewage floating down the river. One hundred thousand mantras later, Jaya crawled out onto the bank of the river, waiting in anticipation for the god of light to appear. No light appeared except the distant light of the rising moon. Jaya was beside himself—what had he done wrong? Discouraged, he gave up the search for two years.

At age sixteen, a holy man passing through the village came to stay with his family, and Jaya asked him about the god of light. This guru told Jaya he would take him to a Hindu high priest who lived 800 miles away, who knew the god of light. With the longing still burning within him to know the truth, Jaya decided to secretly run away with this holy man to see the high priest, willing to face the consequences when he returned.

Halfway through the weeklong train ride, Jaya discovered the holy man and his assistant had disappeared, and with them all Jaya's possessions and money. Jaya got kicked off the train for having no ticket. Too ashamed to return home, too dismayed to hope, despair set in as he decided to end his life.

Jaya laid his body across the train tracks. In one last prayer of desperation he cried, "God of light, if you are real, reveal yourself to me now for I am about to take my life." Jaya cannot explain exactly what happened as he lay on the tracks that night, except he thought he was seeing the light of the oncoming train, but brighter than any light he'd ever seen. A voice from the light said, "Jaya, I am the God you are seeking. I am the God of light. My name is Jesus."

Jaya came to faith in Jesus, the God of light, before he ever met a Christian or saw a Bible. For the last twenty-five years, he and his wife have served among the poorest of the poor in India, starting an orphanage to take in street kids, providing job skills for women who are prime targets for sex slavery, founding a hospital to provide care for those who can't afford it, and starting churches to help others in his country know the God of light.

Jesus is the God of light, of love, of forgiveness. He wants all people from all nations to turn back to him, but he won't force us. He respects our free will. As we will see in coming chapters, there's a purpose for his remaining hidden and for us choosing to seek him, love him, and follow him, even when we haven't seen him.

Mary Neal, the surgeon who died kayaking, asked Jesus why all people were not allowed the same experience she was having. Jesus repeated the same answer to Mary that he had offered Thomas: "'Because you have seen me, you have believed; blessed are those who have not seen and yet have believed' (John 20:29 NIV)."[11]

Jesus said, "If they do not listen to Moses and the Prophets [the Scriptures], they will not be convinced even if someone rises from the dead" (Luke 16:31)—or has a near-death experience! I think this largely explains why God does not just tell NDErs his identity. God looks at the heart, and he wants people who truly seek him and love him. God has put lots of evidence in the Scriptures and in history for all who are truly seeking him. If you want to see examples of the amazing, verifiable, historical evidence that convinced me, I've put a few in "Appendix A: Reasons to Believe."

His promise is that all who seek him wholeheartedly will find relationship with him, because God created you and me for a uniquely special relationship. We don't have to wait for eternity. You enter into that relationship by faith. Just like my wife and I entered marriage by faith—by pledging our lives with a simple "I do." That's all God requires: turning to him in faith, saying, "I want what Jesus did to count for me—I want your forgiveness and leadership—I want to spend eternity with you."

You don't have to wait for eternity to grow in that relationship either. God can speak straight to our thoughts right now. We can learn how to listen spiritually, and as we respond in trust, we grow to know God in a more personal way. If you don't know how to hear God's thoughts in your thoughts, read my book *Soul Revolution* and do the sixty-day experiment. You'll begin to see just how real and relational God is right now!

You can't even imagine how special you are to the Light of the World, but let's try!

12

Light of the World

"ODAY I MET GOD," whispered four-year-old Akiane to her mother.

"What is God?" asked her mother, Foreli, who was raised as an atheist in Lithuania.

"God is light—warm and good. It knows everything and talks with me. It is my parent."

The family had never talked religion, never gone to church, they didn't even own a TV, and so this shocked Foreli. "Who is your God?" questioned her mother.

"I cannot tell you."

"Me? You cannot tell your own mom?"

"The Light told me not to." Little Akiane held firm. "You won't understand."

About the same time Akiane claimed to have visits with God, she began to draw. But her drawings at age four and five surpassed high school–level art students—it seemed miraculous. After drawing "her angel," she explained, "She doesn't smile in my picture, because paper is not white enough to show how white her teeth are, and I wanted to show how she talks to me with her eyes [through her thoughts]. You see, where God takes me, He teaches me how to draw."

Akiane claimed God took her to Heaven where she saw a "house of light with walls like glass" where God lives, a place of beautiful grass, trees, plants, and fruit. She claimed God gave her fruit in Heaven: "It tastes good, better than anything you've ever tasted. The Light gives me fruit."

"What fruit?" asked her mom.

"To breathe."

"What do you mean?"

"To live . . . God says many will need to eat that. The tree will always be there on a new earth." Though only four years old, her descriptions matched what Scripture describes (see Ezekiel 1:22; Revelation 2:7; 21:11, 21), but her mother did not know this.

"I am good there, and I listen there," explained Akiane. "Everyone listens there—God is there. . . . The music there is alive." Akiane's talk of God the Father, Jesus, and the Holy Spirit combined with her supernatural gift for art eventually led her family to faith. As Akiane grew, her miraculous artistic abilities expanded from drawings to paintings, and at age seven she began composing miraculously mature, spiritual poems.

By age eight, Akiane's paintings of Jesus were gaining worldwide recognition. She claimed to see Jesus in Heaven and painted the renowned works *The Prince of Peace* and *Father Forgive Them* as a result. Every major news program in America and many around the world began to recognize her as the only binary child prodigy alive (for art and poetry). She says the purpose of her amazing art is "to draw people's attention to God, and I want my poetry to keep their attention on God."

At age nine, she painted another picture of Jesus in the cosmos. Her mother asked her about a planet. "Oh, that's the new earth. I just felt that I had to include it. I don't remember where, when, or how, but the earth will change. All I know is that everything will be different. There will be no fear, no hatred, and no hunger or pain. Only love" (see Revelation 21:4).

"Is your Jesus looking at the galaxies?" her mother questioned as they looked at the painting.

"He is talking with his Father in heaven . . . about the future of our world. I think Jesus will come back in full power very soon. In the back of him you can see the whole birth process of our new universe."

World-renowned by age ten, she began to get tough questions. One day someone asked Akiane why she had decided on Christianity rather than a different world religion. "I didn't choose Christianity," Akiane replied. "I chose Jesus Christ. I am painting and writing what God shows me. I don't know much about the religions, but I know this: God looks at our love."

At an art exhibit, one man confronted her. "I am a Buddhist. You called Jesus the 'Prince of Peace,' yet in his name so many people were massacred. How do you explain that?"

"Jesus is peace, just like calm water," ten-year-old Akiane answered, "but anyone can drop a stone into water and make it muddy."[1]

Imagine Jesus

Though this sounds somewhat like a modern-day NDE, it's not:

> I was exiled to the island of Patmos. . . . Suddenly, I heard behind me a loud voice like a trumpet blast. It said, "Write in a book everything you see. . . ." When I turned to see who was speaking to me, I saw seven gold lampstands. And standing in the middle of the lampstands was someone like the Son of Man. He was wearing a long robe with a gold sash across his chest. His head and his hair were white like wool, as white as snow. And his eyes were like flames of fire. His feet were like

polished bronze refined in a furnace, and his voice thundered like mighty ocean waves. . . . And his face was like the sun in all its brilliance.

When I saw him, I fell at his feet as if I were dead. But he laid his right hand on me and said, "Don't be afraid! I am the First and the Last. I am the living one. I died, but look—I am alive forever and ever! And I hold the keys of death and the grave." (Revelation 1:9–18 NLT)

John, one of Jesus's disciples, saw this several decades after Jesus's crucifixion. When we think about Jesus only as a meek, mild-mannered religious figure, stain-glassed into obscurity and mostly out of touch with our real lives today, we have been deceived. Jesus revealed the almighty, all-knowing, ever-present, infinite Creator of the universe in a form we could relate to because God wants relationship.

But Jesus is not only fully man; he is fully God in all his majestic brilliance today. That's what NDErs see: the majesty of God in the form of a man. And those who already know him, recognize him. Like Jesus said, "I am the good shepherd; I know my own sheep, and they know me. . . . They will listen to my voice" (John 10:14, 16 NLT). Dean recognized him immediately:

Jesus is pure light! His brightness was before me, around me, part of me, and in me. He is brighter than the noonday sun, but we can still look at Him in Heaven. . . . Jesus is more beautiful, wonderful, and glorious than I can explain. . . . Everything about Jesus is love. His love for you is so personal it seems as if it is only for you. You come to realize that He has cared for you forever and will continue to care for you forever. His love is alive. It is more than just a sense. You are becoming His love. You are His love. Jesus loves us completely. . . . It was like I was the only one He loved in all of His creation. I knew He loved others, but it seemed as if I was the only one.[2]

172

During their peek into Heaven, many NDErs report the very thing Scripture says: "The city does not need the sun or the moon to shine on it, for the glory of God gives it light, and the Lamb [Jesus] is its lamp" (Revelation 21:23). While on earth, Jesus told his followers he is the light who came to reveal the love of the unseen God:

> "Don't let your hearts be troubled. Trust in God, and trust also in me. There is more than enough room in my Father's home. If this were not so, would I have told you that I am going to prepare a place for you? When everything is ready, I will come and get you, so that you will always be with me where I am. And you know the way to where I am going."
>
> "No, we don't know, Lord," Thomas said. "We have no idea where you are going, so how can we know the way?"
>
> Jesus told him, "I am the way, the truth, and the life. No one can come to the Father except through me. If you had really known me, you would know who my Father is. From now on, you do know him and have seen him!" (John 14:1–7 NLT)

Jesus did not reveal all there is to see of God's invisible power, but the exact representation of God's character in a form we could relate to (Hebrews 1:3). The triune nature of God as only One, yet revealed as Father, Son, and Spirit is a mystery that seems paradoxical to our finite, three-dimensional minds. How can three persons be one God? We can only understand partially by analogy.

God of Flatland

To help us understand, I want to adapt English schoolmaster Edwin Abbott's concept of Flatland. Imagine if you created a flat two-dimensional world—Flatland.[3] The flat people of your created world could only move in two directions, forward and back or left to right: there's no up or down (no third dimension). Because you (their creator) are three-dimensional, they could not see you as you are unless you "ripped" them off their two-dimensional flat plane and changed them into three-dimensional creatures (and that would be death—death means "separation" from their 2-D world).

But you could choose to reveal a two-dimensional "slice" of yourself to them. You could put your arm through their Flatland and they'd see a round "2-D slice" of you. It's not fully you, but it's as much as these 2-D people can see and still live in Flatland. If you tried to explain that you're not actually one circular slice, but multiple slices that form one Being—that would be a paradox to them. Multiple 2-D circular slices are always separate in Flatland. They can never be one—why? Because they have no third dimension where circular slices can be "stacked up" into one unified Being.

Jesus was called "the Arm of God revealed" (Isaiah 53) by the Jewish prophets who foretold his arrival into our 3-D world. How God can be three separate persons, yet One God, is a mystery that only resolves somewhere beyond Heaven's extra dimensions. Though all analogies fall short, Jesus revealed a 3-D slice of God's Being: "If you've seen me, you've seen the Father" (or as much as you can see in this 3-D life). That's why Scripture says, "No one has ever seen God, but the one and only Son, who is himself God and is in closest relationship with the Father, has made him known" (John 1:18).

Does this Scripture reject the possibility that NDErs are seeing God? I don't believe so. Just as many Old Testament prophets had visions of God (Moses, Isaiah, Daniel), NDErs may also be seeing God by having been temporarily ripped away from this world and taken into Heaven's dimensions. As one of Dr. Pim van Lommel's Dutch NDErs stated, "I must admit that human language is woefully inadequate for conveying the full extent, the depth, and the other dimension I've seen."[4]

Old Testament Light of the World

The Jewish prophet Ezekiel appears to have seen Jesus's preincarnate glory in his vision of Heaven:

> High above on the throne was a figure like that of a man. I
> saw that from what appeared to be his waist up he looked like
> glowing metal, as if full of fire, and that from there down he
> looked like fire; and brilliant light surrounded him. Like the
> appearance of a rainbow in the clouds on a rainy day, so was
> the radiance around him.
>
> This was the appearance of the likeness of the glory of the
> LORD. When I saw it, I fell facedown, and I heard the voice of
> one speaking. (Ezekiel 1:26–28)

Ezekiel had this vision nearly six hundred years before Jesus's
birth, yet what he describes sounds like a modern NDE. Five
hundred fifty years before the birth of Jesus, Daniel was told
by an angel exactly when Jesus the Messiah would come and be
killed. "The Anointed One [Messiah] will be put to death and
will have nothing. The people of the ruler who will come will
destroy the city and the sanctuary [Jerusalem and the temple]"
(Daniel 9:26). The Romans destroyed the temple in 70 CE and
it has never been rebuilt! So this Messiah had to come and die
before 70 CE.[5]

Then Daniel had a similar vision of Messiah's preincarnate
glory: "On the twenty-fourth day of the first month, as I was
standing on the bank of the great river, the Tigris, I looked up
and there before me was a man dressed in linen, with a belt of
fine gold from Uphaz around his waist. His body was like topaz,
his face like lightning, his eyes like flaming torches, his arms
and legs like the gleam of burnished bronze, and his voice like
the sound of a multitude" (Daniel 10:4–6).

From Old Testament times to New Testament times to NDEs
today—this same Man of Light who shines brighter than the

sun has revealed the unseen God in a relatable form. The night before his crucifixion, Jesus prayed that his disciples would see him "with the glory I had with you [the Father] before the world began" (John 17:5). Saul the Pharisee (later called Paul) had Christians arrested and even killed for blasphemy—because they equated Jesus with the One true God, Yahweh. Then Saul saw Jesus in his glory:

I persecuted the followers of the Way [of Jesus], hounding some to death. . . .

> As I was on the road, approaching Damascus about noon, a very bright light from heaven suddenly shone down around me. I fell to the ground and heard a voice saying to me, "Saul, Saul, why are you persecuting me?"
>
> "Who are you, Lord?" I asked.
>
> And the voice replied, "I am Jesus the Nazarene, the one you are persecuting." . . .
>
> "What should I do, Lord?"
>
> And the Lord told me, "Get up and go into Damascus, and there you will be told everything you are to do."
>
> I was blinded by the intense light and had to be led by the hand to Damascus by my companions. A man named Ananias lived there. He was a godly man. . . . He came and stood beside me and said, "Brother Saul, regain your sight." And that very moment I could see him!
>
> Then he told me, ". . . Get up and be baptized. Have your sins washed away by calling on the name of the Lord." (Acts 22:4, 6–8, 10–14, 16 NLT)

Seeing the Light

While on earth Jesus declared, "I am the light of the world. Whoever follows me will never walk in darkness, but will have the light of life" (John 8:12). Paul encountered this same brilliant Light who declared himself as Jesus. Paul went on to write many of the books of the New Testament. But notice, just because Jesus appeared to Paul in a blinding light, it did not mean Paul was right with God. Paul still had a choice—as Ananias indicated. Paul still had to call on the name of the Lord to have his sins forgiven and be set right with God, just like the thief on the cross hanging next to Jesus did, just like Ian, Howard Storm, and other NDErs realized.

Those who have NDEs may truly be seeing Jesus himself, but that does not guarantee they will be with him in Heaven eternally. They must choose just as Paul still had to choose. After all, Jesus appeared and did the miraculous right in front of the Pharisees, "but the Pharisees and experts in religious law rejected God's plan for them" (Luke 7:30 NLT), and they had Jesus crucified. Judas was chosen by Jesus, saw his miracles, felt his love, yet he did not submit to God's leadership. Judas tried to force Jesus to do his own will (overthrow the Romans). That's probably why he betrayed Jesus. Seeking his will above God's will backfired on Judas, yet perfectly accomplished God's plan.

Love and Knowledge

Dr. Long talks about how the unified theme of thousands of NDEs is the importance of love first. Muhammad in Egypt said after his NDE, "I felt that love is the one thing that all humans must feel towards each other."[6] The second thing most NDErs take back with them is the importance of seeking knowledge. Wouldn't seeking knowledge about this God of love NDErs encounter be the most important knowledge to seek? "You will seek me and find me when you seek me with all your heart" (Jeremiah 29:13). That's what some do—like Katie.

Three-year-old Katie inhaled a cashew nut that lodged in her windpipe. She turned blue and passed out. Her grandfather, a firefighter, was unable to revive her and pronounced her dead. The ambulance arrived nearly thirty minutes after the 911 call. What Katie experienced still motivates her years later. She explains,

> When I died, I rose above my body and saw my grandfather working on my body. . . . I went toward this presence, which was within a brilliant, sun-light-bright space—not a tunnel, but an area. The presence was unbelievable peace, love, acceptance, calm, and joy. The presence enveloped me, and my joy was indescribable—as I write this I am brought back to this emotion, and it delights me still. . . . I knew without a doubt that I was a made creature, a being that owed its existence to this presence.

When little Katie revived, she couldn't stop pestering her mother with questions:

> "Who made me? What was eternity? And what was God?" [Mom] was unable to answer my questions. . . . Even now, when I recall the experience, it is more real than anything I have ever experienced in my life. I recall not only the memory but also the emotion. This still motivates me to ask questions. This experience moved me so deeply that I have dedicated my life to looking for answers. . . . I am currently working on a doctorate in theology.[7]

Who Rules?

Some seek knowledge of God after an NDE, but some don't. Some seek knowledge to re-create the experience rather than seeking God, and as a result, they go off into practices the God of the Bible warns against. Seeing is *not* believing. Seeing God does *not* ensure full trust or loving faithfulness to God, and yet that's what God wants most—to be loved and trusted.

Well-known atheist A. J. Ayer had a cardiac arrest and clinically died. "The only memory that I have . . . encompassing my death, is very vivid. I was confronted by a red light, exceedingly bright, and also very painful even when I turned away from it. I was aware that this light was responsible for the government of the universe. . . . I also had the motive of finding a way to extinguish the painful light."[8] God gives us freedom to choose him, or to rule our own lives without him. Perhaps the loving light of the world is painful to those who reject him?

It's not surprising that people who do not recognize Jesus or even believe in him would see him. Revelation tells us, "Every eye will see him—even those who pierced him" (Revelation 1:7). So it would be a very *bad assumption* to presume that people who have seen God in an NDE will automatically be with him forever. It still requires a choice. Will we give up playing God of our lives, ask his forgiveness, and invite him to come rule again?

The Bible teaches that there's room for only One ruler in Heaven. "The kingdom of the world has become the kingdom of our Lord and of his Messiah, and *he will reign* forever and ever" (Revelation 11:15, italics mine). We've all experienced what life is like with everyone trying to "rule" and play god of their own lives; it's not pretty. Imagine how different life could be if we all turned to the Light of God's love and truly let him lead us. It would be amazing! With such an incredible offer extended to each one of us by God, I sometimes struggle to understand why more people don't turn their lives over to him. I can only guess it's because they still don't see how wonderful it is (and will be!) to live with Jesus!

13

The Highlight of Heaven

IMAGINE THAT DAY, in the beauty of God's world like many
have described, experiencing a living Light that feels like
Love coming out of all that is beautiful. Imagine experiencing such an eruption of joy from your inner being that
spontaneous praise cannot be contained—like Eben Alexander
noticed among the angels, like Samaa and others felt in Jesus's
presence; they'd explode if they didn't praise him. Imagine
being with the Highlight of Heaven.

> Jesus is more beautiful, wonderful, and glorious than I can ex-
> plain. . . . How do I tell you what His face looks like? His face
> was as if it were liquid crystal glass made up of pure love, light,
> and life. . . . His face had the colors of the rainbow and colors I
> cannot describe inside it. All these colors appeared at the same
> time in His face. . . . They came out and off Him as the waves
> of the ocean coming on to the shore. I was seeing the colors
> and I was part of the colors. I was in the colors, and the colors
> were coming out of me. I was seeing Jesus, and I was a part of

Jesus. I was in Jesus, and Jesus was shining out of me. . . . All of it was life. I just wanted to praise Him forever.[1]

There's something in us that wants to associate with greatness—a famous celebrity, powerful CEO, beautiful supermodel, influential politician—it's exciting to be around them for some reason. Compared to the heavenly glory of Jesus, all of the outer glory and beauty, all of the power and prestige, all of the fortune, fame, or greatness of humanity will appear as a candle against the sun. There is no one you'll ever want to be around more than Jesus! And even more amazing—he wants to be around you!

Piercing Eyes

So many accounts of NDErs who looked into the eyes of Jesus make it clear: there seems to be something amazing about his eyes—piercing, magnetic, alluring, kind, and beautifully captivating like nothing you can imagine. Many people said they could get lost for eternity in his eyes! The writers of Scripture use similar descriptions. Daniel said "his face [was] like lightning, his eyes like flaming torches" (Daniel 10:6). John said "his eyes were like blazing fire" (Revelation 1:14). Yet not like fire as we know it—imagine eyes so magical, you can't stop staring.

Dean commented that the changing colors appeared as fire:

When I looked into Jesus' eyes, His eyes were like flames of fire with changing colors of red, orange, blue, green, yellow, and many other colors. . . . I experienced in His eyes that they are deep and full of life. I could get lost in His eyes and never want to come out. In His eyes I saw the love for every human and creation of God. At first it seemed as if His eyes had love only for me. But when I thought about someone else, I saw His love for that person. It was like He loved only that person. So

181

I thought about someone else, and the same thing happened. I saw His love for that other person.[2]

Vicki, who had been blind from birth, described Jesus's appearance and said very similar things about looking into his eyes during her NDE:

Vicki: He embraced me, and I was very close to him. And I felt his beard and his hair. They were very close to me. He actually enveloped me—that's the only word I can think of to describe it. He enveloped me with so much warmth and love and with his actual physical presence. . . .

Interviewer: Was [his hair] long or short?

Vicki: Long, it was past his shoulders.

Interviewer: Did you see his eyes?

Vicki: They were piercing eyes. It was like they permeated every part of me, but . . . not in a mean way. It was like you couldn't lie about anything, and he just looked everywhere and he could see everything. Yet I wanted to reveal everything to him.

Interviewer: Was he wearing any kind of clothing?

Vicki: Yes. And his beard had very bright lights in it. . . . It was just light coming out of the beard itself. . . . There was nothing on his feet at all. He had this kind of robe-thing on that didn't come all the way down to his feet. It was below the knees but above the ankles . . . then it had this sash around the waist part.

Interviewer: Vicki, this is not meant to be a skeptical question but I want to forewarn you that it might sound that way. Did the impression of Jesus

> that you had correspond to . . . what you were
> familiar with by reading the Bible and perhaps
> from other forms of your religious training?
>
> Vicki: I don't really know because I couldn't picture
> it. I know that sounds really stupid possibly,
> but never having seen, I have no real image of
> it. I couldn't really comprehend what the Bible
> said about it anyway.[3]

It's fascinating how many people, even blind people, describe this same Man of Light, shoulder-length hair, beard, wearing a robe of brilliant white light down to his ankles, held together by a gold sash, piercing eyes that see right into your soul, yet also draw you in with a magnetic warmth and love.

Lisa stated, "When I looked into his eyes all the secrets of the universe were revealed to me. I know how everything works because I looked into his eyes for a moment."[4] When people look into his eyes, they feel like they see and understand everything. "Then we shall see face to face. Now I know in part; then I shall know fully, even as I am fully known" (1 Corinthians 13:12). We will never know all God knows (he alone is uncreated), yet we may know all the mysteries that currently confound us. Imagine looking face-to-face into the all-knowing eyes of Love.

The Color of Love

Four-year-old Colton Burpo was in the backseat as they passed the hospital where he'd almost died earlier that year. When Todd jokingly asked if he wanted to go back, Colton blurted out that the angels sang to him there. When asked what songs they sang, he explained that they sang "Jesus Loves Me" and "Joshua Fought the Battle of Jericho," but when he asked them to sing "We Will, We Will Rock You," they wouldn't sing that song.

Then Colton grew solemn and said, "Dad, Jesus had the angels sing to me because I was so scared. They made me feel better."

Todd and Sonja were shocked to hear their son claiming to have seen Jesus when he nearly died. Todd asked where Colton met Jesus.

Colton replied nonchalantly, "I was sitting in Jesus' lap."

As Todd and Sonja probed more, they discovered that Colton claimed he'd left his body, and while watching the doctor from up in the air, he could also see Todd locked in another room shouting at God for letting his son die, and Sonja on the cell phone in the lobby. As more and more details came forth, details a four-year-old couldn't know, they started to believe Colton had actually experienced something real.

Days later as Colton played with his X-Men action figures, Todd asked him what Jesus looked like. Colton set his toys down and looked up at Todd. "He has brown hair and he has hair on his face." Colton didn't yet know the word *beard*. "And his eyes . . . Oh, Dad, his eyes are so pretty!" As he said this, Colton looked as if he was enjoying a wonderful memory. Colton said that Jesus's eyes were blue. They figured Colton was just projecting blue eyes on Jesus since Colton had blue eyes. Jesus was Jewish. Jews' eyes are usually brown!

Every time Todd or Sonja saw a portrait of Jesus, they would ask Colton if that's what Jesus looked like. For over two years and hundreds of portraits, Colton always saw something wrong with every Jesus picture. Several years later, Todd saw a CNN report on artist prodigy Akiane Kramarik (whom I wrote about in chapter 12), who reported seeing Heaven when she was four years old. She described Heaven's amazing colors and Jesus, who was "very masculine, really strong and big. And his eyes are just beautiful." It struck Todd that two four-year-olds both mentioned all the colors of Heaven and the amazing eyes of Jesus. When Colton saw Akiane's *Prince of Peace* painting that night on CNN's website, he stared at the screen and declared, "Dad, that one's right!"[5]

After reading two adult NDEs that described Jesus's blue eyes, it struck me—why would you make up seeing blue eyes on a Jewish man? Maybe Jesus's eyes *are* blue. A woman interviewed by Rita Bennett said: "I recognized [this Being] as Jesus Christ. . . . I looked into his eyes. They were piercing but loving and as clear *as blue* water. . . . When he looked at you, he looked straight through you and into you. You realized immediately that he knew all there was to know about you."[6]

Gary Wood brought it all together for me: "When He looked at me, His eyes pierced me, they went all the way through me. Just pure love! I melted in His presence. [Jesus's] eyes were deep, beautiful pools of love, and they *were blue*. I have since learned that Jews from the tribe of Judah are known to have blue eyes."[7] When I read this, I recalled Colton's comment about Akiane's painting, which we've had in a book on our coffee table for years. I'd never noticed until now, but Akiane painted Jesus with blue eyes!

Jesus was from the tribe of Judah, but does he have blue eyes? I really have no idea. Maybe his eyes can change from "a flaming fire" of many changing colors to blue, but either way, how fascinating that two adults who apparently didn't know of the other people's NDEs would make the same observation as two four-year-olds!

A Fun Person

Not only do people describe Jesus's awesome glory and palpable love, they describe him as a fun person to be around. Some people can't imagine Jesus being the most joy-filled, exciting, adventurous, fun person to be with because they've never really contemplated what the Scriptures say. You'll never find a better best friend in the universe! Jesus shocked his closest followers while on earth because as busy and important as he was, he took time to be with little children. Jesus said, "Let the little children come to me, and do not hinder them, for the kingdom of heaven belongs to such as these" (Matthew 19:14).

There's an innocence and playfulness that gets squeezed out of most adults, but Jesus will restore it to us and model it for us in Heaven. Colton says he sat on Jesus's lap, and when he came back, he kept telling his father how much Jesus loves the little children, over and over again, presumably making sure as a pastor, Todd reminded people to invest in children. My doctor friend's son said when Jesus came to get him in the hospital, he was running and playing in the fields with Jesus. If Jesus invented play, adventure, fun—why wouldn't he enjoy it with us just like we love to enjoy our own children's fun?

Richard noted how Jesus, as God, is also omnipresent. He can commune with the Father, play with little children, interact with groups of adults, and be with you and me personally in Heaven—simultaneously. "The closer I got to the throne, the more everything became transparent. Everything is absolutely transparent, with purity closest to God [as Akiane observed]. I saw Jesus walk up to the throne and disappear into the enfolding fire that surrounds the Being on the throne. Later, after leaving the throne room, I did see Jesus again from afar talking to different groups of people here and there. He seems to be everywhere. Children run to him continually, and he loves them all."[8]

One of the things that blows my mind is imagining a Being more powerful than the sun, but who feels like a close friend! Jesus said to his disciples while on earth, "I no longer call you servants, because a servant does not know his master's business. Instead, I have called you friends" (John 15:15). John, the youngest disciple, called himself "the one Jesus loved," and during the Last Supper John was kicked back, reclining on Jesus's chest like he would on an older brother (see John 13:22–25).

Researchers Osis and Haraldsson report an Indian Christian nurse who mentioned how friendly Jesus was and how comfortable she felt in his presence. "I felt myself going up. There was a beautiful garden full of flowers. I was sitting there. Suddenly I felt beaming light and Jesus Christ came to me. He sat and talked to me. Light was all around."[9]

Eben Alexander did not seem to recognize Jesus (though he seemed to make a connection in church after his NDE), but he affirmed what Scripture says. People are mistaken when they think of God as impersonal, he explains. "Yes, God is behind the numbers, the perfection of the universe. . . . [But God] is 'human' as well—even more human than you and I are." God, says Dr. Alexander, empathizes with humans much more than we can possibly imagine.[10]

Scripture explains what Dr. Alexander experienced:

> Because God's children are human beings—made of flesh and blood—the Son also became flesh and blood. . . . It was necessary for him to be made in every respect like us, his brothers and sisters, so that he could be our merciful and faithful High Priest before God. Then he could offer a sacrifice that would take away the sins of the people. Since he himself has gone through suffering and testing, he is able to help us when we are being tested. . . .
>
> [Jesus] understands our weaknesses, for he faced all of the same testings we do, yet he did not sin. So let us come boldly to the throne of our gracious God. There we will receive his mercy, and we will find grace to help us when we need it most. (Hebrews 2:14, 17–18; 4:15–16 NLT)

Talk Normally

Jesus understands you and me more than we can ever imagine. In fact, it shocks people to realize that he not only knows our languages, but even our colloquialisms. When Samaa decided to return, Jesus said colloquially in her native tongue, "Okay, see ya soon." Khalida found him speaking to her in Arabic in a conversational way:

> He didn't preach to me; He was just talking to me like another person, but with a beautiful and strong voice. . . . It was revealed to me that He is truly the Son of God and that He had died on the cross. . . . I also knew that He is a Father and I was His daughter and His chosen one. All the pain in my life He already knew about, and He was already pleased with me. I knew that all is forgiven by the blood of Jesus. . . . I was begging Him not to leave me there. "I need You," I told Him, not wanting to ever be without Him again. He said to me in Arabic, "I'm going to come back and get you."[11]

During Vicki's life review, Jesus showed her a scene where in a fit of jealousy, Vicki had ripped off the buttons and all the lace from a fancy dress of another blind classmate:

> Vicki: It was like, you know, I could feel from Jesus [his] understanding and compassion about how I felt that way, and why I did it. But, you know, it was sort of like he talked to me during that time. He says, "Yeah, that wasn't too cool."
>
> Interviewer: Really?
>
> Vicki: The thought that came into my mind that he was giving me was—"Yeah, that wasn't too cool."
>
> Interviewer: You're not kidding me?
>
> Vicki: No. That's exactly what he said.[12]

One with God

The intimacy of love God has for us is hard to comprehend. The only comparison comes by analogy—the connection we feel with a best friend, the oneness we want with a spouse, our tender love and desire for our children—and yet there's an intimacy that we seek with each other that always eludes us. We can never be as close, as intimate, or as one with another person as our souls crave. That's because the oneness we crave will only be found when we are united by God with God. God likens it to his own marriage to all of us together.

> "The time has come for the wedding feast of the Lamb,
>   and his bride has prepared herself.
> She has been given the finest of pure white linen to
>   wear."
>   For the fine linen represents the good deeds of God's
>   holy people.
>
> And the angel said to me, "Write this: Blessed are those who are invited to the wedding feast of the Lamb." (Revelation 19:7–9 NLT)

Many NDErs talk about this oneness they experience in Heaven. It's not surprising that even those who do not believe would experience this, because "in Him we live and move and have our being" right now (Acts 17:28). "The Son is the radiance of God's glory and the exact representation of his being, sustaining *all things* by his powerful word" (Hebrews 1:3, italics mine). The unity talked about in Eastern worldviews probably comes from the underlying truth that all *is* sustained by him and intended to be unified in him, yet also remain distinct.

Maybe NDErs experience Reality as it is now and is meant to be forever. That only happens through a unity with God that Jesus prayed for the night before he was crucified, and as his prayer indicates, this ultimate unity still requires a choice:

> I am praying . . . for all who will ever believe in me through their message. I pray that they will all be one, just as you and I are

one—as you are in me, Father, and I am in you. And may they be in us so that the world will believe you sent me.

. . . I am in them and you are in me. May they experience such perfect unity that the world will know that you sent me and that you love them as much as you love me. Father, I want these whom you have given me to be with me where I am. Then they can see all the glory you gave me because you loved me even before the world began! (John 17:20–24 NLT)

Listen to the ecstasy NDErs describe from tasting this unity God intended: "One of the most fascinating things I experienced was being connected to everything there at the same moment. Because of this, I came to understanding life in heaven fast. It is like the electricity that connects power to run anything that needs electric energy here. It is like our computer system that is connected to the Internet, which connects us to every computer in the world. God connects every one of His creations together."[13]

Samaa described what oneness and intimacy means: "Being with Him in heaven, though, made me one with Him in a way I could never have imagined. I thought what He thought, I dreamed what He dreamed, I felt what He felt."[14] Dr. Eby describes an intimacy that's hard to convey: "This will be hard for people on earth to understand, but I was instantly in Messiah, in Him. . . . I knew I was me, and yet I was in Messiah. . . . His love is in a different dimension than our idea of love. There is no question of his love. . . . We are in him and he is in us (see [1 John 4:12–13]). Yet we don't lose our identity."[15]

What if we were created for an intimacy, a oneness, with God and each other beyond all our finite human intimacies? Imagine it if you can. "The angel said to me, 'Write this: Blessed are those who are invited to the wedding supper of the Lamb!'" (Revelation 19:9). It will be the greatest party ever thrown in the universe when all who love God are united in him forever.

Isaiah describes that party:

> On this mountain the LORD Almighty will prepare
> a feast of rich food for all peoples,
> a banquet of aged wine—
> the best of meats and the finest of wines.
> On this mountain he will destroy
> the shroud that enfolds all peoples,
> the sheet that covers all nations;
> he will swallow up death forever.
> The Sovereign LORD will wipe away the tears
> from all faces;
> he will remove his people's disgrace from all the earth.
> (Isaiah 25:6–8)

Imagine the joy and ecstasy of being united with the Highlight of Heaven. At the age of five, Mary Olivia didn't want to leave the one she called "THE MAN" in Heaven. "[His love] was just so warm, accepting, understanding, being with someone who just knew. Knew you inside and out, and outside down. It's like the closest you could ever be to being one with someone. It was a feeling of oneness. I don't have the words!"[16] Imagine an intimacy and oneness that trumps all other relational intimacies, unites all people, and takes away all the mourning, crying, and pain of our past. It's coming.

But then, why not take it away now? Why did Mary Olivia have to come back and face the struggles of being a single mother with three children, then have to battle through a seemingly hopeless terminal illness? Why does God allow all our current mourning, crying, and pain? There *is* a reason, and that's what we will explore next!

14

No More Mourning, Crying, or Pain

BEFORE HER NDE, the concept of God as a loving Father made no sense to Crystal. Why didn't he protect her at age three when the sexual abuse began? Why did he let other men abuse her continually if he loved her? Why would he allow all the pain and suffering and chaos from her father leaving, an abusive stepfather, and a partying mother who left her with questionable company? By age nine, doubts about God's love or existence had a stranglehold, but something about Jesus sounded different to young Crystal.

The fact that Jesus was human appealed to Crystal, as well as the fact that he had died on the cross for her sins, to save her. As Crystal grew to love Jesus, she yearned to be closer to him, so at the age of nine, she told her mother she wanted to be baptized. She wanted to feel clean, and after her baptism, she recalls, "I felt like my soul had been scrubbed."

Unfortunately, the feeling didn't last because the abuse continued. Crystal had expected to be saved from the abuse that was happening in the present. As Crystal entered her teen years, all that shame, hurt, and anger felt like her identity. She blamed herself for the abuse. When her mom got back together with her abusive stepfather, she felt rejected. If her mom chose a violent ex-husband over her, she felt she must be worthless, so she decided to act that way.

At age sixteen, she got involved with a twenty-two-year-old man and started partying. She and her mom fought constantly, until finally her mom kicked her out. Crystal lived in her car for months until her dad rescued her. Later that year, she unsuccessfully tried to kill herself. She got pregnant at seventeen. She had the baby. Two years later, she got pregnant again and this time had an abortion. She felt unforgivable. She had affairs with married men and broke up marriages. She married a guy who had a worse past than she did. They had two kids, but then divorced when his constant drunkenness and drug abuse turned him abusive.

Several years later, a guy Crystal was dating came to take JP, her six-year-old son, for a ride on his motorcycle. Crystal said, "No." But when she went inside to check on another child, he took JP riding anyway. He crashed into a truck and almost killed her son. JP survived being thrown from a motorcycle and wedged into a truck's wheel well, but not without brain stem damage that required four months of inpatient therapy. As if that weren't enough, at age thirty-three, Crystal went to the hospital for pancreatitis. Due to complications, she died for nine minutes and found herself in Heaven.

"I was instantly aware of two beings in front of me and to my left, and I knew right away who they were—they were angels. But they weren't just any angels—they were my angels. I recognized them immediately." She knew her angels were there to greet her and guide her back home. As she stood in front of them, an immense love for these beings swept through her. The angels felt like the closest friends she could ever have, Crystal remembers, "as if they had been by my side for every tear I ever cried, every decision I had ever made, every day I ever felt lonely." She felt an immediate connection, a sense of deep communication with them, and a complete lack of shame, secrets, misunderstanding, or negativity. Instead, there was only a deep, beautiful, sustaining sense of knowing.

Crystal also sensed another profusion of brightness coming from a Being on her right, whom she knew without a doubt was God. She was immediately overcome with a profound, persistent desire to praise and worship him. Although she had always referred to God as a him, she understood, in that moment, that God was neither a him nor a her, but simply God. She also understood that God, Jesus, and the Holy Spirit "were all One—the One before me now," she says.

> I'd spent my life doubting His existence and disbelieving His love for me, but in that instant I knew God had always, always been there—right there with me. . . . There was another sensation—a sensation that I wasn't just aware of God; I was feeling Him. His radiance wasn't simply something I could observe; it was something that overwhelmed every sense I had. In heaven we don't have just five senses; we have a ton of senses. . . .
>
> That is what I experienced in the presence of God—a beautiful new way of receiving and sending love. I was completely infused by God's brightness and His love, and I wanted to enter into His brightness and intertwine myself completely with it. I felt a miraculous closeness to God but wanted to feel even closer.[1]

Crystal always assumed her experience of Heaven would be different. She had imagined herself asking God a barrage of questions—like why, for example, he had allowed her to be molested as a child. Or how he could allow brutality against children or starvation or cruelty against the weak. Crystal says,

I wanted to know why He didn't love me. Or why He lets bad things happen. And yet as I stood in front of Him and I faced Him and I fell to my knees, and I raised my hands, the question I called out to Him was, "Why didn't I do more for You?" Because in an instant, He revealed His true self to me which is love. I had never truly worshipped God ever in my entire life. But I fell in front of Him and I worshipped Him. And as I lay there in worship in awe of this Creator, I remember saying, "I could worship You for eternity."[2]

In Heaven, Crystal's questions had been answered before she had even asked them. In God's presence, Crystal understood God's plan as perfect. She readily admits that back on earth, she can't explain it all. Instead, she believes that we aren't meant to comprehend on earth what we will understand in Heaven. "All I can tell you," she says, "is that I know God's plan is perfect. In his radiance, it all makes perfect, perfect sense."[3]

God Suffers

God suffers with us! That single statement can profoundly change how you view suffering. Even though God has a plan that will one day make perfect sense when we "know fully, even as [we are] fully known" (1 Corinthians 13:12), that doesn't make it feel better now. Yet God is not indifferent when this cruel, evil world stabs us with pain. David said, "You keep track of all my sorrows. You have collected all my tears in your bottle. You have recorded each one in your book" (Psalm 56:8 NLT). God keeps records because all our loss and sufferings will one day be restored in Heaven.

Job went through horrific suffering, lost everything—all ten of his children were killed. He had all kinds of questions he demanded to ask of God, but when he saw God, he too had no questions. Like Crystal, Job discovered that seeing God somehow answers everything. But God said he would restore all Job lost twofold. As Steve Stroope pointed out, Job got twice the sheep and cattle and possessions but only had ten more children. In Heaven, though, he will have twenty! Nothing is lost when Heaven is your destination.[4]

When we suffer, God suffers with us. "In all their suffering he also suffered, and he personally rescued them. In his love and mercy he redeemed them" (Isaiah 63:9 NLT). Paul was persecuting Christians, yet Jesus asked him, "Why are you persecuting Me?" Jesus feels our pain. He tells us on the final day God will say, "I was hungry, and you fed me. I was thirsty, and you gave me a drink. I was a stranger, and you invited me into your home." *When?* they will ask. "When you did it to one of the least of these my brothers and sisters, you were doing it to me!" (Matthew 25:35, 40 NLT). God enters into our suffering with us in a very personal way, and even though he allows it for a time, he does so for a purpose.

I will never forget that horrible, high-pitched squeal. I was sitting on the couch as I watched from the corner of my eye. My five-year-old daughter was passing through a doorway on my wife's shoulders, grabbed the frame, and toppled backward headfirst onto tile. It was excruciating hearing her in pain as I ran and held her. At the hospital, they had to inject dye into her veins to do a CT scan. It really hurt her, and I hurt with her. But I'll never forget how it felt when they said they'd need to inject her again.

The doctors feared she might be bleeding under the skull and told us that if pressure built up it could kill our little girl. My daughter fought and screamed for them not to hurt her again with the needle in order to inject the dye. The doctor looked at me and said, "Dad, you have to hold her down." As I held her down, Ashley looked into my eyes, crying and pleading, "Daddy, don't let them hurt me. No—stop them, Daddy. Why are you doing this to me, Daddy? They're hurting me."

She was crying, I was crying, and it killed me to look into her pleading eyes knowing I *could* stop the doctors, but for her long-term safety, she had to go through this. If I didn't allow this temporary suffering, it could mean something much worse! But I suffered too.

Maybe that's how God suffers with us. He knows this is necessary for a while, because he knows of greater dangers, but it doesn't mean it's easy for him. The only way he can allow it is he already knows and simultaneously experiences the joy of the day when he will remove it forever. "And I heard a loud voice from the throne saying, 'Look! God's dwelling place is now among the people, and he will dwell with them. They will be his people, and God himself will be with them and be their God. "He will wipe every tear from their eyes. There will be no more death" or mourning or crying or pain, for the old order of things has passed away.' He who was seated on the throne said, 'I am making everything new!'" (Revelation 21:3–5). God enters our suffering to lead us through it to the other side.

Markers

Still playing with action figures on the floor, four-year-old Colton Burpo showed his dad a plastic horse. He asked his dad if he knew that Jesus had a horse. After answering a couple questions that Todd asked about his experience of Heaven, Colton made a curious comment: "Jesus has markers."

Todd asked if, by markers, he meant the kind Colton colored with.

Colton said, "Yeah, like colors. He had colors on him." When asked what color, he answered, "Red, Daddy. Jesus has red markers on him."

Todd felt overwhelmed with emotion as he suddenly understood what Colton was trying to say. He asked Colton where

Jesus's markers were. Colton stood up, pointed to both hands, then at the tops of his feet. "That's where Jesus' markers are, Daddy."[5]

Jesus came as God's Suffering Servant (Isaiah 53) to overcome evil, pain, suffering, and death one willing person at a time, and he still has the "markers" to prove it. When Jesus's disciples saw him after the resurrection, Thomas was not present. Filled with doubt, Thomas said, "I will not believe unless I stick my hands in the nail holes." The next week Jesus appeared and "he said to Thomas, 'Put your finger here; see my hands. Reach out your hand and put it into my side. Stop doubting and believe.' Thomas said to him, 'My Lord and my God!' Then Jesus told him, 'Because you have seen me, you have believed; blessed are those who have not seen and yet have believed'" (John 20:27–29). Apparently, Jesus's "markers" remain a permanent reminder that he loved us enough to enter our suffering and redeem it.

As Gary stood before Jesus during his NDE, he noticed "where nails had been driven into His hands, not His palms as some paintings depict, but into His wrists."[6] Probably where palm and wrist meet to bear the weight. It's hard to fathom the cruelty of humanity, and even more difficult to imagine how Jesus could say as they pounded the nails through his flesh and sinew, "Father, forgive them, for they do not know what they are doing" (Luke 23:34).

Richard, a Jewish man who believed in Jesus, died in an auto accident and claimed he observed light coming out of the nail holes: "[Jesus] held out His hands in front of me, and I saw the nail scars. The wounds were open, shining with a beautiful light."[7]

David foresaw what Jesus would suffer, describing a vision of Messiah's crucifixion one thousand years beforehand (before crucifixion was even invented). "All my bones are out of joint. My heart has turned to wax; it has melted within me. . . . You lay me in the dust of death. Dogs surround me, a pack of villains encircles me; *they pierce my hands and my feet....* All the ends of the earth will remember and turn to the LORD, and all the families of the nations will bow down before him" (Psalm 22:14–16, 27, italics mine). This is how God would bless all nations just as he promised to Abraham; he would become the Suffering Servant who, like a judo master, takes the hardest punch evil can throw and turns it into the greatest good. Jesus proudly wears his scars of love in Heaven for a reason—*we need to remember!*

Why Suffering?

But why suffer at all? If he is God, why not just create a world that bypasses all mourning, crying, pain, and suffering? I've come to believe this world and its suffering *is* necessary. In order to accomplish God's goal for humanity—to love God and love each other as his family forever—we must start from the knowledge of good *and evil* (see Genesis 2:16–17). Why? Because love must be free. The freedom to choose or reject God's leadership is necessary for love.

Imagine if a rich and powerful man fell in love with a beautiful woman, and he longed for her to fall in love with him. He could shower her with good gifts, and she may decide she wants more of the goodies he can provide, but will that mean she loves him for who he is? No! Maybe his prestige and power give her access to the finest luxuries that make her want to be with him, but does that mean she loves him for who he is? No! And what if no amount of good gifts or reputation could win her heart, and he got so desperate, he kidnapped her and put a gun to her head, trying to force her to love him. Can love be forced? No! Love cannot be bought, coerced, or forced. It must be freely chosen.

Love that is not free to choose is not love at all. For God to create an eternally loving family, God chose to create creatures who can choose freely to reject him and thwart his love. His good gifts, his prestige, his power can't force our love. We must be free to choose. It's risky business, because free-willed creatures who turn from God and thwart his love hurt each other. And when we get hurt, we often blame God and turn from the One who can heal us. Then hurting people hurt people, and evil propagates from person to person, all of us feeling justified.

Fork in the Road

I was sixteen and on the floor in my room in horrible agony. If there really was a God and he loved me, why had he let my father die? Downstairs I could hear the post-funeral gathering, but I couldn't be with them. I'd just lost my father, my rock, my best friend—I needed to think. It felt like I'd hit a fork in the road and this choice felt heavy. Part of me wanted to curse God and just live life however I wanted—after all, if he didn't care about me why should I care about him? But then another thought pushed through my pain: "If there's no God, there's no hope anything good will ever come from this pain—life sucks, then you die! If I trust what Scripture says, that God does love me, maybe one day he will make it right."

My choice that day felt pivotal in my life. God never took away the pain, but as I cried out to him in trust from my bedroom floor, I felt a peace and had a new thought: *Okay, you'll have to be my Father now.* Years later I read, "A father to the fatherless . . . is God in his holy dwelling" (Psalm 68:5). I now know who put that thought in my head.

Jesus told his followers the night before his crucifixion, "I have told you these things, so that in me you may have peace. In this world you *will have trouble*. But take heart! I have overcome the world" (John 16:33, italics mine). God never promises us a pain-free, trouble-free life. We live in a world where most of us pursue "our will and ways" more than "God's will and ways." When we choose to go our own way, we create ripples of pain, hurt, and suffering that reverberate through humanity and down the generations. Much human suffering is caused by humankind's own choices. But we can overcome evil through him, and he promises something good will come from our sufferings in the end. During his NDE, Dr. Alexander felt he understood the reason suffering and evil exist. Without free will, evil is impossible, he explains. But without free will, humans cannot grow or move forward. Without free will, there is no opportunity for us to grow into what God yearns for us to be. The Creator allows evil to exist as a necessary consequence of the gift of free will. But, he adds, "Free will comes at the cost of a loss or falling-away from [God's] love and acceptance."[8]

Pains of Birth

God promises to overcome evil one willing heart at a time. And when we turn back to him, he will even make something good of all our suffering:

> Yet what we suffer now is nothing compared to the glory he will reveal to us later. For all creation is waiting eagerly for that future day when God will reveal who his children really are. Against its will, all creation was subjected to God's curse. But with eager hope, the creation looks forward to the day when it will join God's children in glorious freedom from death and decay. For we know that all creation has been groaning as in the pains of childbirth right up to the present time. . . .
>
> God causes everything to work together for the good of those who love God and are called according to his purpose for them. (Romans 8:18–22, 28 NLT)

All of life is a birth canal into eternal life. One day all creation will come alive with God's life—it's what NDErs notice. But for now, earth is mixed with the knowledge of good—God's good gifts wooing us to him—alongside the pain, death, and decay of the knowledge of evil, constantly warning us that something's wrong. God doesn't want us to think we are okay without him and miss the whole purpose of our existence—to choose God so we might live with him forever. And when we make that choice, he wants us to grow in faithfulness so he can trust us with eternal rewards and responsibilities.

Professor Howard Storm recalls during his NDE that Jesus and the angels told him God not only knows everything that will come to pass in the future, but also, more importantly, God knows everything that *could* happen. He is aware of every possible variation and every possible outcome. God gives each of us free will—he won't violate our free will or dictate the outcome of everything—yet at the same time, Jesus told Storm, the outcome will always serve God's purpose in the end, no matter how long it takes to unfold or how impossible it might seem.[9]

That's why Jesus taught us to pray, "Your will be done [Father], on earth as it is in heaven" (Matthew 6:10). God's *individual* will for us *is not* always done on earth, or he wouldn't have us pray for it. But God's *ultimate* will can be accomplished whether we choose his individual will or not.

But why does God remain so hidden? It seems if we could see God, then we could better choose God. But even seeing God does not eradicate our need to walk in faith. Captain Black reflects how confusing it was to realize this: "I had clearly seen heaven and was so changed by the experience, why did I fail again and again to be the man I truly wanted to be? Why did I fail often to be a reflection of what I had seen and heard and learned? I guess seeing heaven didn't change the fact that I'm human."[10] Life is all about learning to love God and trust him while we can't see him, because then we will forever choose to love and follow him throughout eternity when we can see him. That's why we don't see him face-to-face now. But why not just create free-willed creatures who do see him?

He did! Understanding their story helps make sense of ours.

15

Angels

ELEVEN-YEAR-OLD JENNIFER was in a severe car accident and left her body. She saw her "limp and lifeless body" below. A spiritual being told her, "His nose is cut off his face; you will need to go back and help him; he is bleeding to death."

Jennifer said, "No, let somebody else do it. He will be fine without my help. I do not want to go back down there. No!"

The voice said, "I will tell you what to do. You take off his shirt after you pick his nose up off the floorboard of the car. It will be next to your feet and his right foot. Place his nose on his face, pressing down to stop the bleeding. It's just blood, so do not be afraid. . . . So then, Jennifer, you will begin to walk him up the right side of the road, and a car will come. Tell the man to take you to the nearest hospital. . . ."

When Jennifer returned to her body everything happened as she was told. A car stopped and carried them to the hospital. She was able to calm both the anxious driver and the man who lost his nose. And there was a happy ending: a skin graft was used to reattach the nose with "barely a scratch left to notice." The astonished emergency room doctor said, "I cannot explain what kind of miracle I just witnessed in this emergency room today."[1]

We know when evil, pain, or suffering hurt us, but we do not know how often God orchestrates his angels to care for us. Angels are God's servants sent to help people. Are they real beings or just mythological? Well, just imagine God's unlimited creativity. There seems to be no end to it—billions of stars clustered in billions of galaxies, and on just one planet orbiting one star, he's created over seven million species of creatures (as best scientists can estimate—we've only catalogued 1.2 million). God has also created spiritual creatures who do not live confined to time and space as we do—one species we call angels. *Angel* literally means "messenger." Angels are referred to 196 times in Scripture. Humans do not become angels—meaning we don't go through a species change—but we can be messengers.

As you've probably noticed, NDErs often report seeing angels. Marv Besteman noticed, "My angels looked like regular guys, except regular guys usually don't wear white robes. Both looked in their mid-forties and stood about 5'8" to 5'10". One had longish brown hair, and the other one had shorter hair . . . neither one of them had wings [though he later saw winged creatures]."[2] They can appear much like human beings, or they can shine with a radiant light, less brilliant than the radiance of God, but still quite impressive. Most do not have wings, though some creatures do (Ezekiel 1).

Dale Black reported angels coming in pairs. "I moved effortlessly along the road, escorted by my two angelic guides."[3] Marv and other NDErs noted the same: "Beside me stood two angels who would always accompany me."[4] After noticing this trend, I recalled Jesus's statement: "See that you do not despise one of these little ones. For I tell you that their angels [plural] in heaven always see the face of my Father in heaven" (Matthew 18:10).

What are angels and what do they do? With so much increased interest in angels come many diverse opinions. I'd like to show you what the Scriptures say and how our world of suffering may tie in to their story in Heaven. "Are not all angels ministering spirits sent to serve those who will inherit salvation?" (Hebrews 1:14). Scripture teaches that angels are spirit creatures who live in God's realm, but they can interact with earth in order to serve people and accomplish God's will. Even in Heaven, God accomplishes his will through free-will cooperation of angels. Some are guardian angels assigned to individuals, some are assigned to churches (Revelation 2), some are over cities or nations (Daniel 12:1). And some were cast out of Heaven.

Fallen Angels

Not every spiritual being is benevolent. Jeffrey Burton Russell, professor of history, emeritus, at the University of California, Santa Barbara, is a leading historian on the topic of evil. He says, "The problem of evil exists in every single world-view and religious tradition except radical relativism."[5] Russell points out that although modern people have tended to believe less and less in a supernatural evil force, the practical experience of evil has not decreased but maybe even increased in our society.

The Hebrew Old Testament prophets taught there are unseen spiritual beings at work in the world. The Hebrew word that is translated *Satan* means "adversary, accuser." Devil, *diabolos*, means "one who divides." In the New Testament, Jesus confronted demonic forces, and Russell notes how most cultures have attested to demonic spiritual forces at work throughout history.

Now, this is where people conjure up all kinds of silly images of devils in red suits with tails and pitchforks. What Scripture teaches is nothing like characterizations we've seen, but evil would love for us to laugh it off. After all, the best terrorist is the one you don't know about. Russell, as a historian, says, "The suggestion that Jesus' belief in the Devil was merely part of a primitive world view poses serious difficulties. The notion that the first century was a benighted age [not as enlightened as we are] . . . is mere chronocentrism—ethnocentrism shifted to time."[6]

Former atheist and college professor Howard Storm experienced evil messengers and benevolent angels firsthand, an experience that changed him forever. He says angels move through time and space at will, not bound by laws of physical nature. They also protect us from evil we can't see and aren't even capable of imagining. "Our angels are ever vigilant to protect us from evil that originates from other dimensions of the unknown universes. . . . They are keeping us safe. There exist supernatural beings that seek chaos. They have no power over us except the power we give them. They are known as demons, the devil, or evil spirits."[7]

Angels were created to love and serve God. And they were created with a free will—before humans. Some of the angels followed the most beautiful, powerful angel created, Lucifer—which means "lightbearer." Lucifer was created good. He's not God's equal opposite, nor the only source of evil. Created by God with a free will, Lucifer's downfall was his pride. God says through Ezekiel the prophet, "You were anointed as a guardian cherub [high-ranking angel], for so I ordained you. You were on the holy mount of God. . . . You were blameless in your ways from the day you were created till wickedness was found in you. . . . Your heart became proud on account of your beauty, and you corrupted your wisdom because of your splendor. So I threw you to the earth" (Ezekiel 28:14–17). When Lucifer fell, he persuaded a third of Heaven's angels to follow him (Revelation 12:3–7). He wanted to be God, and as Ezekiel 28 indicates, his evil angels' most powerful lie is to persuade us to play god of our little universe (my will be done) instead of allowing God to be God (God's will be done).

Deceptive Liars

Jesus tells us, "If you hold to my teaching, you are really my [followers]. Then you will know the truth, and the truth will set you free" (John 8:31–32). But some of the religious leaders who would later crucify Jesus said, "We're already free. We're children of God." Jesus replied, "You are the children of your father the devil, and you love to do the evil things he does. He was a murderer from the beginning. He has always hated the truth, . . . there is no truth in him. . . . For he is a liar and the father of lies" (John 8:44 NLT).

Fallen angels are liars and deceivers. Shut off from the light, love, and truth of God by their own choosing, they seek to deceive us into following them. Moses explained that when people seek guidance from spiritual beings instead of seeking God, something more deceptive is happening: "They stirred up [God's] jealousy by worshiping foreign gods. . . . They offered sacrifices to demons, which are not God" (Deuteronomy 32:16–17 NLT). Scripture warns that when people follow idols or spirit guides or the dead, deceptive demonic angels are really leading them astray.

"Someone may say to you, 'Let's ask the mediums and those who consult the spirits of the dead. With their whisperings and mutterings, they will tell us what to do.' But shouldn't people ask God for guidance? Should the living seek guidance from the dead? Look to God's instructions and teachings! People who contradict his word are completely in the dark" (Isaiah 8:19–20 NLT). So God says, "I will set my face against anyone who turns to mediums and spiritists to prostitute themselves by following them" (Leviticus 20:6). Scripture teaches that God wants us to seek his guidance so we won't be deceived.

Paul says, "Satan himself masquerades as an angel of light. It is not surprising, then, if his servants also masquerade as servants of righteousness" (2 Corinthians 11:14). Which leads to a troubling question: Could the Being of Light that people think is God or Jesus actually be a deceptive fallen angel? Yes. That's possible. I don't think it is true in the majority of cases. As I've tried to demonstrate, this Being of Light people encounter reflects the Scripture's description of the God revealed by the prophets and Jesus. That doesn't mean people can't misinterpret or shoehorn their experience into their own worldview. I think that happens. Also, if NDErs claim Jesus told them things contradicting the Scriptures, the real Jesus would never do that (see Matthew 5:17, 20; Galatians 1:8).

But some Christians adamantly say all NDEs are satanic deceptions. If so, it seems Satan is doing a poor job of misrepresenting God. Plus, God is allowing little children and Christ-followers (including his pastors) to be deceived. Of course, all of us *can be* deceived, so it's wise to check all claims against Scripture, and as Jesus said, look at the fruit it produces in a life (Matthew 7:16). Though some past NDE researchers claimed the NDE experience led people away from a biblical view of God and church and toward more Eastern views, Dr. Sabom challenges this conclusion. Sabom makes a strong case that many of these early researchers in IANDS* studied the same group of NDErs who already had this worldview.[8]

Dr. Bruce Greyson, the research director of IANDS, even admitted that the IANDS research pool, which has been heavily

---

* Dr. Sabom was a founding member of the International Association of Near Death Studies (IANDS), which became a gathering place for NDE stories used by many early researchers. Chapter 7 of Sabom's *Light and Death* gives an important historical context explaining how IANDS research leaned toward a more Eastern interpretation, which Sabom claims influenced the interpretations of actual accounts.

used by NDE researchers, is "not comparable to the general population."[9] In his study, Sabom found NDErs became more committed to their local congregations, not less.[10] In Dr. Sartori's study, "All patients reported an increased tendency to pray, go to church, and read the Bible."[11]

Though some interpret the oneness they experience within a more Eastern framework, Sabom's study found that "a belief in reincarnation and in Eastern, universalist religion is not a direct aftereffect of the near-death experience."[12] Dr. Moody originally reported the same. Ultimately, we are told, "do not believe every spirit, but test the spirits to see whether they are from God" (1 John 4:1).

How? By making sure that spirit aligns with what God's already revealed through the prophets and Jesus. In appendix A and in previous chapters, I have given just a few of about sixty prophetic declarations fulfilled by God in actual, verifiable history—showing God has inspired the Scriptures. The Dead Sea Scrolls prove that prophecies Jesus fulfilled were written before Jesus lived. That's why Paul says, "Even if we or an angel from heaven should preach a gospel other than the one we preached to you, let them be under God's curse!" (Galatians 1:8). Jesus said, "If they do not listen to Moses and the Prophets, they will not be convinced even if someone rises from the dead" (Luke 16:31). For these reasons, I believe it's essential to study Scripture more than NDEs. I hope that's what this book motivates you to do.

Truth Sets You Free

Fallen angels lie and deceive. The only power they can gain over us is when we believe them and follow their lies. Then we think we're doing what we want, but we end up hurting ourselves and others. God wants to heal us of the wounds and replace the lies that keep robbing us of life. In Heaven, God helped Crystal replace the lies and wounds inflicted by evil with his truth. He showed her a beautiful three-year-old girl playing with an Easter basket.

> She wore a bonnet on her head and she had a little white basket in her hand. I watched her pick her basket up and dip it in the light. She would scoop it and then she would dump the light out as if it was water. And the light would cascade out of her basket and she would throw her head back. And she would laugh. And every time she laughed, every time she moved, my spirit began to swell, as if it was a balloon with love.[13]

Watching the little girl play with the Easter basket prompted an immense feeling of love and pride in Crystal's spirit. The feeling grew and intensified, "radiating waves of love" that were so deep, intense, and endless, she felt her soul would burst. Crystal remembers wanting nothing more than to run toward the little girl, embrace her, and tell her how much she loved her.

Suddenly God revealed his intentions. As if a pair of magic glasses was removed from her eyes, Crystal instantly knew who the child was. The little girl with the golden Easter basket was her.

"I knew God was allowing me to see myself as He saw me," Crystal says. In God's eyes, she was perfect, and that would never change, no matter what happened to her on earth, no matter what bad decisions she had made that had filled her with a sense of worthlessness. None of it mattered. Until this moment, Crystal had believed God couldn't possibly love her, especially after the abuse she had suffered and the sins she had committed. Now, however, she knew she had based her beliefs on a lie—a lie God obliterated with his love.[14]

Because she had been three years old when her abuse began, God took Crystal back to that very age:

211

[The little girl] was me at the moment the enemy stepped into my life and whispered that I was worthless, that I was broken, that I was disgusting, and that I got everything I deserved. She was the 3-year-old that heard that God didn't love her, that He had abandoned her, that He had forsaken her, and that God didn't exist. And, He had allowed me to look through His eyes and to see the truth. And the truth set me free.[15]

We don't have to wait for Heaven to be set free. The way we fight evil is with truth—taking thoughts captive, resisting lies, and trusting God's truth. Do you see yourself as God's masterpiece? I wrote a book called *Unshockable Love* (formerly *Mud and the Masterpiece*) to help you understand that God sees you as his masterpiece he wants to restore, and he wants you to see the same in others.

Choose Life

The Scriptures teach there are many fallen angels—demonic spiritual beings who followed Lucifer. They are void of the love of God; they are consumed with their own desires. They lie to us about God and the path to life. Their decision to turn from God was eternal—so there's no second chance for them. Their choice was eternal. Ours is temporal.

This answers the question of why earth with its pain and suffering is necessary. Lucifer and the fallen angels made a choice to reject God in his presence. Because they are eternal beings, their choice was eternal. They wanted to rule instead of God, but they had no idea what that choice meant. God honored their free-will choice. He created a place where God would not rule—an eternal place absent of God—a place called hell. Jesus said that hell was "prepared for the devil and his angels" (Matthew 25:41). He gave them what they wanted—free reign without God's love, light, or life.

God created our space-time temporal (temporary) world in order to create eternally free creatures who will forever choose to love and follow God. Why? Because we start from the knowledge of *good and evil* (see Genesis 2:17). We live in a world where we taste Heaven—God's love and goodness, and we also taste hell—the absence of God and his ways. This is why God stays hidden.

We experience a taste of both Heaven and hell greatly reduced. NDErs tell us our spiritual senses are about a hundred times more intense than the five senses we currently experience. God starts us in a time capsule, a birth canal called earth, and even though we all sin and turn away from God, he gives us time—a second, third, hundredth chance to turn from our willful ways and turn back to him.

In Heaven, we will still have free will. We must, or we couldn't love God. Theoretically, we could still sin in Heaven,* but unlike the angels, we will forever choose God, remembering what it was like to live without God's will and ways on earth. And God is teaching the angels as they serve us—"God's purpose in all this was to use the church to display his wisdom in its rich variety to all the unseen rulers and authorities in the heavenly places" (Ephesians 3:10 NLT)—so we will all remember the pain and suffering of turning from God and what it cost him to win us back. Through earth's sufferings, God is birthing eternally free children who will forever choose to love him. That's why Jesus still has the markers. Angels and humans all need to remember forever why suffering was necessary.

Dean worked as a psychologist counseling traumatized people. He said during his NDE,

You can see the nail piercings that took place in His hands. But again, it was the love that was coming out of them to me

---

* I say "theoretically" because I think God perfects us in Heaven so that we will not sin. How he perfects us is a much-debated question.

that expressed His love for me. . . . I had worked with children and teenagers over the past 33 years. During that time, the one issue that came up a lot with the children I had worked with was sexual abuse by adults. This one issue, to me, seems to do more damage than all the other issues I faced as a counselor. . . .

I asked Jesus, "What about child abusers?"

Jesus said back to me, "When you place a person in jail, they get out. They either get out when their time is up, or they get out when they die, but they get out. But when we put a person in hell, they are there for eternity." Then His eyes looked at me with a fiery red flame that said, "WHO ARE YOU TO NULLIFY WHAT I HAD DONE!" This came across to me very stern. I also saw His arms outstretched like He was on the cross and He paid the price for everyone who sinned, or ever will sin, implying that we do not have a right to condemn anyone, since He does not. I knew that I knew—He wanted all people there with Him. He truly wants us there with Him. All people![16]

Honestly, there's only one explanation that makes sense of a loving God allowing so much pain and suffering: he knows there's something much, much better or much, much worse ahead. He wants to save us all—the abused, the abuser, and everyone in between (see Luke 7). We are eternal creatures, tasting Heaven and hell so we will choose God. As Oxford scholar C. S. Lewis once said, "God whispers to us in our pleasures, speaks in our conscience, but shouts in our pains: it is His megaphone to rouse a deaf world."[17] Jesus said, "It is not my heavenly Father's will that even one of these little ones should perish" (Matthew 18:14 NLT). That leads to the next question: What do we make of hellish NDEs?

16

What about Hell?

Howard Storm, professor of art at Northern Kentucky University, was taking students on a tour of Paris's museums when a stomach ulcer perforated his duodenum. Little did he know, but from the time of perforation, life expectancy was typically five hours. The hospital had only one surgeon on duty that weekend, so he and his wife, Beverly, had to wait. Ten hours later, a nurse informed them the doctor had gone home, and they would have to wait until morning. Howard had fought to stay alive, but now he had nothing left. Howard shared with me in an exclusive interview what happened next.[1]

> I never thought to pray, never thought about God. I knew that there was no life after death, and so the thought of death . . . certainly terrified me because it just means, "END." I told my wife, "It's time for us to say goodbye." I told her to tell my mother and father that I loved them, tell my kids that I loved them, tell my friends that I was thinking about them, and, I said, "Kiss me." She kissed me and said goodbye to me and I said goodbye to her and she sat down and wept like I didn't know a

person could weep. . . . It was so horrible to see her suffer. I just wanted to be gone, I wanted it to be over with. . . .

Howard closed his eyes and passed. He expected oblivion, but instead, he found himself standing up beside the bed. He opened his eyes.

I felt more alive than I ever felt in my entire life. . . . "Why do I feel so good?" I just felt the worst I had ever felt in my entire life, and then I couldn't breathe, and now I'm like Superman. . . . My eyesight, my hearing, my taste . . . my peripheral vision has greatly expanded, and my depth of field is without any limitation. I'm an artist so I'm really aware of the visual things. . . . So, I try to speak to my wife who was on the other side of the bed with her head on her hands, bent over, and I get no reaction from her. So, I start to yell and scream at her because she's not responding to me. I'm yelling and cussing and swearing at her and—nothing. So, I turned to Monsieur Fleurin [the patient in the adjacent hospital bed] (who had been extremely kind to us) and I'm yelling and screaming and had my face inches from his face and he's just staring as if he can't see me which, of course, he couldn't.

At this point, Howard still did not realize he was actually dead. He recognized his lifeless body, yet felt so alive. His only thought was about how critically he needed surgery.

I heard people calling me in English, kind of nicely, you know? "Howard, Howard. Come here, come here." So, I go over to the doorway of the room and the hallway is gray, it's very unclear like a terrible black and white TV picture . . . men and women standing far away from the light of the doorway. And, I said, "I'm sick. I need to have surgery. I've been waiting all day for a doctor," and, they said, "We know all about you. Hurry, come with us now. We can't wait any longer. Come, come. Hurry!" And, I'm thinking, "*Okay. They've come. They've come to take me to the doctor. This is great! I need the surgery.*"

The people—as I left the light of the room, going into the hallway—encircled me and kind of started leading me in this direction as we journeyed. At first, I thought I was in the hospital but then as we walked in this grayness with these people around me, I became aware that this hospital was not this big because we've gone miles and miles and miles now. . . . As the grayness got darker and darker, they moved in closer and closer but, initially, they stayed far enough away from me so that I couldn't see them. All that I could see was . . . v-neck shirts with short sleeves, you know, unadorned slacks. They looked exactly like hospital staff. . . .

Now, as I asked them questions like, "Where are we going? How much further?" things like that, they started to become more rude and say things to me like, "Shut up! Don't ask questions! You'll find out! You don't need to know! Keep moving! Keep moving! Move it!" . . . I'm getting pretty intimidated. That becomes fear. That becomes terror. And, now, this is over a journey of miles and miles and miles and, eventually, it's so dark, I'm aware I can't see anything anymore. It's pitch black. And, I figure, "I'm done," you know, "I've had it." And, so, I said, "I'm not going any further," and, they said, "Oh, yes, you are. You've got further to go." And, I said, "I'm not going," so they started to tug at me and push at me. I played football and wrestled in high school, so I knew how to play that game. . . . So I'm trying to fend them off by punching and slamming them. And, they're pulling and tugging at me and there's a lot [of them] . . . judging by the voices and the touching . . . dozens, hundreds . . . maybe more than that. And, what they were doing was just playing with me, toying with me.

At first, it was pushing, kicking, pulling, hitting. And, then, that became biting and tearing with their fingernails and hands. And they were taking pieces of me and there was a lot of laughter, a lot of very foul language. And, then, they became more invasive . . .

Howard had to pause in the interview just to fight back the traumatic memories, which he later told me he had spent years trying to forget.

I don't ever go further with this because it was so demeaning. I mean, I don't talk about it. There has never been a horror movie or a book that can begin to describe their cruelty because their cruelty was . . . purely sadistic. . . . They were so empty, so without compassion or feeling for me, that it was just amusement for me to scream and yell and fight back. And, the less that I had the strength and the ability to fight back, the less interested they were in me. Eventually, I was eviscerated. . . . I definitely lost one of my eyes, my ears were gone, and I'm laying on the floor of that place. And, I just want to say that the emotional pain of what they had done to me was worse than the physical pain. The physical pain was pain from head to foot; just, solid, horrible, acute pain. On a scale of 1 to 10: 10, total. It didn't begin to match what I felt on the inside . . . having been taken down to nothing. I mean, the worst things that you could possibly imagine had happened to me and more but for no reason. . . .

And, in that place, I heard a voice, which I identified as my voice except that it did not come out of my throat. . . . It's strange but I feel like it came out of my chest. This voice said, "Pray to God," and I thought, "I don't believe in God. I don't pray." The voice said, "Pray to God," and I thought, "I don't even know how to pray. I couldn't pray if I wanted to pray." The voice said, "Pray. To. God." And, I thought, "When I was a boy and had gone to Sunday school, we'd been taught prayers. What were those prayers?"

Howard struggled to remember any prayers from childhood, anything with God's name in it, so he pieced together all he could recall into a ragtag prayer of desperation, shouting out,

> "Yea, though I walk in the valley of the shadow of death, I will fear no evil, for thou art with me. For purple mountain majesty, mine eyes have seen the glory of the coming of the Lord. . . . One nation under God. God Bless America."

To my amazement, the cruel, merciless beings tearing the life out of me were incited to rage by my ragged prayer. It was as if I were throwing boiling oil on them. They screamed at me, "There is no God! . . . Nobody can hear you! Now we are really going to hurt you." They spoke in the most obscene language, worse than any blasphemy said on earth. But at the same time, they were backing away. . . .[2]

Now, this made me want to pray more because for the first time, I was able to hit back at them. The prayers were clobbering. And, I also noticed that the more I muttered and tried to articulate anything that had "God" in it, like, "Glory, glory, hallelujah! His truth goes marching on," they would retreat further and further away.

Once the beings retreated, Howard lay on the ground in despair, contemplating his situation. He felt completely alone, nearly destroyed, yet painfully alive and intensely aware in this terrifying, horrible place.

So, now, I have eternity—time without measure—to think about my situation. . . . Since I had no religious or theological understanding, I had to put it in the only way that I could think of it which was: septic systems. . . . Because I had lived a garbage life, I had gone down the toilet, down the septic system. . . . And, I realized, this is the horrible part: that the people that had met me were my kindred spirits. Now, I do not know if I knew any of those people in this world prior to this experience . . . [but] they were my brothers and sisters in spirit. They denied God, they lived for themselves, and their lives were about manipulation and control of other people. That's what drove them, that's what motivated [them] . . . that's what they really lived for.

My life was devoted to building a monument to my ego. My family, my sculptures, my painting. . . . All of those things were gone now, and what did they matter? I wasn't far from becoming like one of my own tormentors for all eternity.[3]

As Howard lay alone in the dark, feeling himself slipping away into hopelessness, a few words from a song he hadn't heard since childhood came into his head. He could remember but three words, "Jesus loves me," and the tune, yet it tapped deep into a longing and ignited a tiny spark of hope.

And, now, all of a sudden it was all I had. I had nothing else. I'm scraping the bottom of the barrel of what might be possible . . . and I thought, *Why would [Jesus] care about me? Even if he is [real] why would he care? He must hate me. I'm so sorry.* I thought, *Enough of this! I'm done! I don't have anything else.* I wanted it to be true that Jesus loved me. . . . I yelled into the darkness, "Jesus, save me!" I have never meant anything more strongly in my life.[4]

And, when I said that, I saw a light. A tiny, little speck of light and it, very rapidly, got very bright and came over me. And, I saw out of the light: hands and arms emerge out of this impossibly beautiful light . . . so intense, it's way brighter than the sun. . . . And, these hands and arms came out and they reached and they touched me and when they touched me, in that light, I could see me and all the gore. And, I was road-kill. All that gore began to just dissolve and I became whole.

And, much more significantly to me than the physical healing was that I was experiencing a love that is beyond—far beyond words. I have never been able to articulate it, but I can say that if I took all my experience of love in my entire life and could condense it into a moment, it still wouldn't begin to measure up to the intensity of this love that I was feeling. And, that love is the foundation of my life from that moment on. . . .

Those arms went on me and healed me, they went behind my back and he picked me up as if it was no effort on his part. He just gently picked me up and held me up against him real tight, up against his chest. So, there I am: with my arms around him, his arms around me. And, I am bawling like a baby. I am slobbering and snotting and drooling with my head buried in his chest. And, he starts to rub my back, like a mom or dad with

220

a child. And, I knew. I don't know how I knew, but I knew that he loved me very much, just the way I was. *Jesus does love me.* . . . I had called out to Jesus and he came to rescue me. I cried and cried. . . . Joy upon joy billowed through me.[5]

He carried me upward, just straight upward. I wanted to see where we were headed, and I realized that we're moving really, really rapidly because there's all kinds of light . . . beings of light moving past us. And, I am seeing only by his light—by his glory—that I can see that we're moving away. Everything was going at a great rate of speed, and off in the distance is this . . . tremendous center of light. A world of light beyond being able to perceive . . . bigger than galaxies. . . . And, as I looked towards this tremendous center of light [I knew] . . . that's God's house. That's heaven.[6]

Hellish NDEs

As he looked far across space to this great City of Light, Howard said he had a life review in the presence of Jesus and several angels, which we will explore in the next chapter. Howard revived, miraculously, and several years later left his career as a university professor and chairman of the art department to become a pastor. What would motivate an avowed atheist professor to give up tenure and his life's work to make up a story of visiting hell? We could write it off if this were the only NDE story like this, but there are many.

In the 1970s when NDE reports were increasing, very few if any persons experiencing hellish NDEs came forward. In fact, Moody boldly stated, "No one has described the cartoonist's heaven of pearly gates, golden streets . . . nor a hell of flames and demons with pitchforks. So, in most cases, the reward punishment model of the afterlife is abandoned and disavowed."[7] But Moody's declaration was overcharacterized and premature.

Dutch researcher Dr. Pim van Lommel notes that people who experience hellish NDEs sometimes find themselves pulled deeper and deeper into a profound darkness. "The NDE ends in this scary atmosphere. . . . Such a terrifying NDE usually produces long-lasting emotional trauma." The exact number of people who experience this type of NDE, which is often known as a "hell experience," is unknown, because as van Lommel has noticed, shame and guilt prohibit people from sharing about these terrifying experiences.[8]

Sartori notes, "[Research] has served to highlight that negative NDEs are just as real as the pleasant ones and can occur in the absence of anesthetics."[9] Some studies produced no distressing NDEs, but this may result from how the study was conducted. Studies asking for people to come forward if they've had an NDE will produce people excited to tell others of a good experience. On the other hand, people who have experienced a negative NDE may feel embarrassed or ashamed and thus be less likely to share their stories. Many such people have confided in Howard Storm, perhaps because they feel a sense of camaraderie and security with him as someone who has also experienced a negative NDE. These stories of negative NDEs are not uncommon, Storm believes, but because of the associated shame, it's unlikely they will be shared often.[10]

Frequency of Hellish NDEs

Despite that, *The Handbook of Near-Death Experiences* reports that twelve different studies involving 1,369 subjects found that 23 percent "reported NDEs ranging from disturbing to terrifying or despairing."[11] Dr. Rawlings, the cardiologist from chapter 3, revived a patient having multiple hellish experiences that the patient could not recall afterward. Rawlings postulates that these experiences produce such trauma that they get suppressed in the subconscious mind, and unless a patient is interviewed immediately after resuscitation, we should not expect as many accounts to come forward.[12] Rawlings quotes other doctors reporting a similar blocked-memory response.

A fourteen-year-old girl became despondent over her life and decided to end it. She swallowed a bottle of aspirin. In the hospital, the doctor reported resuscitating her from a cardiac arrest, during which she kept saying, "Mama, help me! Make them let me go! They're trying to hurt me!" The doctors tried to apologize for hurting her, but she said it wasn't the doctors, but "them, those demons in hell . . . they wouldn't let go of me . . . it was just awful!" The doctor reports, "She slept for another day, and her mother hugged her most of the time. After the various tubes were removed, I asked her to recall what had happened. She remembered taking the aspirin, but absolutely nothing else! Somewhere in her mind, the events may still be suppressed. . . . She subsequently became a missionary several years later."[13]

Similarly, in other cultures, not all NDEs are pleasant. In India, Yamdoots are considered "messengers" like angels. "Yam doots are supposed to appear at the bedside of the dying to take them away to their Lord, Yamaraj [the god of death]. The appearance of the Yamdoot depends upon the Karma of the patient. If he has accumulated good deeds, a pleasant Yamdoot appears, but if he has not acquitted himself well in his lifetime, a fearful Yamdoot might come."[14]

A Hindu clerical worker said, "Somebody is standing there! He has a cart with him so he must be a Yamdoot! He must be taking someone with him. He is teasing me that he's going to take *me*! . . . Please hold me; I'm not going."[15] His pain increased and he died.

Osis and Haraldsson report, "One out of every three (34 percent) Indians who experienced the take-away hallucination refused to consent [were afraid of the Yamdoot coming to take them away]."[16] Enough "hellish" accounts have been documented for researchers to categorize them into three categories that I'm labeling "the void," "hell on earth," and "the pit."

The Void

Some NDErs find themselves leaving their bodies but either entering a void like they are somewhere in outer space or experiencing a falling sensation through outer darkness. Gary was a young artist who lost control of his car on a snowy winter evening. He described leaving his body and watching as icy water filled the car.

> I saw the ambulance coming, and I saw the people trying to help me, get me out of the car and to the hospital. At that time I was no longer in my body. I had left my body. I was probably a hundred or two hundred feet up and to the south of the accident, and I felt the warmth and the kindness of the people trying to help me. . . . I also felt the source of all that kind of kindness or whatever, and it was very, very powerful, and I was afraid of it, and so I didn't accept it. I just said "No." I was very uncertain about it, and I didn't feel comfortable, and so I rejected it. And it was at that moment that I left the planet. I could feel myself and see myself going way, way up into the air, then beyond the solar system, beyond the galaxy, and out beyond anything physical. . . . It became unbearable, it became horrific, as time goes on when you have no feeling, no sensation, no sense of light. I started to panic and struggle and pray and everything I could think of to struggle to get back.[17]

Some reject the love or light of God, or like A. J. Ayer, they experience the Light as painful or they want to resist it. Others simply find themselves in a void that becomes terrifying; others experience an outer darkness often accompanied by a falling sensation. My friend Paul Ojeda died of a cocaine overdose and found himself suddenly sober, but in a situation he never expected. He explained to me what happened:

> When I died, I didn't see a light, I saw a black tunnel like some-
> one had dropped me into an outer darkness and I was free-
> falling. I realized I was no longer high. I was in a different place
> and there was a different sense of time, but I was rapidly going
> deep into this and I thought, *I'm a good person, I shouldn't be
> going here.* But nothing made it stop, and I realized I'm going
> to hell, and I'm not gonna get out of here. That's when I cried
> out, "Please Lord, I don't want to go to this place, please save
> me." I didn't see a face or a figure, I just felt the presence of the
> Lord beside me, and he asked in my spirit, "Paul, what have
> you done with the life I've given you?"

Paul saw his entire life play out before him from birth to thirty (his age at that time), and God revealed every hidden dark secret in his heart that nobody knew about except him. He said to God, "I realize I've done nothing with my life. I know I deserve hell, but I know this isn't about me, now. If you give me the chance, I'll go back and I will tell others this is real."

He woke up in the hospital, and the first thing he said was, "I saw hell, and I'm not going back. I want to find the God that pulled me out of hell." Several years later, Paul ended up leaving a lucrative business he founded to start a church to serve the Hispanic community in Austin. Did Paul and others experience the various "chains of darkness" (2 Peter 2:4) or the "bottomless pit" (Revelation 9:1 NLT) warned about in Scripture?

Hell on Earth

Like Howard Storm, George Ritchie from chapter 1 observed what felt like some level of hell on earth. George claimed Jesus took him on a tour of what seemed to be "levels" of hell. He showed him people on earth working in a city factory, a guy standing over another one still barking orders at him. A group of women on earth were standing around smoking, and one of the women was begging for a cigarette. When one woman took one out and lit it, the begging woman ravenously snatched at it, but her hand went right through it. Then he watched a man walking along the street, his deceased mother right by his side, hounding him about why he married Marjorie, how he needs to take better care of himself. People permanently invisible to the living, yet permanently wrapped up in their affairs. Ritchie had the thought hit him, "Lay not up for yourselves treasures on earth! For where your treasure is, there will your heart be also!" He recalls,

> I had never been any good at memorizing Scripture, but those words of Jesus from the Sermon on the Mount sprang into my mind now like an electric shock. Perhaps these insubstantial people—the businessman, the woman begging cigarettes, this mother—although they could no longer contact the earth, still had their hearts there. Did I? . . . To be cut off for all eternity from the thing they could never stop craving . . . surely that would be a form of hell. . . .
>
> But if this was hell, if there was no hope, then why was [Jesus] here beside me? Why did my heart leap for joy each time I turned to Him? . . . Whichever way I looked, He remained the real focus of my attention. Whatever else I saw, nothing compared with Him.
>
> And that was another of the things baffling me. If I could see Him, why couldn't everyone else? . . . How could they not help but see the burning Love and Compassion in their midst? How could they miss Someone closer, more brilliant than the noonday sun?
>
> Unless . . .
>
> For the first time it occurred to me to wonder whether something infinitely more important than I ever believed could have happened that day when at age eleven I walked forward to the

altar of a church. Was it possible that I, in some real way, had actually been "born again," as the preacher said—given new eyes—whether I understood any of it or not? . . . "Where your heart is . . ." As long as my heart had been set on getting to Richmond by a certain date, I had not been able to see Jesus either. Maybe whenever our center of attention was on anything else, we could block out even Him.

George seemed to move again, still somewhere on the surface of the earth, but distant from any cities or living people. Hordes of discarnate people were jammed together on the plains.

"Lord Jesus!" I cried. "Where are we?"

At first I thought we were looking at some great battlefield: everywhere people were locked in what looked like fights to the death, writhing, punching, gouging. . . . They could not kill, though they clearly wanted to, because their intended victims were already dead. . . . These creatures seemed locked into habits of mind and emotion, into hatred, lust, destructive thought patterns.

Even more hideous than the bites and kicks they exchanged were the sexual abuses many were performing in feverish pantomime. . . . And the thoughts most frequently communicated had to do with the superior knowledge, or abilities, or background of the thinker. "I told you so!" "I always knew!" "Didn't I warn you!" were shrieked into the echoing air over and over. . . . In these yelps of envy and wounded self-importance I heard myself all too well.

Once again, however, no condemnation came from the Presence at my side, only a compassion for these unhappy creatures that was breaking His heart. Clearly it was not His will that any one of them should be in this place.[18]

George wondered why they didn't just get away from each other—no one was making them stay and take such abuse, but then he had a sick thought. What if they actually seek out others like themselves, with kind of a sick consolation of finding like-minded people, yet all they can do is hurl abuses at each other? It struck him, "Perhaps it was not Jesus who had abandoned them, but they who had fled from the Light."[19] Jesus warned of an "outer darkness, where there will be weeping and gnashing of teeth" (Matthew 25:30 NLT). Is that what Howard Storm and George Ritchie experienced?

The Pit

The last type of hellish NDE usually involves feeling locked or trapped in a dark pit, cave, or under the earth, often accompanied by a putrid smell like feces, sulfur, or death. Demonic or evil creatures are often involved, and in some cases extreme cold, in other cases extreme heat and even fire (see Matthew 13:40–42; Mark 9:43–44). All NDErs report the same heightened senses that make the heavenly experiences so alive, yet here they make the horrific experiences so much worse than earth's evils. Nancy Bush studied distressing NDEs and reports that this last category is the least reported, and probably the most written off, yet these experiences usually result in extreme trauma emotionally.

One NDEr Bush interviewed said, "Hell is a pit and there is darkness, but there is also fire. I was in a place to which the Bible refers as 'outer darkness' and it is not pretty. . . . After my experience, I could not talk about it. I did not want people to know that I had gone to hell. . . . Some people may just want to laugh this 'hell business' off, but as real as this letter is, so is that place."[20]

Fran died of a drug overdose at age twenty-six, but was then revived. She recalls, "I then felt my body slipping down, not straight down but on an angle, as if on a slide. It was cold, dark, and watery. When I reached the bottom, it resembled the entrance to a cave. . . . I heard cries, wails, moans, and the gnashing of teeth. I saw these beings that resembled humans, with the shape of a head and body. But they were ugly and grotesque. . . . They were frightening and sounded like they were tormented, in agony. No one spoke to me."[21]

The New Zealand surfer stung by the box jellyfish first found himself completely disoriented.

> It was so dark I couldn't see my hand in front of my face and it was bitterly cold. . . . It was a terrifying experience. I knew right there and then, I was myself, Ian McCormack, standing there, but without a physical body. I had the sensation and the feeling that I had a body, but I couldn't touch it. . . . A terrifying encroaching evil seemed to pervade the air around me.
>
> Slowly I became aware that there were other people moving around me, in the same predicament as I was. Without my saying a word out loud, they began to answer my thoughts. From the darkness I heard a voice screaming at me: "Shut up!" As I backed away from that one another yelled at me, "You deserve to be here!" My arms came up to protect myself and I thought, "Where am I?" and a third voice shouted, "You're in hell. Now shut up." I was terrified—afraid to move or breathe or speak. I realized that maybe I did deserve this place. . . .
>
> I'd prayed [in the ambulance] just before I died, and asked God to forgive me for my sins. I was weeping by now and I cried out to God, "Why am I here, I've asked you for forgiveness, why am I here? I've turned my heart to you, why am I here?"
>
> Then a brilliant light shone upon me and literally drew me out of the darkness.[22]

Ian found himself rescued by the light of Jesus, much like Howard Storm.

What Do They Mean?

Are these people actually in hell? Not fully, because just like Heaven experiences, all of them came back to life. They didn't die; they tasted death. They see what appears to be levels of a hellish afterlife. Remember, many NDErs found a barrier or boundary they knew they could not cross or they could not return to life. Maybe that's why they still had the ability to choose—their choice would not be "eternalized" until they crossed that boundary. So what people experience is a warning of the reality of hell.

Jesus warned about hell just as much as he taught about Heaven. He taught that God goes after wayward people like a shepherd leaves ninety-nine sheep to find the one lost sheep: "In the same way, it is not my heavenly Father's will that even one of these little ones should perish" (Matthew 18:14 NLT). That's why Jesus gave his life. "[God] wants all people to be saved and to come to a knowledge of the truth. For there is one God and one mediator between God and mankind, the man Christ Jesus, who gave himself as a ransom for all people" (1 Timothy 2:4–6), so that "everyone who calls on the name of the Lord will be saved" (Acts 2:21).

Then why would anyone end up in hell? Jesus said, "People loved darkness instead of light because their deeds were evil" (John 3:19). Oxford scholar C. S. Lewis, an atheist turned believer, wrestles with the idea of hell in his book *The Problem of Pain* and concludes that God does not *send* anybody to hell: "I willingly believe that the damned are, in one sense, successful, rebels to the end; that the doors of hell are locked from the *inside* . . . [to] enjoy forever the horrible freedom [from God] they have demanded."[23]

Hell's Welcoming Committee

Howard Storm found not every "welcoming committee" is benevolent, though they may seem kind at first. "There are as many entry points into heaven as there are individuals," he explains.

"God and the angels, for the specific comfort and beginning edification of that person, individually create each setting. . . ." Storm believes that a person who has rejected God's love cannot be welcomed into the journey to heaven. However, they are not alone after they die, but instead are welcomed by a group of like-minded spirits who wait for them and then guide them on a journey away from God's light and love. The degree of suffering and distress is unique to the individual, Storm contends. "Hell is separation from God," he says. "How it is experienced is proportionate to the life of the individual." God gives us free will; neither he nor the angels will intervene. He will respect a person's choice to embark on an eternal journey without him.[24]

As I thought about it, some positive NDEs, had the person not come back, might have become negative as the person journeyed away from the light and love of God. Jesus taught there are different "levels" or degrees of hell depending on the kind of life a person lived (Luke 20:47). I do not think the fact that someone has a peek into Heaven or a glimpse of hell is determinate of where they will end up. Some people seemed to get an intentional tour of both, presumably for the purpose of both inspiring and warning others. Some Christians like Dr. Eby claim Jesus showed them a tour of both for this purpose.

Harvard neurosurgeon Eben Alexander also realized he was given "some kind of grand overview of the invisible, spiritual side of existence. And like all good tours, it included all floors and all levels."[25] He started in a place he calls "the earthworm's view," which sounds more sophisticated than "hell," but what he described is very similar to what others called "the pit." Alexander describes it as . . .

> Darkness, but a visible darkness—like being submerged in mud . . . transparent, but in a bleary, blurry, claustrophobic, suffocating kind of way. . . . [I hear] the sound of metal against metal, as if a giant, subterranean blacksmith is pounding an

anvil somewhere off in the distance. . . . Grotesque animal faces bubbled out of the muck, groaned or screeched, and then were gone again. I heard an occasional dull roar. Sometimes these roars changed to dim, rhythmic chants, chants that were both terrifying and weirdly familiar. . . . My time in this realm stretched way, way out. Months? Years? Eternity? . . . The faces that bubbled up out of that darkness became ugly and threatening. The rhythmic pounding off in the distance sharpened and intensified as well—became the work-beat for some army of troll-like underground laborers, performing some endless, brutally monotonous task. The movement around me became less visual and more tactile, as if reptilian, wormlike creatures were crowding past, occasionally rubbing up against me with their smooth or spiky skins. Then I became aware of a smell: a little like feces, a little like blood, and a little like vomit. A biological smell, in other words, but of biological death. . . . I edged ever closer to panic.[26]

God Is Love?

Why would a loving God punish people for eternity for a limited number of earthly offenses? That's what makes no sense to people, but I don't believe that's what is happening. When we think we are temporal creatures being punished eternally for finite offenses, we are wrong. We are, in fact, eternal creatures like the angels. But unlike the angels, we are being given many, many finite, temporal chances on earth to choose Life instead of Death eternally (see Deuteronomy 30:19–20).

Why would a loving God allow so much evil, pain, and suffering on this earth? Because it's a warning and a chance to choose him! There's something much, much worse when we choose to follow ourselves and reject him as God. Hell is God giving free eternal creatures what they want—freedom from him. All the sufferings and evils of earth are meant to warn us.

God did not create hell for humans. He created hell for eternal angels who made an eternal choice to rule themselves—hell is where they rule. Currently, the Holy Spirit keeps our evil inclinations in check on earth through our consciences and law (John 16:8). For now, our choices are temporal; they can change with time. When we die finally, our choices become eternal. Not that we have no choice in eternity, but all choices "eternalized" have eternal ramifications. And remember, NDErs have not died finally during their experience—they can still choose and find rescue. But why can't God just bring everyone into Heaven—just change them?

Hitler's Heaven

What would God do with Hitler, or anyone who really did not want to submit to God's rule? Force him? Take away his free will? But then he'd be a slave, a prisoner in Heaven, not a loving child. If left with free will, it would only be a matter of time until he chose eternally his will over God's, and he'd be cast out of Heaven just like the angels. God knows all this, and this earth is perfectly suited to shape us into eternally free, loving children. All we have to do is choose to follow him now. But in God's presence, wouldn't everyone choose him? No!

Nancy Bush reports about a Jewish woman who was given about as clear a choice as possible. Describing her NDE she said, "I know that it all happened, and yet, logically, I cannot account for the happening—or possibly I just can't totally accept the reality of it—because I am Jewish and I do not believe in Jesus Christ. I only believe in God." One snowy winter night she was with her husband and children in the car when they had a bad head-on collision and she found herself out of her body, viewing the accident from above.

I was in a circle of light. I looked down upon the accident scene. I looked directly into the car that struck ours, and I saw a young woman . . . and I knew that she was dead. I looked into my car and saw myself trapped and unconscious. I saw several cars stop and a lady taking my children to her car. . . . I heard [my husband] talk to me, and I saw me never moving and never answering. . . .

[A] hand touched mine, and I turned to see where this peace and serenity and blissful feeling was coming from, and there was Jesus Christ—I mean the way he is made out to be in all the paintings, with white robe and beard . . . and I never wanted to leave this man and this place. I never looked or thought back upon the accident scene or earth again, until the final experience prodded me to do so.

I was led around a well, because I wanted to stay with [Jesus] and hold his hand. He led me from a side of bliss to a side of misery. I did not want to look, but he made me look, and I was disgusted and horrified and scared. It was so ugly. The people were blackened and sweaty and moaning in pain and chained to their spots. I had to walk through the area back to the well. . . . He led me to it, but he made me go through it alone as he watched . . . and I knew that I would be one of these creatures if I stayed, because of what I saw in the well. I knew that if I elected to stay because of the greatest, most serene feeling, that I would only have misery because he didn't want me to stay.

I leaned over the well, and this young Jesus look-alike (maybe it was God himself, or maybe the Christians aren't as peculiar as I think they are) put his hand on my back as I looked in. There were three children calling, "Mommie, Mommie, Mommie, we need you. Please come back to us." There were two boys and a girl. The two boys were much older than my two little ones, and I didn't have a little girl. . . . And then all at once I was in the circle again (his hand still on my shoulder) and I saw the accident scene again, and I cried that I did not ever want to leave him [Jesus]—and then I heard my babies cry and saw the lady taking them to her car—and I knew I had to leave and get back.[27]

She knew she had to go back and raise her children. Several years later, she had a little girl—the little girl she saw in the well. What's peculiar is that even seeing Jesus wasn't enough. Having seen she still says, "I am Jewish and I don't believe in Jesus Christ."[28] Presumably, Jesus didn't want her to stay because she had rejected him. Maybe she was getting another chance.

Jesus said, "I tell you the truth, those who listen to my message and believe in God who sent me have eternal life. They will never be condemned for their sins, but they have already passed from death into life. . . . The dead will hear my voice—the voice of the Son of God. And those who listen will live" (John 5:24–25 NLT). "But whoever rejects me rejects [God] who sent me" (Luke 10:16).

God does not want us to fear death or condemnation. He has made entrance to Heaven so simple that anyone, anywhere, can call on his Name and be saved—set right with God (Romans 10:13). The only thing that can keep us out of Heaven is our pride. What about those who have never heard his Name? Ultimately, we don't know. But we do know God looks at the heart, he's just, and Scripture tells us it is by faith, not by our deeds, that a person is saved (Ephesians 2:8–10).

Salvation is found in no one else but Jesus (Acts 4:12), yet many people who never knew the name of Jesus will be in Heaven (Abraham, Moses, Rahab, and others according to Hebrews 11). The Old Testament "faithful" will be there because of Jesus's payment—yet they lived before his Name was known (Matthew 8:10–12). God somehow applied Jesus's payment (still to come) based on their faith in the light and knowledge they did have.

Maybe he does the same for those who have never heard his Name. "The eyes of the LORD search the whole earth in order to strengthen those whose hearts are fully committed to him" (2 Chronicles 16:9 NLT). And God promises, "If you look for me wholeheartedly, you will find me" (Jeremiah 29:13

NLT). He wants all to hear so that they will not fear death or judgment, but know they have life with God now and forever (1 John 5:13). But if faith makes us right with God, then what about our good or bad deeds? Do they matter? Absolutely! It's time to explore the life review and rewards for a life well lived.

17

The Life Review

OWARD STORM HAD BEEN RESCUED from the horrors of the outer darkness, and now he found himself with Jesus, paused in space looking toward what he knew to be God's City. Jesus called in a melodic tone, and seven lights shot across the vast distance from the City of Light to join them. Howard recognized them as angels or saints, more brilliant and beautiful than he could imagine, trumped only by Jesus himself. Jesus asked him if he wished to view his life; unsure of what to expect, Howard agreed. Here's how he described the life review to me:[1]

> There are these angels in a semicircle around us. I'm being held. I'm now facing them with Jesus' arms still around me, holding me . . . hanging in space outside of heaven. They gave me a life review. . . . Jesus wanted them to play out, in chronological order, the scenes of my life. Mine was not as some people describe: panoramic, instantaneous. Mine was chronological from when I was born up to the present, moment by moment, life by life . . . in detail; including, knowing, experiencing the

feelings of the people that I was interacting with. . . . The entire emphasis was on my interaction with other people—of course, initially, starting out with my mother and father, my sisters . . . school and friends.

The review of his life was not what Howard expected. It seemed to be presented not from his own memory, but from the perspective of a third party. Together he and the angels watched scenes from his life unfold, many of which he had forgotten. He was shown not only the events themselves, but also their effects on other people's lives and the thoughts and feelings of the people with whom he had interacted—details Howard had not known about at the time the events had taken place.

I learned in my life review [regarding] the relationship with my father . . . [that] I had participated in the breakdown of that relationship as much as he did. He was not a good father to me and I resented it, and I was angry at him. So, I did everything I could, subconsciously and sometimes consciously, to be as rebellious and as cold-hearted towards him as possible; which, only aggravated him more and made him more of a hostile father. So, the things that I had seen in my life where I was the victim and everybody else was the bad guy, I came to find out was a two-way street. We were both playing this game . . . as a son to my mother and father; I had failed them. My father and I had no relationship and my poor mother . . . because of my dad and [me] not speaking to each other . . . we couldn't have much of a relationship. I hardly ever saw her. I had a very poor relationship with my sisters. I had not been a good husband to my wife.

The whole emphasis was on people and not on things. . . . As my life progressed, my adolescence into adulthood, I saw myself turning completely away from God, church, all that, and becoming a person who decided that life was all about [being] the biggest, baddest bear in the woods. . . . As a matter of fact, there were some instances where I had won promotions, honors, awards, and they skipped them. And, I said to Jesus, "You're skipping the most important thing in my life! This is what I lived for, to get this award! Kentucky Artist of the Year: big banquet in my honor and a big cash prize and everything." And, he said, "That's not what we're here for you to see. That's not important. What I want you to see is how you treated the students."

Howard could barely watch some of the scenes from his life as they were replayed by the angels. He was particularly distressed by how he had treated his children, when he neglected them to focus on his own career and accomplishments, rather than on their need to feel loved by him.

And, now I began to experience Jesus' and the angels' literal pain, emotional pain with watching the sins in my life. . . . I had not been the father to my kids that I should have been, and I knew I hadn't—because I was *busy*. I was trying to *be somebody*. . . . [Their] football games and the band concerts and the choral concerts and the theater performances; they could all wait, because I was busy being important. I was doing stuff making myself into somebody. The emotional abandonment of my children was devastating to review.[2]

Watching his life review, Howard understood how his self-centered nature had dominated his entire life, causing him to put his own desires before the needs of the people around him. At one point Howard was so ashamed by how much his cruel and selfish behavior grieved Jesus and the heavenly beings, he begged them to stop the review. Yet he persisted in continuing to watch it for one reason: in spite of the fact that they were disappointed in the way he had lived his life, Jesus and the angels continued to communicate only unconditional love for him.

No matter what we watched me do in life, they communicated their deep love for me, even as they expressed their disapproval of things I did. . . . To use vulgar words is only poor taste. To use the name of God in crude or empty ways is an insult to our

Creator. I was horrified at how it hurt my heavenly company when we witnessed me blaspheming God and Christ Jesus. . . . [3] Here is the nicest, kindest, most loving being I've ever met who, I realized, is my Lord, my Savior, even my Creator; holding me and supporting me, trying to give me more understanding of my life. [And] Jesus is a very feeling man. God is a very feeling Creator, and they feel about us. . . .

The reason why he didn't love what I did was because it distracted from who I was meant to be . . . [like] when you see someone that not only is *not living up* to their potential but actually *denying* their potential. . . . I was made for one purpose and one purpose only, and that's what I was missing.

The angels showed me that we do not earn our love of God by the things we do. God's love is given without cost or strings attached. We live lovingly because God loves us so much. Thank God there is a way to change our lives and be forgiven our mistakes. . . . Jesus is God's redemptive act for a fallen world. . . . If a person is not ruled by the love of God, he or she is ruled by hatred of God. The greatest hatred of God is to be indifferent to God.[4]

For Howard, everything became crystal clear after his NDE, and he is simply grateful that he has been given another chance to live his life, be forgiven for his mistakes, and love the God who so dearly loves him.

The Butterfly Effect

The life review in the presence of God often has the most dramatic impact on the life of a person according to NDE researchers. It clarifies what really matters to God as he shows them that every little action has relational reverberation, person to person, down through the generations. Some people experience their life flashing before them as they are dying, like Ian McCormack. Gary experienced it right when his car crashed: "I slipped out of my body. It was like slipping out of my clothing. I was above the car now; it was as if the top of the car had been removed. I could see my body; I could hear Sue crying. My life passed before my very eyes . . . like a rerun. Everything, in just an instant, flashed before me. I had no fear, and there was no sorrow or confusion."[5]

Most experience the life review in God's presence as he gently guides them to see what matters. The majority of life reviews start with a question from this Being of Light. They may phrase it in different ways but they all hear basically the same thing: "What have you done with the life I gave you?" It's not said in judgment, but in love, to prompt reflection and learning.

Imagine when your earthly life ends and you relive your whole life—every moment. Imagine the day God shows you how your faithful, loving acts of service produced an unseen ripple effect of good in God's economy. Dr. Mary Neal felt Jesus's embrace as she relived her whole life while trapped underwater in her kayak.

> My life was laid bare for all its good and bad. One of the things we did was look at many, many, many events throughout my life that I would have otherwise called terrible or horrible or sad or bad or tragic. And, instead of looking at an event in isolation, or looking at how it impacted me and my little world, I had the most remarkable experience of seeing the ripple effects of the event when seen 25, 30, 35 times removed . . . [and how it] changed me and changed others such that again and again and again, I was shown that indeed, it is true: beauty comes of all things. It was really a life-changing experience.[6]
>
> Through this experience, I was able to clearly see that every action, every decision, and every human interaction impacts the bigger world in far more significant ways than we could ever be capable of appreciating.[7]

God records every thought, every act, and every motive. He promises to reward those who love him and have been faithful to him. Jesus reminds us what to live for: "What good will it be for someone to gain the whole world, yet forfeit their soul? Or what can anyone give in exchange for their soul? For the Son of Man is going to come in his Father's glory with his angels, and then he will reward each person according to what they have done" (Matthew 16:26–27). The life review NDErs experience seems to be a preview. It's not the judgment, but it is an opportunity to live for what truly lasts. Don't wait for your life review to live for what matters!

The Best Feeling

I did the funeral for eighteen-year-old Ben Breedlove, whose YouTube video of him sharing his NDE the week before his actual death went viral. Kid Cudi and Kim Kardashian tweeted about it, *People* magazine reported on it, and Ben's message impacted millions of people around the world. Ben and his family were part of our church and personal friends. Ben had lived on the edge of heart failure his whole life. When he would come to spend the night at our house, we had to make sure the boys didn't get too crazy or his heart could fail. Ben's physical heart was weak, but his spiritual heart was strong. Ben loved God, loved his friends well, and loved life, and I'll never forget hearing about his life review after his NDE.

Ben told his sister, Ally, that every moment he'd ever experienced played out before him in an instant, and "it was the *best* feeling!" In *When Will the Heaven Begin*, Ally says, "Ben knew he was ready for something more important."[8] To those who are faithful, God will one day say, "Well done, good and faithful servant! You have been faithful with a few things; I will put you in charge of many things. Come and share your master's happiness!" (Matthew 25:21).

Imagine a day when you see the positive ripple effects and the negative ripple effects. The life review makes it really clear that Jesus was telling the truth when he said, "There is nothing concealed that will not be disclosed, or hidden that will not be made known" (Matthew 10:26). Dr. Pim van Lommel notes that the life review usually takes place "in the presence of the light or a being of light. During a panoramic life review, people experience not just their every action or word but also every thought from their past life." The NDEr is able to see how their thoughts, words, and actions impacted others. Van Lommel says a cardiac arrest may last minutes, yet people can talk about their life review for days.[9]

Mark was a passenger in a Jeep driving on snowy mountain roads in Lake Tahoe. When the car lost control and crashed, Mark was crushed between the Jeep and a telephone pole. He left his body and had a life review:

> I would describe this as a long series of feelings based on numerous actions in my life. The difference was that not only did I experience the feelings again, but I had some sort of empathetic sense of the feelings of those around me who were affected by my actions. . . . I was adopted as an infant. I had been somewhat of a troublemaker. I sometimes hurt other children when smaller and had taken to drug and alcohol abuse, stealing, crazy driving, bad grades, vandalism, cruelty to my sister, cruelty to animals—the list goes on and on. All of these actions were relived in a nutshell, with the associated feelings of both myself and the parties involved. But the most profound was a strange sense coming from my mother. I could feel how she felt to hear of my death. She was heartbroken and in great pain. . . . I got a sense that it was such a tragedy to have had this life end so soon, having never really done much good. This feeling left me with a sense of having unfinished business in life.[10]

Secrets Revealed

Regardless of cultural or religious upbringing, the life review appears consistent around the globe. Steve Miller studied non-Western, non-Christian NDEs: "In my nonwestern sample, I saw no significant difference in life reviews compared to western life reviews."[11] Different people have described it differently, one as a "movie of myself and of my entire life," another as a "panoramic review of my life," another "like a PowerPoint" presentation. All of them were shocked to experience not only a living, three-dimensional observation of their whole lives, but even their secret thoughts and motives. Such an experience aligns with what Scripture predicts will happen: "Judge nothing before the appointed time; wait until the Lord comes. He will bring to light what is hidden in darkness and will expose the motives of the heart. At that time each will receive their praise from God" (1 Corinthians 4:5).

Rene hydroplaned on the streets of Sydney, Australia, hit a piling, and "died":

> I arrived in an explosion of glorious light into a room with insubstantial walls, standing before a man about in his 30s about 6 foot tall, reddish brown shoulder length hair and an incredibly neat, short beard & moustache. He wore a simple white robe, light seemed to emanate from Him and I felt He had great age and wisdom. He welcomed me with great Love, Tranquility, Peace (indescribable), no words. I felt "I can sit at your feet forever and be content," which struck me as a strange thing to think/say/feel. I became fascinated by the fabric of His robe, trying to figure out how light could be woven!
>
> He stood beside me and directed me to look to my left, where I was replaying my life's less complimentary moments; I relived those moments and felt not only what I had done but also the hurt I had caused. Some of the things I would have never imagined could have caused pain. I was surprised that some things I may have worried about, like shoplifting a chocolate as a child, were not there whilst casual remarks which caused hurt unknown to me at the time were counted. When I became burdened with guilt I was directed to other events which gave

joy to others. Though I felt unworthy, it seemed the balance was in my favor. I received great Love.[12]

Jesus promised that it's not the things people see that matter most, but the unseen things done to please God that will ultimately be rewarded. "Don't do your good deeds publicly, to be admired by others, for you will lose the reward from your Father in heaven. . . . Give your gifts in private, and your Father, who sees everything, will reward you. . . . Don't be like the hypocrites who love to pray publicly on street corners and in the synagogues where everyone can see them. . . . Pray to your Father in private. Then your Father, who sees everything, will reward you" (Matthew 6:1, 4–6 NLT).

Not everyone can succeed in the world's eyes. Most will not be rich, famous, or powerful, and the world's glory will pass away with death; yet every single person can succeed in what God put them here to do. He looks at the heart and motives most. "And without faith it is impossible to please God, because anyone who comes to him must believe that he exists and that he rewards those who earnestly seek him" (Hebrews 11:6). George Ritchie, the soldier in chapter 1, stood in Jesus's presence as every scene from his life was relived before him, including his secret thoughts and motives:

> What emanated from this Presence was unconditional love. An astonishing love. A love beyond my wildest imagining. This love knew every unlovable thing about me—the quarrels with my stepmother, my explosive temper, the sex thoughts I could never control, every mean, selfish thought and action since the day I was born—and accepted and loved me just the same. . . . I saw myself turning away when my stepmother bent over to kiss me goodnight, saw the very thought itself: *I'm not going to love this woman. My mother died. Miss Williams went away. If I love her she'll leave me, too.* I watched myself at age ten, standing at that same dining room window while Dad went to the hospital

to bring home Mother and our new brother Henry, saw myself deciding before I ever saw him that I was not going to like this newcomer. . . . Every detail of twenty years of living was there to be looked at. The good, the bad, the high points, the run-of-the-mill. And with this all-inclusive view came a question. It was implicit in every scene and, like the scenes themselves, seemed to proceed from the living Light beside me.

What did you do with your life?[13]

Moody notes this all-encompassing reflective question is common among NDEs. The wording is obviously unique to each experience, but it generally involves a question related to whether or not the person is prepared or ready to die, and what the person has done with the life he or she had been given. The main emphasis is to lead NDErs to think about their lives.[14]

Jesus told us, "The time is coming when everything that is covered up will be revealed, and all that is secret will be made known to all. Whatever you have said in the dark will be heard in the light, and what you have whispered behind closed doors will be shouted from the housetops for all to hear!" (Luke 12:2–3 NLT). The message is clear: Live now for what really matters.

Relational Matters

The world tells us money matters, power matters, prestige matters—and we drive ourselves crazy trying to prove to one another that we're successful enough, important enough, powerful enough; yet in the end it's relationship that truly matters. How ironic that in trying to prove we are worthy of love through accomplishments, we could miss accepting God's love and sharing it with those around us—and in the end, that matters most for true success!

Everybody wants to change the world; nobody wants to love their neighbor! Yet all God needs us to do to change the world is to love God so we can love our neighbor as much as ourselves. We may accomplish big things in the world's eyes, build huge corporations, lead sweeping political change, or even lead large nonprofits or churches in God's name—and that can all be good. But if we fail to love our families, our neighbors, our co-workers, and those in need whom God puts in our path, we've failed in the primary task God's given us.

Jesus told us that in the final day God will say, "When you failed to love, serve, clothe, feed, care for the least, the forgotten, the unimportant . . . you failed to do it to me. When you *did* love, serve, clothe, feed, care for the least important, you did it to me—now come and receive your reward" (Matthew 25, my paraphrase). As Jeffrey Long notes, NDErs found that some of the most seemingly insignificant actions—a small kindness, for instance—turned out to be important or meaningful in their own or another person's life. Likewise, people saw in their life review they had overvalued unimportant, insignificant things.[15]

Jesus said it's the little, unseen things that matter: "When you give a banquet, invite the poor, the crippled, the lame, the blind, and you will be blessed. Although they cannot repay you, you will be repaid at the resurrection of the righteous" (Luke 14:13–14). As a pastor of a large church, I refocused after reading Steve Sjogren's life review. We can do lots of great things, but "without love, we are nothing" (1 Corinthians 13:1–3, my paraphrase). Steve was leading a large church doing lots of good, yet during his NDE God redirected him:

> As the clock ticked, I heard God speak. He told me about my life and all that He wanted to change in it. It was as if we had taken a trip to the woodshed, in the most positive sense of the expression. God gave me a number of life-altering, unforgettable messages that I will take to my grave. Some I can share, some are more personal. . . . We did not communicate just with

words, but also with memories and images. God let me know how much He valued me. It's almost impossible to describe the perfect sense of acceptance that surrounded me, yet even in the midst of this very personal embrace, part of me knew that not everything in my life had matched what God had intended for me. I had fallen down so often that the angels probably had headaches. Despite my list of fiascos, God extended His total acceptance and absolute love to me—and showed me how He was going to give me another chance. I got the sense that God was going to give me an opportunity to let go of the things that had become idols in my life and allow me to begin to embrace people instead. I was to become the husband and father that I was supposed to be. Right there in the ICU ward, I realized that I didn't know the names of any of my children's friends! I was to become the employer, neighbor and friend that I was intended to be.[16]

"Whoever does not love their brother and sister, whom they have seen, cannot love God, whom they have not seen" (1 John 4:20). Jesus makes it clear: it's not how great we become in the world's eyes or what we accomplish that matters most—it's how we go about these things, and why we do them. Are we motivated by love for God and to serve others? Jesus told us, "Whoever wants to be a leader among you must be your servant, and whoever wants to be first among you must be the slave of everyone else. For even the Son of Man came not to be served but to serve others and to give his life as a ransom for many" (Mark 10:43–45 NLT).

Responsibility

One thing NDErs recognize is that you can't pretend or hide, cover up or mask anything. In the light of God's eyes, the truth about ourselves is fully known, and there's no one to blame, nowhere to hide, no excuses to make. We will fully realize the truth even if we spent a lifetime fooling ourselves. The only thing left to do is take responsibility for it. And God wants us to do that now, so that we can be free of all pretenses. Then, with his help, we can grow into the people he intended.

One NDEr noticed, "I lingered at those incidents where I had trouble recognizing my responsibility until I was ready to accept it." He wanted to explain his reasoning to those he hurt, but needed to just own what he had done. Yet he also observed that no one condemned him. He even felt "a warm support," although he struggled to understand how this "support" could possibly love him. "Could it not see how naïve I had been in life?" he wondered. "And that I had been motivated by ambition, selfishness, fear—and, yes—even by joy or euphoria?" He also saw how his thoughts, words, and actions had positively impacted others. "Everything was shown simultaneously—my entire life!" he remembered.[17]

Jeffrey Long observes that NDErs were typically the ones who judged themselves.[18] Maybe that's why Jesus said, "A good man brings good things out of the good stored up in him, and an evil man brings evil things out of the evil stored up in him. But I tell you that everyone will have to give account on the day of judgment for every empty word they have spoken. For by *your words* you will be acquitted, and by *your words* you will be condemned" (Matthew 12:35–37, italics mine).

One woman said, "I saw how selfish I was and how I would give anything to go back and change." [19] Another man recalls, "Next he showed me my life review. Every second from birth until death you will see and feel, and [you will] experience your emotions and others that you hurt, and feel their pain and emotions. What this is for is so you can see what kind of person you were and how you treated others from another vantage point, and you will be harder on yourself than anyone to judge you."[20]

Judgment

Lindi, a woman who attends our church, told me, "I was always afraid of judgment. I know there's no condemnation for those in Christ, but because of all my past sin, I knew I'd be held to account. So honestly, I wasn't really excited about Heaven. But when I was there, it wasn't like that—I was *so* excited for my life review."

Lindi heard a Voice [she assumed from Jesus] giving another person a life review, saying, "Let's look at all the things you've done to serve Me, to love other people well; let's look at the relationships in your life and how you've loved them well and therefore served Me through them." Lindi recalls, "What was interesting is it was all about relationships. There was nothing about accomplishments, nothing about our 'successes'—all about how you've loved other people." Then came the part she had feared, but the Voice said, "Let's look at the missed opportunities to love Me better. Let's look at how you could have loved other people better, and the missed relationships and how you could have loved them better and therefore served Me better." Then the Voice said, "Welcome home, thank you for loving me so well throughout your life." She realized there's truly no condemnation, and it motivated her to not miss opportunities. She's since started working to free women from sex trafficking.

What those who experience the life review also realize is that God's love and compassion for us is not based on our good or bad deeds: it's unconditional—there to receive as a free gift. "God saved you by his grace when you believed. And you can't take credit for this; it is a gift from God. Salvation is not a reward for the good things we have done, so none of us can boast about it" (Ephesians 2:8–9 NLT).

As we will see in the next chapter, there are two judgments. One determines whether we've accepted or rejected God's free gift of love, forgiveness, adoption, and salvation; the other judgment is to reward us. Ephesians chapter 2 continues: "For we are God's masterpiece. He has created us anew in Christ Jesus, so we can do the good things he planned for us long ago" (Ephesians 2:10 NLT). God wants us to have confidence that we will never be cast out from his presence—we are safe and secure in Christ. But that doesn't mean our good or bad deeds don't matter; they affect our experience of eternity!

The life review is not either of these judgments. It is simply a clarifying reminder that God knows everything about us, and we will all one day give an account. When near-death researchers proclaim there is no judgment because of the life review, they don't understand what the Scriptures reveal. But also, when Christians say NDEs can't be of God because NDErs don't face judgment, and quote, "People are destined to die once, and after that to face judgment" (Hebrews 9:27), they don't understand the Scriptures either. There's no judgment *at all* until the story of earth is complete, and human history, as we know it, ends (see Revelation 11:15–18).

It's no surprise people don't feel judged by this Being of Light if he is Jesus. Jesus told us, "God sent his Son into the world not to judge the world, but to save the world through him. There is no judgment against anyone who believes in him. But anyone who does not believe in him has already been judged" (John 3:17–18 NLT). Every human feels judged already—it's why we judge others, compare ourselves, and justify ourselves to ourselves—but it's all counterproductive.

God wants to set us free from proving ourselves, judging ourselves, or comparing ourselves to each other so we can be free to accomplish the wonderful things he created us to do. At the end of time, there are two judgments, and as we'll discover in the next chapter, the bema seat judgment that's coming will not be like a sentencing—it will be like the greatest cosmic awards ceremony ever imagined!

18

Rewards and Judgments

GARY'S SISTER was driving while the siblings sang "Silent Night" on the way home during Christmas break. Suddenly, Gary heard a scream and an explosion. Searing pain shot across his face; just as fast, the pain was gone. His life flashed before his eyes, then he found himself transported through a brilliant tunnel-like pathway that led to a world beyond imagination.

"I then began walking on a green, lush carpet of grass that covered the hillside. Looking down, I noticed that the grass came all the way through my feet and that there were no indentions where I had just walked. From the hill, I viewed the outer portion of a magnificent city." After marveling at the beauty of Paradise, Gary made his way up to the City gate.

[An] angel came through the gate, and he was checking the pages of a book that he was carrying. He then nodded to the giant angel, confirming that I may enter into the city. Suddenly, there in front of me stood my best friend, John [who had been decapitated but was now whole]. His eyes sparkled with life as we embraced. . . .

John told me he had many wonderful things to show me. John took me into a very large building that looked like a library. The walls were solid gold and sparkled with a dazzling display of light that loomed up high to a crystal, domed ceiling. I saw hundreds and hundreds of volumes of books. . . . Many angels were there reading the contents of the books. John explained to me that these books contain a record of every person's life that has ever been born, throughout all history. Everything we do here on earth is recorded in these books—good or bad—everything.[1]

The Great White Throne

When near-death researchers proclaim that the life review shows there is no judgment, they are naively ignorant of what the Scriptures teach. The Old Testament prophets and Jesus talk about two separate judgments. The great white throne judgment is a judgment of faith and determines who belongs to God. The bema seat judgment is actually a rewards ceremony for all who belong to God. As Scripture makes clear, neither judgment takes place until the end of human history as we know it: "The kingdom of the world has become the kingdom of our Lord and of his Messiah, and he will reign for ever and ever. . . . The time has come for judging the dead, and for rewarding your servants the prophets and your people who revere your name, both great and small—and for destroying those who destroy the earth" (Revelation 11:15, 18).

One of the most fascinating observations of NDErs correlates with Scripture's teaching of books in Heaven recording all our deeds. Marv Besteman recalls seeing these during his NDE: "Piled on top of this shelf or table made of stones were books upon books upon books, stacked up three to four books high, all along the surface both left and right."[2]

Moses alluded to the Book of Life, which indicates who belongs to God (Exodus 32:32–33). An angel told the prophet Daniel during his vision of Heaven, "Everyone whose name is found written in the book . . . will be delivered. Multitudes who sleep in the dust of the earth will awake: some to everlasting life, others to shame and everlasting contempt. Those who are wise will shine like the brightness of the heavens, and those who lead many to righteousness, like the stars for ever and ever" (Daniel 12:1–3).

NDEs confirm what Scripture says—there are books in Heaven recording all our deeds, and the Book of Life which records the names of those who gave their lives to God. Both come into play after the end of time, at the great white throne: "Then I saw a great white throne and him who was seated on it. . . . And I saw the dead, great and small, standing before the throne, and books were opened. Another book was opened, which is the book of life. The dead were judged according to what they had done as recorded in the books" (Revelation 20:11–12).

People dismiss the idea of judgment; it's not a popular idea today. But it's been a common idea in most all cultures for all time. What's uncanny is how many NDErs refer to the books of Heaven. Jeffrey Long's website contains the story of a thirteen-year-old girl who died in a pool accident and found herself at the City gates where she sees books and an "old" friend:

> I was waiting in line at first, behind all these people. And then it was my turn. And I was standing in front of this BIG guy, who I think was an angel. He was holding this BIG book. . . . The angel guy asked me for my name, and I told him. When he looked for it he said, "I'm sorry but it is not your time." So I said to him, "Why is it not my time?!?! I'm ready to die! My life sucks!! My best friend died [five] years ago!! Why is it not my time?!?!" And then he turned around as if someone was

talking to him and turned back around to me again and said, "Someone wants to talk to you." Then he pointed to the gate with the city behind it. . . . It was Jake. You see, Jake, my best friend, died in a car accident five years ago. We were both seven years old, and when I saw him there I ran to the gate as fast as I could! We both reached out and grabbed each other's hands and cried. He looked my age, but I knew it was him. And I feel stupid in saying this, but he got cute since the last time I saw him! ha ha ha! Then we talked for a while, about things that happened, about each other, and then the angel said, "It's time for you to go back."[3]

Another teenager who drowned explains on the same website that he also saw books:

[My angels] did not like my response of, "I don't want to go back down there; it is painful." "You must! Your mission is not yet complete!" We communicated telepathically; no lips or mouth movements; all thoughts. Moment by moment you discover how quickly you are gaining knowledge; and how easy it is to accept. My three angels sought permission from above to show me something. . . . What looked like a HUGE four foot thick book, of LIFE. MY Life. Just as my life had passed before my eyes when I was being drowned, I was now being shown my future life.[4]

The psalmist says, "Your eyes saw my unformed body; all the days ordained for me were written *in your book* before one of them came to be" (Psalm 139:16, italics mine).

Written in the Book

At first, it seemed strange to me why God would need to have books in Heaven. But maybe they are there for us—as a record and reminder. Just like we have historical movies and books, Heaven seems to have both a panoramic visual replay and books of record. Across the globe, NDEs confirm books in Heaven. As Osis and Haraldsson reported, Hindu Indians never experienced "reincarnation and dissolution in Brahma, the formless aspect of God which is the goal of Indian spiritual striving. [But] the concept of Karma—accumulation of merits and demerits—may have been vaguely suggested by reports of a 'white robe man with a book of accounts.'"[5] They miss the connection to the Bible completely, but report that multiple Indians mentioned this man in white some called "God," and "books of account."

An Indian doctor said, "The [Indian] patient seemed to die. After some time, he regained consciousness. He then told us that he was taken away by messengers in white clothing, and brought up to a beautiful place. There he saw a man in white, with an account book."[6] Another Indian "saw a beautiful scene, lovely flowers. In there he saw a man dressed in white sitting with an open book."[7]

At the great white throne, every person will see clearly their need for Jesus's payment for their debt. Like Jesus said, God will accept, forgive, and take back any person who wants God's leadership. God does not send anyone out of his presence; he gives them what they want. If they did not want God's forgiveness and leadership, they will be judged by their own words. As Jesus said, "But I tell you that everyone will have to give account on the day of judgment for every empty word they have spoken. For by your words you will be acquitted, and by your words you will be condemned" (Matthew 12:36–37).

Remember though, what NDErs experience is not the judgment, because NDErs didn't "die"—not fully! Long says 31 percent of NDErs report some border or boundary: "I reached the point where I felt I had to make the choice whether to go back to life or onward into death. My best friend was there (who had died of cancer two years before), and she told me that this was as far as I could go or I would not be able to turn back."[8]

Heaven and Hell Will Change

After the great white throne, Heaven and hell will change. "Then death and Hades were thrown into the lake of fire. The lake of fire is the second death. Anyone whose name was not found written in the book of life was thrown into the lake of fire" (Revelation 20:14–15). Death and Hades (or hell, the holding place of the dead) and all who did evil and rejected God will undergo the second death. Some think this is a type of annihilation; others argue that eternal creatures cannot be annihilated. Whatever the case, evil, sin, pain, and suffering will never plague humanity again.

God cannot allow those unwilling to submit to his rule into his eternal kingdom or they would corrupt it like we did the earth and humanity. "Nothing impure will ever enter [the City of God], nor will anyone who does what is shameful or deceitful, but only those whose names are written in the Lamb's book of life" (Revelation 21:27).

If you're not sure what your verdict would be at the great white throne, you can be sure right now. As Jesus said, "I tell you the truth, those who listen to my message and believe in God who sent me have eternal life. They will never be condemned for their sins, but they have already passed from death into life" (John 5:24 NLT).

The Bema Seat

At some point after earth's history concludes, another judgment happens called the *bema seat*. It's a judgment for God's children. Yes, there is a judgment of believers: "For we must all appear before the judgment seat of Christ, so that each of us may receive what is due us for the things done while in the body, whether good or bad" (2 Corinthians 5:10). The word translated "judgment" is the Greek word *bema*, which refers to the judge's seat at the ancient games—like the Olympic judge's stand. This was the place where the judges would award the gold or silver medals (crowns in their day) for a race well run. It's a judgment of rewards.

God loves to reward every faithful act, deed, even motive, and that's what will happen at the bema seat judgment. We don't earn God's love or acceptance into Heaven; that's a gift we receive or reject. But all our deeds determine our *experience* of Heaven—what we take with us from this life. Paul uses an analogy of building a house:

> [Each person] will be rewarded for their own hard work. . . . No one can lay any foundation other than the one we already have—Jesus Christ. Anyone who builds on that foundation may use a variety of materials—gold, silver, jewels, wood, hay, or straw. But on the judgment day, fire will reveal what kind of work each builder has done. The fire will show if a person's work has any value. If the work survives, that builder will receive a reward. But if the work is burned up, the builder will suffer great loss. The builder will be saved, but like someone barely escaping through a wall of flames. (1 Corinthians 3:8, 11–15 NLT)

Paul pictures some people who came to faith and lived their lives investing in things of eternal value, and what they built with their life will stand and bring great reward eternally. Others received God's gift but lived mostly for themselves. Imagine a person running out of a burning house—they're safe, but all they worked for just went up in smoke. What you do with your life really matters—every moment of this life matters more than you ever imagined.

The bema seat is where Jesus rewards us—it's like a huge Oscars celebration for all of God's children across human history! You thought the red carpet was a big deal—you ain't seen nothing yet! God promises to recognize and reward every single person, personally.

It's gonna be the most rewarding thing you've ever imagined. Isaiah looked forward to it, saying, "See, your Savior comes! See, his reward is with him" (Isaiah 62:11). Jesus said, "For the Son of Man is going to come in his Father's glory with his angels, and then he will reward each person according to what they have done" (Matthew 16:27). So let's imagine that day, and live for the things that God rewards.

What Gets Rewarded Eternally?

When you think about life, it's really not fair at all. Half of humanity lives on less than $2 per day, the powerful oppress the powerless, suffering and injustice come with the territory for most. Yet God promises that one day those who persevered out of love for God will be rewarded. All those unseen times you wondered, "Is it worth it? Is it worth resisting temptation? Is it worth being mocked, shunned, cast out among peers? Is it worth it to love God when I hurt so badly? Is it worth it to love people when they're so mean and evil? Is it worth it?" One day you will see—the answer is a resounding yes!

Perseverance Matters

"Blessed is the one who perseveres under trial because, having stood the test, that person will receive the crown of life that the Lord has promised to those who love him" (James 1:12). God personally promises to reward our perseverance. When no one else could see how hard it was for us, yet we clung to him and endured—he knows, he sees, and he's keeping track of everything: "I know about your suffering and your poverty—but you are rich [eternally]! I know the blasphemy of those opposing you. . . . Don't be afraid of what you are about to suffer. . . . Remain faithful even when facing death, I will give you the crown of life" (Revelation 2:9–10 NLT).

Ken Ring interviewed Carla, a blind NDEr who finally saw the truth during her life review. Carla clinically died during surgery, left her body, and accurately described the operating room: "The operating table was in the center of the room. And the telemetry was on the ceiling, you know, the screen for the telemetry was on the ceiling." During her life review she saw the truth about bullying she endured:

Interviewer: Were you able to see details of people that you had never been able to see?

Carla: Oh, yeah. But I saw, you know, myself [and] how I was dealing with people and the exact things that I had said, you know, to these people throughout each experience. . . . I grew up tall and grew physically before my age, and so the kids who were partially sighted used to call me "big barn." And I think that through this, as I could see myself on the playground or swimming or doing whatever it was I was doing, that I was not the way they depicted me. That in actuality some of the kids who made fun of me were bigger and fatter than me, you know, and I could see this. . . . It doesn't sound like a big deal [but] it really was to me. . . . I thought that I looked like a really graceful person. Like "a lady."[9]

I think about my friend Kate, born with cerebral palsy. Inside she's just like you and me, but outside she's bound to a wheelchair and speaks mostly through a computer. Kate told me at one point she became suicidal due to the rejection and hurt inflicted on her by well-functioning people. That's when she found faith in Jesus and began to live for him. It changed her perspective, and she now looks for ways to love and serve

260

others and is writing a book to encourage others with disabilities. Imagine Kate's reward! Whenever you're struggling or suffering or going through trials, remember—be faithful to God, endure, and he will reward it!

Seeking God Matters

While confined to a Roman jail cell and facing execution, Paul declared, "Now there is in store for me the crown of righteousness, which the Lord, the righteous Judge, will award to me on that day—and not only to me, but also to all who have longed for his appearing" (2 Timothy 4:8). God promises to reward those who diligently seek him, walk by faith with him, and long for him. "Without faith it is impossible to please God, because anyone who comes to him must believe that he exists and that *he rewards* those who earnestly seek him" (Hebrews 11:6, italics mine).

Faith is another word for trust. You can't have a relationship without trust. That's why faith matters so much to God. We show our love for him by seeking him, seeking his will and ways, and trusting what he says in Scripture. No one else can see all those decisions made by faith each day, yet God records every one. He will one day reward them all.

Jesus promised, "I tell you the truth, until heaven and earth disappear, not even the smallest detail of God's law will disappear until its purpose is achieved. So if you ignore the least commandment and teach others to do the same, you will be called the least in the Kingdom of Heaven. But anyone who obeys God's laws and teaches them will be called great in the Kingdom of Heaven" (Matthew 5:18–19 NLT). How awesome to know that you may never be rich, powerful, or on the cover of a magazine, but if you faithfully seek God, know the Scriptures, and lovingly obey his will—one day you will be one of the great ones for eternity!

Developing People Matters

It should not surprise us that developing people and spiritually building into people matters to God—we can't love God unless we also love his children (1 John 4:7–21). Yet we forget so quickly. The world tells us to build up ourselves. When we obey that, we neglect building up others. As Professor Howard Storm realized during his life review, "The whole emphasis was on people and not on things. . . . I said to Jesus, 'You're skipping the most important thing in my life!' . . . And, he said, 'That's not what we're here for you to see. That's not important. What I want you to see is how you treated the students.'"[10]

We've all wanted people to see us, believe in us, and develop us into the people God intended; yet most of us didn't get that, so we don't give it. When we take time to build into our kids, God will reward it—it's our first duty! But it's fairly easy to care about developing *our* kids. When we take time to also help others find faith, or develop God's other "kids"—he will reward us!

Jesus used an agricultural metaphor to teach this: "Wake up and look around. The fields are already ripe for harvest. The harvesters are paid good wages, and the fruit they harvest *is people* brought to eternal life. What joy awaits both the planter and the harvester alike!" (John 4:35–36 NLT, italics mine). Helping people find faith and grow spiritually might get you mocked or persecuted in the short run, but it will one day bring you great, great joy! You don't have to be far along to simply reach back and help someone two steps behind you. Ian McCormack got this message after Jesus rescued him from the outer darkness:

> Directly behind Jesus was a circular shaped opening like the tunnel I had just traveled down. Gazing out through it, I could see a whole new world opening up before me. I felt like I was standing on the edge of paradise. . . .

Through the centre of the meadows I could see a crystal clear stream winding its way across the landscape with trees on either bank. To my right were mountains in the distance and the sky above was blue and clear. . . .

Jesus asked me this question: "Ian, now that you have seen do you wish to return?" I thought, "Return, of course not. Why would I want to go back? Why would I want to return to the misery and hatred? No, I have nothing to return for. I have no wife or kids, no one who really loves me. You are the first person who has ever truly loved me. . . ."

But he didn't move so I looked back one last time to say, "Goodbye cruel world I'm out of here!" As I did, in a clear vision right in front of the tunnel, stood my mother. As I saw her I realised my mistake; there was one person who loved me—my dear Mum. . . . I had mocked her beliefs. But she had been right after all, there was a God and a heaven and a hell.

I began to consider how selfish it would be to go through to paradise and leave my mother believing that I had gone to hell. . . . So I said, "God, there's only one person really I want to go back for and that is my mum." . . .

Then as I looked back again, I saw behind her my father, my brother and sister, my friends, and a multitude of other people. God was showing me that there were many other people who also didn't know, and would never know unless I was able to share with them. I responded, "I don't love those people" but he replied, "I love them and I desire all of them to come to know me." Then the Lord said, "If you return you must see things in a new light."[11]

When you build into others spiritually, no one may even notice or care—but God cares! Paul writes this to the people he spiritually developed in Thessalonica: "What will be our proud reward and crown as we stand before our Lord Jesus when he returns? It is you!" (1 Thessalonians 2:19 NLT). Peter says to all who spiritually shepherd and develop others, "Care for the flock that God has entrusted to you. Watch over it willingly, not grudgingly—not for what you will get out of it, but because you are eager to serve God. Don't lord it over the people assigned to your care, but lead them by your own good example. And when the Great Shepherd appears, you will receive a crown of never-ending glory and honor" (1 Peter 5:2–4 NLT). When you invest in people spiritually, God sees, and he will reward it. One day you will see how one life changed another life, and how your greatest impact on humanity came by developing individuals.

Serving the Least Matters

People matter to God. He cares about those who get neglected, outcast, marginalized, unseen by most because they can't do anything for us. God sees though, and when we act unselfishly to serve those who can't do anything for us, it will be rewarded in Heaven.

After his life review, one NDEr said, "I saw how selfish I was and how I would give anything to go back and change." Jeffrey Long notes how many NDErs say that of all the aspects of the NDE, the life review is by far the one that prompts the greatest personal transformation, because it allows the person to relive his or her own life—to witness mistakes and missteps as well as good deeds and decisions. "Things that seemed insignificant at the time—a small kindness, for instance—turn out to be significant in their own or another person's life."[12] That's why Jesus told us when we serve the least "important" person in earthly terms, we serve him—and it will be rewarded (see Matthew 25:31–46).

Work Matters

So many people hate their jobs. It's a shame, because all our work matters to God when we do it to please him. Imagine how it could transform your purpose for working with excellence if you knew it really will make a difference in eternity. "Whatever you do, work at it with all your heart, as working for the Lord, not for human masters, since you know that you will receive an inheritance *from the Lord as a reward*. It is the Lord Christ you are serving. Anyone who does wrong will be repaid for their wrongs, and there is no favoritism" (Colossians 3:23–25, italics mine). Whatever we do with the motive of doing it well to please God, gets rewarded! Isn't that encouraging to realize? You can succeed anywhere, doing anything. But if we are lazy, dishonest, slacker employees, God sees that too—and we lose a potential reward he wants to give us.

Finances Matter

"From everyone who has been given much, much will be demanded; and from the one who has been entrusted with much, much more will be asked" (Luke 12:48). I used to hate those words of Jesus's—they haunted me. I live in America, where most of us will be in the top 2 percent of the wealthiest humans in history (if you make $25,000/year or more, you're there—over $1 million will pass through your hands over your lifetime!). I'm college educated, which puts me in the top 1 percent of the most learned of humanity. I have more choices, more gadgets, more entertainment, and more discretionary time than most humans have ever had.

So what will I do with all that God has entrusted to me? It matters to God. Jesus told us very clearly that all our money is Monopoly money, and all our possessions—we can't keep one. At the end of the game, it all goes back in the box. What lasts is how you played the game to honor God.

"Use your worldly resources to benefit others and make friends," Jesus said. "Then, when your earthly possessions are gone, they will welcome you to an eternal home. If you are faithful in little things, you will be faithful in large ones. But if you are dishonest in little things, you won't be honest with greater responsibilities. And if you are untrustworthy about worldly wealth, who will trust you with the true riches of heaven? And if you are not faithful with other people's things [i.e., God's things], why should you be trusted with things of your own [eternal possessions]? . . . You cannot serve both God and money." (Luke 16:9–13 NLT)

He Loves to Reward

When we invest our resources in building God's kingdom, making his churches strong, feeding the poor, righting injustices, blessing others as an act of love toward him—he says it will be rewarded with true riches, true possessions, things that can never be taken from us. Imagine what those things might be, because you'll never outgive God. He loves to reward!

But part of the reason people don't invest time, money, or service for the rewards to come is because they just can't picture it. Some people still fear that Heaven will be boring—or less fulfilling. When we get a clear picture of the cost/benefit of possibly sacrificing some earthly rewards to live for eternal ones, it's a no-brainer. The rewards to come are—excuse the pun—out of this world!

19

Exhilarating—Not Boring

THOSE WHO HAVE DIFFICULTY picturing Heaven fear it will be boring. Just imagine the exhilarating future that awaits you as God's reward for a life well-lived. You've never experienced a gift so great.

To experience something so sacred, so profound as the boundless love of God was the most thrilling part of heaven. It satisfied a longing in the deepest part of me. My spiritual family had shared God's perfect love with me. How could I ever be the same? . . . I felt so special, you can't believe how special. After all, all this was for me. Everyone there was there for me. I had no idea what gift I was to receive, but the anticipation on the faces of the people let me know that it was something extraordinary. I felt like a kid again, like that fifth-grade kid who loved God. Like that kid who used to look forward to Christmas like you wouldn't believe. I couldn't wait to open the gifts that waited for me under the tree. And I couldn't wait for the gift that waited for me now. The music continued, such beautiful music, and I became even more excited. It swelled and with it so did my anticipation. And then, as I was about to travel through the entrance and receive the gift . . . I was swept away.[1]

Every NDEr says the life to come is real life—just like we live now—only expanded in experience: more beauty, more thrills, more responsibility, more important assignments, more bliss and adventure. No one wants to come back. So let's imagine what it might be like to gain the greatest gift ever—eternal rewards— because I'm convinced it's worth way more thought, planning, sacrifice, and investment than you're currently giving it.

One thing that's clear: we will all be equally loved and valued by God in Heaven, but there will be differences. As Jonathan Edwards speculated, maybe we will all be completely full to overflowing with God's love, joy, and excitement, but like cups with different capacities, we will experience God and all his wonders to the capacity we developed while on earth.[2] God promises to reward those who faithfully follow and serve him, and the great news is that every one of us can wildly succeed in his eyes and overflow with great capacity in Heaven. What might those rewards be like? Let's imagine . . .

Your Perfect Place

Imagine your dream house—in your dream location. So many people strive and sacrifice and save to get the perfect retirement home in the perfect place. I get it. When I worked as an engineer in Santa Barbara, I got to be friends with people who now own my dream home—a beautiful mansion on the beach, surrounded by lush gardens, with a view of the mountains too! Paradise—almost.

Our friends love God, and they love to share their blessings with many people—including my family! Don't you think God loves to give good gifts, and could bless his children even more? If God were to design a house just for me, he could do even better than that! And he will—for all his children. Jesus promised it: "In My Father's house are many dwelling places; if it were not so, I would have told you; for I go to prepare a place for you" (John 14:2 NASB). You and I want to bless our kids with wonderful homes, special places just for them—how much more does your Heavenly Father want to reward you with the same?

From the composite picture I get from many NDEs, there are homes in the country, homes in the mountains, homes in quaint villages, and homes in the City of God forming a semicircle around the central feature of the universe—God's throne. It's all one big home, one *oikos*—the Greek word not just for a house but also the larger extended family—with many smaller family dwelling places! Imagine being "home" in every place you dwell. That's the picture painted by Jesus. Recall that as Captain Dale Black flew over the great City escorted by his two angels, he described the exquisite architecture of the City homes between God's throne and the great wall:

> Between the central part of the city and the city walls were groupings of brightly colored picture-perfect homes in small, quaint towns. . . . The dwellings in these townships were not arranged in a uniform or symmetrical manner but appeared perfectly balanced somehow. Each home was customized and unique from the others yet blended harmoniously. Some were three or four stories, some were even higher. There were no two the same. If music could become homes, it would look like these, beautifully built and perfectly balanced.[3]

In a fascinating NDE written in 1898, Rebecca Springer reported what other Christian NDErs would report a hundred years later, including homes. Rebecca had a severe illness and hadn't eaten or had much fluid for three weeks. One night, feeling death close, she prayed for Jesus to send comfort. She found herself standing beside her bed. She looked, and Frank, her favorite brother-in-law who had passed away, was right beside her. After a joyous greeting, he said, "Shall we go?" She looked back and saw "on the bed . . . lay a white, still form, with the shadow of a smile on [her] poor, worn face. My brother drew me gently, and I yielded, passing with him through the window, out on the veranda, and from thence, in some unaccountable way, down to the street."

She traveled with Frank to a place described by modern NDErs and Scripture, where she explains she found herself on

the softest and most beautiful turf of grass, thickly studded with fragrant flowers, many of them the flowers I had known and loved on earth . . . others of like nature wholly unfamiliar to me. . . . Away, away—far beyond the limit of my vision, I well knew [with telescopic vision]—stretched this wonderful sward of perfect grass and flowers; and out of it grew equally wonderful trees. . . . I saw, half hidden by the trees, elegant and beautiful houses of strangely attractive architecture, that I felt must be the homes of the happy inhabitants of this enchanted place. I caught glimpses of sparkling fountains in many directions, and close to my retreat flowed a river, clear as crystal . . . and instead of sunlight there was a golden and rosy glory everywhere.[4]

Since there's no scarcity in Heaven, maybe we will have multiple homes to enjoy. Just like the best properties have the best locations, imagine having a view of the most beautiful, exciting place in the universe—God's throne! That could be one of your God-given rewards.

Your Own Property

It's funny how we live for stuff—cars, boats, all kinds of bling—yet forget to live for God who promises to reward us with *lasting property*. On the one hand, it sounds shallow and materialistic to think we'd want or need stuff in Heaven, but on the other hand, maybe we won't be tempted to idolize it like we do now—we'll just enjoy it as a gift, which will give God enjoyment with us. Jesus told us if we are faithful managers of the property that we can't keep, God will give us property that we can keep. Jesus promised, "I assure you that when the world is made new . . . everyone who has given up houses or brothers or sisters or father or mother or children or property, for my sake, will receive a hundred times as much in return and will inherit eternal life. But many who are the greatest now will be least important then, and those who seem least important now will be the greatest then" (Matthew 19:28–30 NLT).

I wonder what lasting property or possessions will be like? Since so much of the world to come seems continuous with this world—but a hundred times more fulfilling—maybe some of the property will be very similar (after all—it is *life* . . . eternal). Then again, with the universe as our playground, maybe some of us will be the proud owners of celestial wonders or cosmic playgrounds that would blow our tiny imaginations. All I know for sure is this—if God says there are treasures in Heaven, they will definitely be a lot better than the things we treasure on earth. Live for it!

Important Responsibilities

One thing that's certain about Heaven—you'll never be bored! In fact, people will have important roles, responsibilities, projects to complete, music to compose, and cities or nations to govern. It will be life, but with the people in charge who fully submit to God's will and ways. Jesus told his twelve disciples, "I assure you that when the world is made new and the Son of Man sits upon his glorious throne, you who have been my followers will also sit on twelve thrones, judging [ruling] the twelve tribes of Israel" (Matthew 19:28 NLT).

271

Jesus told a parable of Heaven, likening it to a wealthy man about to be made king, who went away and entrusted his money to ten different servants, asking them to use it to expand his business interests. When he returned as king,

> The first servant reported, "Master, I invested your money and made ten times the original amount!"
>
> "Well done!" the king exclaimed. "You are a good servant. You have been faithful with the little I entrusted to you, so you will be governor of ten cities as your reward."
>
> The next servant reported, "Master, I invested your money and made five times the original amount."
>
> "Well done!" the king said. "You will be governor over five cities." (Luke 19:16–19 NLT)

The last servant did nothing with what was given him (because he hated the man and didn't want him as king). All he had got stripped away, and he ended up in outer darkness (see Luke 19:20–27).

God watches to see how faithful we are because he's equipping us to take on way more important responsibilities. He even allows all the trials and tests of earth because he's preparing us to rule with him. When we undergo suffering and hardship, there really is a greater purpose. God is training us to govern in eternity. "If we endure hardship, we will reign with him" (2 Timothy 2:12 NLT). "Do you not know that we will judge [rule] angels?" (1 Corinthians 6:3). Some of us will govern angels, others will rule cities—some will be over nations.

And it's not those who powered their way up who will be entrusted with the most important responsibilities, it's those who humbly served and obeyed God who will be trusted with more. Jesus said, "To all who are victorious, who obey me to the very end, to them I will give authority over all the nations. . . . They will have the same authority I received from my Father, and I will also give them the morning star!" (Revelation 2:26, 28 NLT).

Work and Creativity

Todd began to accept the idea that his four-year-old son, Colton, had actually been to Heaven. He wanted to know more, so he asked his son what he did there.

"Homework."

That was certainly not the answer Todd expected. "What do you mean?"

"Jesus was my teacher," Colton said.

"Like school?"

Colton nodded. "Jesus gave me work to do, and that was my favorite part of heaven."[5]

His favorite part of Heaven—the work Jesus gave him to do? Not all of us will rule cities, but I imagine all of us will take on special projects, assignments, work perfectly fitted to how God has wired us. It's what we were created to do before the fall, to steward and govern over creation (see Genesis 1:26). God is a Creator, a Builder, a Developer—and he loves to create through us.

If you love creativity, imagine getting rewarded with an assignment to create and showcase a special exhibit for the president of the United States. Now imagine greater—the President of All Creation rewarding you with the assignment to create for him! Imagine all the time ever needed to create that music or art you never had time for on earth. Imagine the joy of being in the zone as you research, explore, discover, or build something commissioned by the Great Builder.

After showing George Ritchie the realm of self-absorbed beings, Jesus showed him a whole new realm. George thought these might be the outer environs—still far from the center of

Heaven—filled with people enraptured in their projects. "Enormous buildings stood in a beautiful sunny park and there was a relationship between the various structures, a pattern to the way they were arranged, that reminded me somewhat of a well-planned university. Except . . . it was more as if all the schools and colleges in the world were only piecemeal reproductions of this reality."

Jesus led him into one of the buildings with high-ceilinged corridors and people walking around—it was buzzing with excitement as if everyone was enthralled with discovery and on the verge of some great new breakthrough.

> Somehow I felt that some vast experiment was being pursued, perhaps dozens and dozens of such experiments.
>
> "What are they doing, Jesus?" I asked.
>
> But although Knowing flamed from Him like fire—though, in fact, I sensed that every activity on this mighty "campus" had its source in God—no explanation lighted my mind. What was communicated, as before, was love: compassion for my ignorance, understanding that encompassed all my non-understanding.
>
> And something more. . . . In spite of His obvious delight in the beings around us, I sensed that even this was not the ultimate, that He had far greater things to show me if only I could see. . . . We entered a studio where music of a complexity I could not begin to follow was being composed. . . .
>
> Next we walked through a library the size of the whole University of Richmond. . . . *Here*, the thought occurred to me, *are assembled the important books of the universe*. Immediately I knew this was impossible. How could books be written somewhere beyond the earth! But the thought persisted, although my mind rejected it. *The key works of the universe*.

They walked out of that building, across a park between the buildings, and into what he described as "a strange, sphere-shaped structure where a catwalk led us over a tank of what appeared to be ordinary water." It was crowded with techno-logical machinery and appeared to him as what might be a space observatory.

> "Is this heaven, Lord Jesus?" I ventured. The calm, the bright-ness, they were surely heaven-like! So was the absence of self, of clamoring ego. "When these people were on earth, did they grow beyond selfish desires?"
>
> *They grew, and they have kept on growing.* The answer shone like sunlight in that intent and eager atmosphere. But if growth could continue, then this was not all. Then there must be something even these serene beings lacked.[6]

Imagine if in Heaven we keep on learning, growing, discov-ering, and creating because all of it ultimately points back to God—back to the glory of his infinite wonders that will take ages of eternity to explore. Jesus told us Heaven will be life—why do we keep imagining something less exciting than earthly life? Maybe in Heaven we will know fully as we are fully known, in an earthly sense. So we might know and understand all the mysteries of our world, but we will never finish exploring all the depths of God's creative capacities. And I imagine part of the reward of Heaven encompasses the types of projects, roles, responsibilities, creative endeavors, universal exploration, or unimaginably exciting assignments God will give his faithful servants.

My Greatest Reward

"One thing I ask from the LORD, this only do I seek: that I may dwell in the house of the LORD all the days of my life, to gaze on the beauty of the LORD and to seek him in his temple" (Psalm 27:4). "You will fill me with joy in your presence, with eternal pleasures at your right hand" (Psalm 16:11). We may not understand it now like the prophet David who wrote these psalms, but there's no greater reward in the universe than intimacy with God. He's the highlight of the universe and the longing of every person. He is the Greatest Reward of all. No one ever wants to leave his presence. Listen again as NDErs describe being with him:

> I was so consumed by His presence that I dropped to my knees and looked up at Him. He is so glorious, so beautiful. All light inside of Light.[7] —Khalida

> I was filled with awe at His beautiful presence.[8] —Gary

> Seeing the majesty and indescribable beauty of the Lord made me speechless. . . . When I was in His presence, it was all I wanted.[9] —Samaa

> It's the pinnacle of everything there is. Of energy, of love especially, of warmth, of beauty.[10] —anonymous Dutch NDEr

> The magnificence of this Person pierced me like a laser . . . all Power, all Wisdom, all Splendor, all Love. . . . Nothing mattered except to remain in this presence.[11] —Mickey

Moody wrote about an indescribable love and warmth flowing from the divine being toward the person. "He senses an irresistible magnetic attraction to this light. He is ineluctably drawn to it."[12] Imagine the most majestic, beautiful, awe-inspiring Being who possesses such power that one word alone speaks into existence whole universes! Imagine the One to whom all other beauty, joy, and pleasure owe their existence. And now imagine feeling a unique, close intimacy with *that* person—a closeness that rivals that of father and child, a best friend, even a spouse—that's the greatest reward imaginable. I'm convinced there's a closeness, an intimacy, that God has in store for us that all the greatest intimacies on earth merely hint at—a Oneness and an ecstasy that make sex seem trivial and boring in comparison. Why wouldn't that be the case when God himself calls his people his bride?

Different Capacities

Everyone in Heaven will see the Lord and experience the joyful bliss so many NDErs have described, but I'm not sure that everyone will be equally close in the same way. One NDEr surmised that our love and faithfulness to God on earth determines our capacity to experience him in Heaven. People who love God deeply are deeply moved in his presence, while the ones who love him less deeply do not experience the same depth of love. Those who reject God find his presence intensely painful. That aligns with what atheist A. J. Ayer experienced during his NDE.

But I've also noticed how some NDErs knew they could not yet go to the City of God. George Ritchie in his tour visited what seemed like levels of hell on earth, then what seemed like the outer environs of Heaven, and then he claimed Jesus took him through a "tunnel" where he found himself in what felt like another dimension. They stopped, and with his new telescopic vision, George saw a city.

> And then I saw, infinitely far off, far too distant to be visible with any kind of sight I knew of, a city. A glowing, seemingly endless city, bright enough to be seen over all the unimaginable distance between. The brightness seemed to shine from the very walls and streets of this place, and from beings that I could not discern, moving about within it. In fact, the city and everything in it seemed to be made of light, even as the Figure at my side was made of light.
>
> At this time I had not yet read the book of Revelation. I could only gape in awe at this faraway spectacle, wondering how bright each building, each inhabitant, must be to be seen

over so many light-years of distance. Could these radiant be-ings, I wondered, amazed, be those who had indeed kept Jesus the focus of their lives? . . . Even as I asked the question, two of the bright figures seemed to detach themselves from the city and start toward us, hurling themselves across that infinity with the speed of light. But as fast as they came toward us, we drew away still faster. . . . He had shown me all He could.[13]

George apparently could go no closer at that point. It's fas-cinating to me that multiple NDErs say similar things, viewing the City of God, the New Jerusalem, from somewhere far out in space or maybe some dimension containing our space (we'll explore this more in the next chapter). But just as George could not go closer, neither could Howard Storm after being rescued from hell.

Howard remembers that he and Jesus rose up together, slowly at first, and then shot through space toward a large illuminated area in the far distance. It looked like a galaxy, Howard recalls, with a bright concentration of light in the center. In spite of the fact that he was very aware of God's love for him, Howard also began to experience feelings of shame and fear as he remem-bered all the times in his life he had scoffed at the possibility of God and Heaven, as well as all the thousands of times he had used God's name as a curse or an insult. Remembering this about himself, Howard felt too ashamed to go closer to the light.[14]

"I am a terrible piece of garbage," he thought to himself. "They should put me back where I belong, back in that hole of darkness and terror. They made a terrible mistake. I belong back there." Jesus stopped moving and spoke directly into How-ard's mind. "We don't make mistakes," he said. "You belong here." They stopped, still countless light years away from the City. Jesus comforted Howard as he wept, then gave him a life review. After his life review, Howard asked Jesus,

So what happens to people that are going towards this [City] but aren't sure they're ready? He said, "They freeze up," and I said, "What do you mean they freeze up?" And he said, "They just lock up and . . . think about themselves. . . . They want to move forward but they're not ready to." [15]

Another of Heaven's travelers surmised that our reward for deeds on earth determines how much of God's glory we share and how close of an intimacy we share with him. "There are different glories. And by different glory, it means to shine; they actually shine brighter so that those people on the outer environs could not behold a being, for instance, from the most holy place, a person who goes into the most holy place, he'd be very bright to appear to those people." [16] He believes people can learn and grow in Heaven and even increase intimacy with God, "but there's some barrier they can't go beyond, I believe it's the fact that they have no rewards because they didn't do any work [for God on earth]. . . . But a person with more glory, more brightness, spends more time in the presence of God." [17]

The Bright Morning Star

Jesus promised, "To the one who is victorious and does my will to the end, I will give authority over the nations. . . . I will also give that one the morning star" (Revelation 2:26, 28). Why would we want the "morning star" as a reward? Because "I, Jesus . . . am the bright morning star" (Revelation 22:16 NLT). He wants to give us the greatest reward of all—himself! Every believer will see God and experience the loving wonders of his presence, but don't you want to leave this earth with the greatest capacity possible for the greatest reward of all? All it takes is the simple, childlike, trusting obedience we're all capable of displaying.

Sam is a good friend whose grown child, Shane, has autism and severe mental retardation. He doesn't understand abstract things, like Heaven. One Saturday morning, Shane came downstairs and announced, "I'm getting baptized at church Sunday."

That piqued Sam's interest because she was concerned Shane could not understand the significance of baptism. "Maybe someday, but I don't think you have to get baptized," Sam said.

"No, I do! Jesus told me I'm going to get baptized on Sunday," Shane insisted.

Sam was concerned. "Shane, Jesus didn't tell you that!"

Shane, who had never ever mentioned a dream in his life, proclaimed, "No, I had a dream last night and Jesus took me to Heaven, and Mamaw was there [Shane's deceased grandmother], and Jesus was there, and God was there."

Sam knew something strange had happened; Shane couldn't make up abstract ideas like dreams or Heaven. Cautiously, Sam probed. "Well, what was it like?"

Shane excitedly explained, "Jesus built me a house, and it has a red door. He showed me my house and told me I'm getting baptized tomorrow."

Sam didn't even know if there was a baptism the next day. Still not sure what to think, she questioned, "He showed you your house? So Shane, will I live next to you?" Sam knew Shane loved to do everything with her.

"No!" came Shane's surprising answer.

"Well, why not?" Sam asked, quite shocked at his response.

"I'm living right next to God."

Shane got baptized the next day at our church's baptism, just like he said he would.

It would make perfect sense to me if the Shanes of the world had the most special location in the City of God. "Blessed are the pure in heart, for they will see God," said Jesus (Matthew 5:8). Just imagine what life in Paradise and the City of God will be like—let's take a peek.

20

Paradise Found

IN THESE FINAL CHAPTERS, I'm going to stretch beyond the core experience of most NDEs, because I want us to imagine how real and amazing Paradise and the City of God will be. I'm describing sights that three or more Christians claimed to see. These fit within Scripture's framework, but with details I hope will ignite your imagination.

I don't know if the present Heaven will be exactly as these people report, but what each have said forms a composite like the descriptions you'd expect if ten people went to New York City and reported what it was like. They all have different angles and details, but over time, a cohesive picture starts to form. Even if it's not just like this, I'm confident it will be better than you or I can imagine. Why would the Creator of earth's wonders make Paradise and his heavenly City less spectacular? The apostle John did not have an NDE but was taken to Heaven by an angel. Picture this place John and some modern NDErs claim to have seen:

I saw the Holy City, the new Jerusalem, coming down out of heaven from God, prepared as a bride beautifully dressed for her husband. And I heard a loud voice from the throne saying, "Look! God's dwelling place is now among the people, and he will dwell with them. They will be his people, and God himself will be with them and be their God. 'He will wipe every tear from their eyes. There will be no more death' or mourning or crying or pain, for the old order of things has passed away."

He who was seated on the throne said, "I am making everything new!" . . .

And he carried me away in the Spirit to a mountain great and high, and showed me the Holy City, Jerusalem, coming down out of heaven from God. It shone with the glory of God, and its brilliance was like that of a very precious jewel, like a jasper, clear as crystal. It had a great, high wall with twelve gates, and with twelve angels at the gates. On the gates were written the names of the twelve tribes of Israel. There were three gates on the east, three on the north, three on the south and three on the west. The wall of the city had twelve foundations, and on them were the names of the twelve apostles of the Lamb.

The angel who talked with me had a measuring rod of gold to measure the city, its gates and its walls. The city was laid out like a square, as long as it was wide. He measured the city with the rod and found it to be 12,000 stadia [~1,400 miles] in length, and as wide and high as it is long. The angel measured the wall using human measurement, and it was 144 cubits [216 feet] thick. The wall was made of jasper, and the city of pure gold, as pure as glass. The foundations of the city walls were decorated with every kind of precious stone. The first foundation was jasper, the second sapphire, the third agate, the fourth emerald, the fifth onyx, the sixth ruby, the seventh chrysolite, the eighth beryl, the ninth topaz, the tenth turquoise, the eleventh jacinth, and the twelfth amethyst. The twelve gates were twelve pearls, each gate made of a single pearl. The great street of the city was of gold, as pure as transparent glass.

I did not see a temple in the city, because the Lord God Almighty and the Lamb are its temple. The city does not need the sun or the moon to shine on it, for the glory of God gives it light, and the Lamb is its lamp. The nations will walk by its light, and the kings of the earth will bring their splendor into it. On no day will its gates ever be shut, for there will be no night there. The glory and honor of the nations will be brought into it. Nothing impure will ever enter it, nor will anyone who does what is shameful or deceitful, but only those whose names are written in the Lamb's book of life. (Revelation 21:2–5, 10–27)

The New Jerusalem

When I used to hear about the heavenly City of God, called the New Jerusalem in Revelation, with pearly gates and streets of gold, it sounded gaudy to me—kind of like the set of a bad televangelist show. Because of my poor imagination, I assumed much of this description in Revelation was apocalyptic metaphor or a vision not meant to be literal in any way. While much of Revelation is apocalyptic and metaphorical, I'm starting to see that maybe the ancient writers of Scripture saw something real. They made their best fumbling attempt to put into earthly word-pictures a stunningly beautiful Paradise and City beyond description. NDErs describe a similar reality, though I don't think every city NDErs describe is the New Jerusalem (Heaven has other cities as Jesus alluded to in Luke 19:17–19).

One day, the New Jerusalem and the new earth will be united as in John's vision, but the New Jerusalem is ready now in the present Heaven where people live, waiting for that day. "For [Abraham] was looking forward to the city with foundations, whose architect and builder is God. . . . All these people were still living by faith . . . longing for a better country—a heavenly one. Therefore God is not ashamed to be called their God, for he has prepared a city for them" (Hebrews 11:10, 13, 16). God *has prepared* a city for them—past tense. So by faith, let's imagine your first trip to the City of God.

Entering Another Dimension

Maybe you'll instantly arrive in Heaven, or maybe you'll go through a tunnel first. Each person's journey seems unique. Maybe you'll start far off, somewhere in some kind of deep space like those described in the last chapter. Maybe the present Heaven is located in the hidden dimensions of our space that scientists postulate, or maybe in the dark matter of deep space, or maybe our space is located within it.[1] As I write, my father-in-law is fighting terminal brain cancer. He was a founding manager of NASA's Space Station project. Imagine how exciting his journey will be if his starts with a tour from deep space to Heaven's space.

Another person, Ed, did not die, but claimed to be given a vision of Heaven. I include it because Ed eloquently describes much of what Scripture and other NDErs confirm. Imagine the excitement of your first flight home.

> We flew through the starry heavens. On a path, or ladder, or a stairway, we moved forward at a great speed. . . . I asked the angel, "Why did we stop?" "Turn around," the angel said. I turned around to face a most amazing sight. . . . My eyes feasted on a huge spherical globe! I fixed my clouded eyes upon a spectacular, panoramic view of God's house. Our inheritance; paradise lost. The whole thing was bright and rich. Its sacred beauty filled my soul. . . .
>
> "The sphere is of pure gold," the angel stated. He knew what I was thinking, because he answered before I could ask him. . . . It's not like the gold on a watch or the gold on a wedding ring. Heaven's gold is clear, yet having a golden look. I could clearly see through the golden sphere, a transparent gold. . . . Though made of gold there was a changing multi-colored effect playing

upon the sphere. It was an awesome colorful light show. Colors flashed, like sheets of lightning. They shimmered around the golden sphere. . . .

I could see through the golden sphere onto the most beautiful spring-green land. . . . Looking like an electrifying jewel embedded in the center of the circular land stood a city-cube of dazzling, colorful, golden splendor! Awesome rainbows of inexpressible colors flowed over, around, and into the city-cube . . . more enthralling than any sunset or sunrise I have ever seen. The gold sphere itself does not shine. The light originates from a huge and colorful cube-shaped city. . . .

The angel explained to me that, "The city you see inside is New Jerusalem. It is Heaven's Heart. The Father and the Lord Jesus are inside on their thrones. The surrounding land is called Paradise." . . . The city's shape had the look of a colorful, bright cube. Its colors were bright. Its hues were more than the colors of a springtime rainbow. The colors were not those of an Earth rainbow. Other colors dazzled. Colors I have never seen. These new colors were indescribable! . . .

The diameter of the sphere is enormous. I calculated from the center of the sphere to the [edge], there could be fitted twenty New Jerusalems. Therefore, the distance from the city to the outer edge of the sphere would be thirty thousand miles. The diameter of the sphere would be sixty thousand miles across. . . . Earth is only eight thousand miles in diameter.[2]

Beyond the Cosmos

When I first read Ed's account, it sounded like science fiction fantasy (maybe it is). But as I read account after account saying similar things that fit together with other reports, I started to wonder. One person said, "Now these colors are what make heaven interesting. Let me compare it to a sky. You're used to seeing the sky change colors, you know. The sunset, never two alike; always changing. . . . So that's what these colors do in heaven, they make colorful sky but mostly it is gold."[3] If I were making this up I'd say, "Mostly it's blue." Some do see an azure blue sky, but it seems to change much like our atmosphere, and many saw a spectacular golden sky. And remember NDErs (like Marv Besteman) viewing the spectacular light show of Heaven from inside Heaven's atmosphere match Ed's description of a light show he viewed from outside the atmospheric sphere.

After going through a tunnel of dark space with Jesus, Dr. George Ritchie said, "I saw, infinitely far off, far too distant to be visible with any kind of sight I knew of, a city. A glowing, *seemingly endless city*, bright enough to be seen over all the unimaginable distance between. The brightness seemed to shine from the very walls and streets of this place."[4] Howard Storm also found himself in some deep space with Jesus when he glimpsed what looked like a galaxy, a vast area of illumination far off in the distance. In the center of the light was an even brighter concentration of light, which Howard instinctively understood to be God's abode.[5]

Gary Wood found, "As I walked on the pathway, I instinctively knew I was headed north [same as Ed, Dale Black, and others]. Then the swirling mass of a funnel-shaped cloud opened up wide and I saw a *giant golden satellite* suspended in Heaven."[6] Captain Dale Black "traveled through what looked like deep space, almost as if a jet were flying through a snowstorm at night . . . fast approaching a *magnificent city*, *golden and gleaming* among a myriad of resplendent colors."[7]

Scripture doesn't say anything about a transparent golden sphere containing Paradise and the New Jerusalem, which in some ways makes these Christian NDErs' common visions intriguing yet questionable. On the other hand, God told us he has not revealed all his mysteries to us in Scripture (see Deuteronomy 29:29), and what would motivate doctors, professors, and commercial airline pilots to make up (or copy) the same fantastic vision? It sounds crazy—why would they risk their reputations?

Of course, the City of God is not the only place God resides. Scripture tells us, "He is before all things, and in him all things hold together" (Colossians 1:17). So God fills all, is present everywhere by his Spirit, holds it all together, but can also make himself visibly manifest in a place—a City he's created so he can dwell with those who love him.

Paradise

Jesus told the thief who professed faith on the cross beside him, "Today you'll be with me in Paradise" (Luke 23:43). Several mentioned that Paradise is the beautiful, earth-like country surrounding the City of God. It seems to be the port of entry for most. It looks very much like the earth, with trees, animals of all kinds, very high mountains and lakes, all of which make the transition easier as we start in what's familiar, yet spectacularly more vibrant.

Ed doesn't know how, but he found himself traveling toward the sphere, then suddenly inside the sphere standing in Paradise.

> I stood on a carpet of indescribable beauty. In the distance, there were trees growing at the edge of a forest, the tree's branches heavy with bright colorful leaves. . . . My eyes thrilled as I took in the striking wild-hued flowers of all varieties and shapes. They dotted themselves against the vivid green grass. Like the tree leaves, the flowers sparkled from within. I saw that each leaf and petal glowed as if lit by an electric light.
>
> I did not feel cold, nor did I feel hot. The temperature seemed perfect. The crystal air was clear, was pure, and a sweet smelling air. It was a perfect day in Heaven. . . . The beauty of it all was astonishing. Nowhere did I see a dead blade of grass or a wilting flower petal. Infinite rays of colorful light permeated everything. It seemed that every colorful thing I saw seemed to shine from within, [with] colors that excited my eyes. My eyes danced about looking everywhere for new colors, a kid in a candy shop!

I took a deep, deep breath of air. . . . It was invigorating, like fresh spring air just after a morning rain. The whole sky was bright and golden as if the sun had just set. The sky was the inside of the great golden sphere. Like a lightning storm, iridescent colors chased with wild abandon across the sky. Yet there was no thunder. It was more beautiful than any sunset I had ever remembered. . . .

Upon a closer inspection at a blade of grass, it seemed that it was translucent green. Translucent means it lets light through, but you cannot see through it clearly. . . . And the grass and flowers became like wind chimes, as if wired together to ping and ding, tinkle and jingle, and bong. The wind plucked invisible musical strings. A choir of living grasses and flowers rose up in sweet unison, all in harmony. The sound of joyous music arose from around my feet![8]

You have to wonder if that's what Vicki and many others heard when they heard wind chimes. One of Moody's NDErs described the sensation of hearing something like "bells tingling, a long way off, as if drifting through the wind . . . like Japanese wind bells."[9]

Ed asked the angel where they were. "You're standing in Heaven's Paradise," the angel replied. "Look up and straight ahead and you will see New Jerusalem. The city is from where all of God's Light shines." Ed could see that the light came out of everything, but most intensely out of the City, apparently reflecting off the inside of the sphere creating Heaven's amazing atmosphere.[10] "For the glory of God gives [the City] light, and the Lamb is its lamp" (Revelation 21:23).

The City on a Hill

"Let your joy soar with the sight of New Jerusalem," said the angel. "This is your inheritance. It will be yours to walk on and live in with Jesus." Ed noticed,

The city is an immense cube [see Revelation 21:6]. I believe that where I was standing was looking straight at one of its four corners. This gave the illusion the cubed city had a peaked type roof. Its brightness is extraordinary, but its intensity did not hurt my eyes. . . . The land slopes upward toward the city. This awesome sight was unhindered by the hills or the line of forest.[11]

Imagine the vast beauty of Paradise, the suburbs of Heaven—over forty times the size of earth's land surface if Ed's estimates are correct.[12] And in the center a magnificent City, so high (according to Revelation 21:16–17) not even a Mount Everest–sized mountain range can block the view. The City of God is cube shaped just like the Holy of Holies in the tabernacle Moses made and the temple Solomon built. Maybe that's why they were told to pattern it after what they saw—it was a shadow of Heaven (Hebrews 8:5; 9:24 say that). The angel and Ed began to fly slowly toward the City. The angel pointed out to Ed the home he would one day possess in Paradise as they passed over it. Ed had to return before visiting the City, but let's keep journeying in our imaginations, uphill to the New Jerusalem.

I find it fascinating that Scripture never says the New Jerusalem is a City on a hill, as Ed mentioned, yet so many NDErs do. Gary recalls, "I was actually standing on the outside of the city, on a lush green carpet of grass on a hill. I started walking *up the hill* [toward the city]."[13] As one of Dr. Rawlings's NDE patients described, "The whole area was lit with this brilliant, beautiful light. I have never seen anything like it before. I found myself on a rolling green meadow that was *slightly uphill*. I saw my brother and he was alive, and yet I remember when he had died."[14]

Betty Malz found herself walking up to the city wall:

I was *walking up a beautiful green hill*. It was steep, but my leg motion was effortless and a deep ecstasy flooded my body. I looked down. I seemed to be barefoot, but the complete outer shape of my body was a blur and colorless. Yet I was walking on grass, the most vivid shade of green I had ever seen. Each blade was perhaps one inch long, the texture like fine velvet; every blade was alive and moving. . . . All around me was a magnificent deep blue sky, unobscured by clouds. . . . I was arriving at where I had always dreamed of being. The wall to my right was higher now and made of many-colored, multi-tiered stones. A light from the other side of the wall shone through a long row of amber-colored gems several feet above my head.[15]

The City Wall and Gates

Imagine coming up to the great wall and the City gates. Great excitement and anticipation well up from deep within you as you prepare to enter the City of God. Brad Barrows, who was blind from birth, describes details he doubtfully would have made up since he is blind. Listen to how they coincide with Scripture and other people's descriptions. As Brad approached the end of the dark tunnel, he was aware of an "immense field" stretching before him for what seemed like miles. As he took in this scene, he says, "I knew that somehow I could sense and literally see everything that was around me." He noticed, for example, huge palm trees with gigantic leaves, and very tall grass as well.

> When I noticed that I was walking up this field [up the hill to the City], it seemed as if I was so exhilarated and so unbelievably renewed that I didn't want to leave. I wanted to stay forever where I was. . . . It seemed like everything, even the grass I had been stepping on seemed to soak in that light. It seemed like the light could actually penetrate through everything that was there, even the leaves on the trees. There was no shade, there was no need for shade. The light was actually all-encompassing.
>
> Yet I wondered how I could know that because I had never seen before that point. At first I was taken aback by it [by

sight]. . . . I felt like I wouldn't understand it had it happened
. . . on earth. But where I was, I was able to accept it almost
immediately.

As Brad got closer to the city, backlit with the light of God as
Revelation 21:23 says, he heard music and thousands of voices
"singing in a language I had never understood or maybe many,
many languages. The music I had heard was nothing like anything I have ever experienced on earth." Brad never describes
it as a city or a wall or gate—maybe because he started too
close to see it as a city wall—yet his description coincides with
Revelation's description and what other NDErs say:

> As I was going up the hill, I came to a large stone structure. I
> could tell that it was stone without even touching it. I could
> tell with some sort of sight that I had at that time, some sort
> of vision, I knew. They were almost like gem stones [the wall's
> foundation?]. They seemed to literally shine with their own
> particular light. Yet the light itself was actually penetrating
> right through the stones. It seemed that the stone was actu-
> ally heightening that light, the light that was already there,
> to the point where I was almost afraid to touch those stones.
> I thought that they might be fiery hot. In another sense, I was
> very curious about them. The structure I was going into was a
> large tubular structure. I would say that at first the tube seemed
> to be at least a hundred feet in diameter, with the top of the
> tube being well over a hundred feet above my head [a gateway
> arch?]. Right up to the tube, there were palm trees and grass,
> and again this large field that actually existed all the way up to
> the entrance of this tube.[16]

What's amazing to me is that Brad, still blind today, vividly
describes walking up the hilly meadows of Paradise, up to the
gemstone foundation of the City wall, and into the archway
of the City gate; yet he doesn't seem to even know what he's
describing to researcher Ken Ring. He's describing this: "[The

city] shone with the glory of God, and its brilliance was like that of a very precious jewel. . . . The foundations of the city walls were decorated with every kind of precious stone. . . . The twelve gates were twelve pearls, each gate made of a single pearl" (Revelation 21:11, 19, 21).

Several NDErs in Jeff Long's study said similar things: "There was such beauty, beautiful beyond expression. There was also a bright city or something like a city in the distance."[17] Another noticed the same wall: "As far as the eye could see to my left was a beautiful landscape of tulips of every color imaginable. To my right was a wall of a beautiful blue that matched the sky."[18]

Through the Arched Gates

Remember the airline pilot, Captain Dale Black, who came flying in with angels toward the City's southeast side? Listen as he describes getting ready to enter the gates of the City:

> The wall to the city was not a single wall but rather a series of walls layered next to each other. The wall was made of three outer layers, three inner layers, and one higher wall in the center. . . . At its tallest point the wall was a couple hundred feet. And surprisingly, it was as thick as it was tall [Revelation 21 says 216 feet thick]. The wall was massive and stretched out to my left and right as far as I could see in both directions.
>
> The outer wall was greenish in color with a hint of blue and a hint of black mingled within it. It was made entirely of translucent stones. Large multicolored stones were built into the base of the wall in layered rows [Revelation 21 says there are twelve foundation stones]. A powerful light permeated the wall, and you could see all the colors of the rainbow in it. Strangely, whenever I moved, the colors moved ever so slightly as if sensing my movement and making an adjustment.
>
> The two angels that had escorted me there were still with me, moving me along. . . . I was eye-level with the base of the

wall now and no longer hovering above it, but standing in front of an impressive opening. It was an archway that seemed to be approximately forty feet high and thirty to thirty-five feet wide.

A tall, majestic angelic being stood to the right side of the gate. . . . The entrance, or gateway, was opalescent in color, as if it had been made of pearls that had been liquefied, and then solidified onto the wall. The entrance was completely composed of this mesmerizing substance that also coated the entire inside of the opening as far as I could see. The ornamentation around the entrance included phenomenal detail. It was the most astounding sight I had ever seen. As I basked in the beauty that adorned the gateway, I noticed large gold letters emblazoned above the opening. They seemed to quiver with life. The single line of letters formed an arch over the entrance. I didn't recognize the letters but knew the words were as important as any words could be. . . . I was filled with excited anticipation of entering that beautiful gate.

I was immersed in music, in light, and in love. Vibrant life permeated everything. All these weren't just around me, they were inside me. And it was wonderful, more wonderful than anything I had ever experienced. It felt as if I belonged there. I didn't want to leave. Ever. It was as if this was the place I had been searching all my life to find, and now I'd found it.[19]

Imagine an excitement that trumps your best Christmas morning memory as you approach the City gate. Though different people estimated different dimensions of the gate, their descriptions correlate. Scripture never explains that light shines out of everything, including the wall (but it makes sense if God's glory/light shines through everything). It never explains what a gate made of pearl would look like, so we picture ornate wrought-iron-style gates decorated with pearls. Yet NDErs consistently give us the picture of something far more mesmerizing and accurate to Revelation. A wall of gorgeous backlit stone, sitting on twelve foundations made of various gemstones: "The first foundation was jasper, the second sapphire, the third agate, the fourth emerald, the fifth onyx, the sixth ruby, the seventh chrysolite, the eighth beryl, the ninth topaz, the tenth turquoise, the eleventh jacinth, and the twelfth amethyst . . . each gate made of a single pearl" (Revelation 21:19–20).

Pearlescent Gates

Betty Malz recalls the amazing feelings of homecoming as she approached the City:

> My emotion was a combination of feelings: youth, serenity, fulfillment, health, awareness, tranquility. . . . I was arriving at where I had always dreamed of being.
>
> The wall to my right was higher now and made of many-colored, multi-tiered stones. A light from the other side of the wall shone through a long row of amber-colored gems several feet above my head. "Topaz," I thought to myself. "The November birthstone." I remembered this from working in Edwards Jewelry.[20]

Betty feels the same anticipation of home, sees the same light shining out of the stones, and notices topaz—the ninth foundation stone of the New Jerusalem—several feet above her head. If each layer of gemstones was a foot in thickness, topaz would be about three feet above her head! As Betty approached a futuristic, pearlescent gate unlike any entrance you've imagined, she heard music and singing.

> I not only heard the singing and felt the singing but I joined the singing. I have always had a girl's body, but a low boy's voice. Suddenly I realized I was singing the way I had always wanted to . . . in high, clear, and sweet tones. . . . The voices not only burst forth in more than four parts, but they were in different languages. I was awed by the richness and perfect blending of

the words—and I could understand them! I do not know why this was possible except that I was part of a universal experience.

While the angel and I walked together I sensed we could go wherever we willed ourselves to go and be there instantly. Communication between us was through the projection of thoughts. . . .

The angel stepped forward and put the palm of his hand upon a gate which I had not noticed before. About twelve feet high, the gate was a solid sheet of pearl, with no handles and some lovely scroll work at the top of its Gothic structure. The pearl was translucent so that I could almost, but not quite, see inside. The atmosphere inside was somehow filtered through. My feeling was of ecstatic joy and anticipation at the thought of going inside.

When the angel stepped forward, pressing his palm on the gate, an opening appeared in the center of the pearl panel and slowly widened and deepened as though the translucent material was dissolving. Inside I saw what appeared to be a street of golden color with an overlay of glass or water. The yellow light that appeared was dazzling. There is no way to describe it.[21]

The angel asked her if she wanted to go inside. Though she did with all her being, she heard the voice of her father, praying for her to live. She asked if she should check on him, and "the gates slowly melted into one sheet of pearl again and we began walking back down the same beautiful hill."

To me, the mismatched dimensional estimates of this gateway arch lend validation to their testimony: it indicates no collusion—they aren't just copying the same story. They seem to be giving different angles, estimates, and perspectives like the various accounts of Jesus's resurrection. My Harvard-trained lawyer friend told me slight discrepancies of the same story hold more weight in a court of law. It indicates people telling the truth from their slightly different perspectives.

From these NDE witnesses and Scripture, we start to get a picture of this massive wall with a foundation layered with twelve gemstones—1,400 miles long, approximately 200 feet high, and 216 feet thick—and twelve translucent gate-like archways made of pearlescent material you can pass through to enter the majestic City of God.

But why a wall in Heaven? And how is the City 1,400 miles high if the wall is only 200 feet high? These questions plagued me, and I can only guess at the answers. Revelation tells us "its gates will never be closed" (Revelation 21:25 NLT), so the wall must be more for decoration than for protection. And the 1,400-mile-high sides are apparently made of the same transparent gold that you can see, yet also see through. "The city was pure gold, as clear as glass" (Revelation 21:18 NLT). The gates are there for welcoming in rather than keeping out.

Don Piper explains the pearlescent gates like this:

> As we came closer to the gate, the music increased. . . . Looming just over the heads of my reception committee stood an awesome gate interrupting a wall that faded out of sight in both directions. It struck me that the actual entrance was small in comparison to the massive gate itself. [Maybe that explains varied dimensions; some describing the whole gate archway, others the entrance?] I stared, but I couldn't see the end of the walls in either direction. As I gazed upward, I couldn't see the top either.
>
> One thing did surprise me: On earth, whenever I thought of heaven, I anticipated that one day I'd see a gate made of pearls, because the Bible refers to the gates of pearl. The gate wasn't made of pearls, but was pearlescent—perhaps iridescent may be more descriptive. To me, it looked as if someone had spread pearl icing on a cake. The gate glowed and shimmered. I paused and stared at the glorious hues and shimmering shades. The luminescence dazzled me.[22]

Clearly this is an otherworldly entrance into your most exciting, exhilarating experience ever! Imagine the thrill as your new senses come alive with sights, smells, colors, and sounds of music and light—all alive with love—filling your soul with ecstasy as you pass through the great hallway of pearlescent material, through the wall, and into the glorious City of God.

21

The City of God (Pets Allowed)

D ON PIPER WAS JUST ABOUT TO ENTER the City gate. Imagine if you were experiencing this rapturous crescendo of joy:

Everything I saw was bright—the brightest colors my eyes had ever beheld—so powerful that no earthly human could take in this brilliance. In the midst of that powerful scene, I continued to step closer to the gate and assumed that I would go inside. My friends and relatives were all in front of me, calling, urging, and inviting me to follow.

Then the scene changed. I can explain it only by saying that instead of their being in front of me, they were beside me. I felt that they wanted to walk beside me as I passed through the iridescent gate. . . . As we came closer to the gate, the music increased and became even more vivid. It would be like walking up to a glorious event after hearing the faint sounds and seeing everything from a distance. The closer we got, the more intense, alive, and vivid everything became. Just as I reached the gate, my senses were even more heightened, and I felt deliriously happy.

I paused—I'm not sure why—just outside the gate. I was thrilled at the prospect and wanted to go inside. I knew everything would be even more thrilling than what I had experienced so far. At that very moment I was about to realize the yearning of every human heart. I was in heaven and ready to go in through the pearlescent gate.[1]

Imagine going through the gate into the City of God. The angel who greets you at the gate is overpowering in stature, yet you experience the warmth and love of Heaven. Today, your name is in the book—Heaven's long-awaited guest of honor. Imagine watching the pearlescent substance dissolve around you as you and your welcoming party of family and friends, with Christmas-morning anticipation, walk into the long, great hallway as a crescendo of melodies draws you up into its joy.

One person noticed that "inside the gate it looks like a large hallway. . . . The gate is two hundred and sixteen (216) feet thick and that makes a nice long hallway. And on the sides of the hallway, are archways like a third of a circle . . . and in those places are what on Earth would be offices and the records are kept. So when we greet the Angel at the gate, he is there to welcome us."[2] Dale Black noticed the pearlescent substance lining the hallway: "The entrance was completely composed of this mesmerizing [pearly] substance that also coated the entire inside of the opening as far as I could see."[3]

This sounds like the same great hallway Dr. Mary Neal described during her NDE while kayaking: "We were traveling down a path that led to a great and brilliant hall . . . radiating a brilliance of all colors and beauty. I felt my soul being pulled toward the entry . . . the gate through which each human being must pass."[4] It's likely the very place Brad Barrows tries to describe, but being blind and having never seen anything before, he calls the semicircular hallway a "tube": "I could start hearing plainly the music I had heard before. It was as if people were singing in several different languages. . . . When I looked into the tube, I could tell that I was going to step on some kind of stone, the same shiny, brilliant stone that I could see all around the tube. It was smooth stone, very, very smooth."[5]

Smooth like pearl?

Imagine the thrill of passing through the great hallway, and for the first time, experiencing the sights and sounds in the greatest city ever imagined. As you enter the City, the first thing you see is the Tree of Life. "Then the angel showed me the river of the water of life, as clear as crystal, flowing from the throne of God and of the Lamb down the middle of the great street of the city. On each side of the river stood the tree of life, bearing twelve crops of fruit, yielding its fruit every month. And the leaves of the tree are for the healing of the nations" (Revelation 22:1–2).

Trees of Life

The Tree of Life was the tree found in the Garden of Eden. It was the reason God hid Eden from humanity once we sinned against God. God decreed that once we came to know good and evil. "[Man] must not be allowed to reach out his hand and take also from the tree of life and eat, and live forever" (Genesis 3:22). God protected us from eternal life separated forever from him by the knowledge of evil. Now, with the collective knowledge of earth's evil in our past, armed with the knowledge of what it cost God to restore us, we can live in his City with him and forever choose to love and follow God, freely. Now as we enter his gates, we can eat of the Tree of Life and *live*.

But as one person observed, it's not just one tree. "The first thing we see is the tree of life. Now I used to think this was one tree but it is a row of trees that contain the fruit alongside of the River of Life. . . . Now this fruit grows as John says [in

Revelation], different fruit every month and when somebody takes a piece of fruit, another piece appears right away because a lot of people [are] partaking of the fruit."[6] Imagine as you walk over to try a piece, you notice you're not really "walking"—though you can walk—but more like gliding.

"It is possible to move by the speed of thought. You have to go somewhere and just like that you're there. But there is a mode to move slowly. You have the sensation of moving which in itself is delightful. When you ride down a scenic road [in Heaven], you can look out and see the scenery whereas travelling by thought you wouldn't see that because right away you're there."[7] Imagine as you move toward the trees, you realize they're part of a beautifully landscaped garden-boulevard, following the flow of a river winding down the hills through the center of the City. The River of Life is lined by rows of delicious fruit trees, gardens, and flowers on each bank, flanked by streets on either side of the river.

Streets of Gold

As we continue our imaginary tour, you notice the streets look gold, but not like the gaudy yellowish-gold we often imagine. They're made of a substance unlike any we've seen. Betty Malz noticed "what appeared to be a street of golden color with an overlay of glass or water. The yellow light that appeared was dazzling. There is no way to describe it."[8] No one describes the garish yellow-brick-road-to-Oz picture I had in my head, but instead an otherworldly, transparent, crystal-like road alive with golden hues.

Gary notes, "We walked on transparent streets, and I could see all the way through them. A NASA scientist later told me there is an impurity in gold, and when it's removed, the gold is no longer yellow, it's crystal clear."[9] Astronauts' helmets have a thin gold coating that reflects the sun yet allows them to see through the gold-plated visor. How would the ancients have known gold could be transparent? Revelation says it, I just couldn't imagine it before: "The great street of the city was of gold, as pure as transparent glass" (Revelation 21:21). I've never seen a substance like that, yet many NDErs claim they saw the streets described in Revelation. So imagine, you cross the street to taste the fruit trees by the River. Some claimed to taste the fruit, not from the Tree of Life, but from Heaven's other trees:

> As I walked along the golden pathway, I noticed the sky. It was rosette-pinkish in color, but it was also a crystal clear blue. . . . There was a park, which had benches where you could sit and talk to others. . . . [People] were having a wonderful time talking with people who had just come through the veil. . . . The beautifully manicured park was filled with huge, striking trees. They had to be at least two thousand feet tall. And there were many different varieties. Some I knew; others, I had no idea what species they were. . . . I went up to what I thought was a walnut tree, and I was told to take and eat. The fruit was pear shaped and copper colored. When I picked it, another fruit instantly grew in its place. When I touched the fruit to my lips, it evaporated and melted into the most delicious thing I had ever tasted. It was like honey, peach juice, and pear juice. It was sweet but not sugary.[10]

Child prodigy artist Akiane mentioned how good the fruit of Heaven tastes: "better than anything you've ever tasted. The Light gives me fruit. . . . God says many will need to eat that. The tree will always be there on a new earth."[11] The fruit and the leaves heal and strengthen you. I've wondered before, will there be adventure, excitement, risk in Heaven? Maybe there will still be a need for healing, but in Heaven God always heals, meets our needs, and wipes away our tears. I'm not sure. But I am sure of this—Life will be thrilling.

The Cultural Center of the Universe

With the taste of new strength, you're ready for a tour of the cultural center of all creation. The City is huge, so there's a lot to explore. Some think the measurement of New Jerusalem is metaphorical, and maybe it is, but John does say, "the angel measured the wall *using human measurement*" (Revelation 21:17, italics mine). The City is expansive according to that measurement—1,400 miles on each side—which would make it approximately half the size of the United States, so there's plenty to explore. But that's not difficult because, if NDEs are right, you can see across a lot of it with telescopic sight, travel instantly by thought, or slowly stroll through gardens, quaint mountain villages, or to the City center taking in all the attractions.

And there are so many sights to take in—the parks, rivers, fountains, lakes, libraries, art galleries, museums, music events, sporting events. Wait a second, sporting events? Art galleries? I'm speculating now, but why would we think the Originator of all human creativity, culture, and fun would take that away from his children once they are finally home? Randy Alcorn writes, "We have every reason to believe that the same activities, games, skills, and interests we enjoy here will be available [there]."[12] God didn't say he's destroying all things, he said he's renewing all things (Matthew 19:28; Revelation 21:5).

If "all things" really means *all things*, then the same culture, creativity, fun, and excitement you'd find in the best of earthly endeavors will be resurrected to trump our wildest dreams. So dream big! I imagine much of what we created on earth motivated out of love for God will also be enjoyed for eternity.

There will be no end to the excitement of this City. Just think, the City's also 1,400 miles high! I wonder if there are levels, or stories—like earth's terrain plus its atmosphere, layered one on another? This could be, since we can move anywhere, including up and down at will. Just think, the New Jerusalem could have our earth's atmosphere, with something like our sky and clouds that make up our seven-mile-high troposphere, and be two hundred "atmospheric stories" high. That's twice the surface area of the earth, just within the City, and that doesn't count the countryside of Paradise (not to mention entire universes to explore). Heaven will be endless excitement, enjoyment, and exploration . . . even before God renews, re-creates, and rejoins the new Heaven with a new earth somehow remade to fit perfectly together!

Gary met his best friend, John, at the gates of Heaven. John had been decapitated in a horrible accident on earth, but now fully alive and fully restored, John took Gary on a tour of the city. Imagine it one day.

> John told me he had many wonderful things to show me. John took me into a very large building that looked like a library. The walls were solid gold and sparkled with a dazzling display of light that loomed up high to a crystal, domed ceiling. I saw hundreds and hundreds of volumes of books. . . .
>
> We left the library, and I was taken to a grand auditorium. Everyone was clothed in glowing robes, and as I entered into the arena, I found I was clothed in a robe also. Looking up, I saw a beautiful, spiral staircase winding up loftily into the heights of the atmosphere [like in Solomon's temple, 1 Kings 6:8]. A beautiful, crystal clear river of water flowed directly in front of me. My eyes followed the river that flowed from the throne of God! It was an awesome sight to see the source of the river that was the throne of almighty God! . . .
>
> Growing along the crystal river were orchards of fruit-bearing trees. . . . The hills and mountains before us towered in breathtaking beauty. I noticed a host of people on the hillside. They were observing things that were taking place on earth.[13]

Gary noticed that the landscape of the City is as varied as the United States, since it's half that size. And he saw people from

Heaven observing earth. Scripture hints that those in Heaven still have knowledge of earth's happenings (Luke 15:7; Revelation 6:10–11). In light of Heaven's joys, all of earth's sorrows will gain new context within the knowledge of God's perfect plan.

The Plunge of Your Life

Dale had noticed this River that "stretched from the gathering area in the middle of the city to the wall. It flowed toward the wall and seemed to end there."[14] As Gary marveled at the River of Life, flowing down from God's throne,

> John told me to drink of the water. Tasting the water, I found it to be very sweet. John then guided me into the water. Stepping in, I discovered it was only ankle deep, and then it began to rise. It covered my thighs and my shoulders, until my entire being was eventually submerged. . . . The beautiful water was actually cleansing me of any debris that may have clung to me in my transition from earth to glory. In the water, John and I could communicate with one another without verbally expressing ourselves. . . . The water receded, and we came out on the other side of the bank.[15]

Gary emerged from the River completely dry! Imagine plunging into the River of Life, with characteristics unlike any water you've experienced. Four people spoke of swimming in the River of Life and reported the same mysterious discovery: "As we walked into the river it got deeper and deeper until finally the surface of the river was over the top of our head[s], we were still breathing and so then I got the understanding, this is the flowing of the Spirit of God; it is a manifestation of the Spirit of God."[16]

God says through Jeremiah the prophet, "They have forsaken me, the spring of living water" (Jeremiah 2:13). Is that why Jesus equated the Holy Spirit with Living Water? "Jesus stood and said in a loud voice, 'Let anyone who is thirsty come to me and drink. Whoever believes in me, as Scripture has said, rivers of living water will flow from within them.' By this he meant the Spirit" (John 7:37–39). Is it more than just a metaphor in Heaven? I don't know. But it's interesting that when the angel directed Ed into the River, he discovered the same surprising qualities.

> "I can breathe!" I said, astonished. I spoke to the angel underwater, in clear tones without the words sounding bubbly.
> "You are standing in the River of Life. It is of the Spirit of God. It washes away the scars of sin. . . . You shall never thirst with this water. It flows from the Spirit of the Living God, feeding the Trees of Life."
> As we emerged from the River of Life, I noticed that I was not dripping wet![17]

Rebecca Springer, who had an NDE in 1898, surprisingly writes of the same cleansing properties when her deceased brother-in-law, Frank, took her in the water of Heaven:

> To my surprise and delight, I found I could not only breathe, but laugh and talk, see and hear, as naturally under the water as above it. I sat down in the midst of the many-colored pebbles, and filled my hands with them, as a child would have done. My brother lay down upon them . . . and laughed and talked joyously with me.
> "Do this," he said, rubbing his hands over his face, and running his fingers through his dark hair. I did as he told me, and the sensation was delightful. . . . As we neared the shore and my head once more emerged from the water, the moment the air struck my face and hair I realized that I would need no towel or brush. My flesh, my hair, and even my beautiful garments, were soft and dry as before the water touched them. . . .
> I turned and looked back at the shining river flowing on tranquilly. "Frank, what has that water done for me?" I said.

"I feel as though I could fly." He looked at me with earnest, tender eyes, as he answered gently, "It has washed away the last of the earthlife, and fitted you for the new life upon which you have entered."

"It is divine!" I whispered.

"Yes, it is divine," he said.[18]

Revelation 22:2 says the leaves of the trees fed by the River of Life are to heal the nations. Though I believe we retain the memory of earth's lessons and God's forgiveness washes away our guilt, perhaps some healing from the scars of sin will still take place as four people indicated. It's interesting that earth's water is a one-of-a-kind polar liquid, giving it unique cleansing properties, and water sustains all life—making up 65 percent of our bodies and covering 70 percent of earth's surface. Could it be a shadow of Heaven? Maybe our sun and earth's water are artificial life support to the Light of Heaven and the Water of Life that give eternal life support.

Children and Pets Allowed

As we continue to explore the new City, we notice people of all ages, and the tragedies of young lives lost on earth find redemption as they grow and thrive in the Life to come. And good news for people whose pets were like children to them—it seems in this City, pets are allowed!

> John then took me [Gary] by what looked to be a school-area playground, with golden fountains and marble benches. Flowers grew everywhere, producing a fragrance like sweet-smelling perfume. I marveled at the brilliant colors that the flowers had, each one was different from the other flowers, and no two were alike. . . . I saw a tiny little girl with long, brown hair that hung in ringlets down her back. She wore a white robe that glistened in the light of our Lord. She had sandals on her small feet. When

she saw Jesus, she began to run towards him with her arms stretched out. Jesus stooped down and caught her as she leapt into his arms. Then from all directions children came running to see Jesus. There were children of every race and color. They all wore robes of white and sandals. . . . While Jesus was ministering to them, all sorts of animals were with the children. It was an awesome sight to see a magnificent lion frolicking with the children, as if it were a kitten, and seeing birds of elegant beauty sitting on shoulders and tops of heads. I saw teenagers who had left this earth prematurely. They were playing in crystal pools of water, laughing and singing.[19]

Isaiah foresaw God's heavenly restoration of all creatures: "The wolf and the lamb will live together . . . the calf and the yearling will be safe with the lion, and a little child will lead them all" (Isaiah 11:6 NLT). People often wonder if they will see their pets in Heaven. Clearly there will be animals in Heaven, and if God uses animals to teach children (and even adults) how to love, don't you think renewing all things would include pets we've loved as well? I imagine so. Van Lommel noted that NDE "children do encounter favorite pets that have died more frequently than do adults."[20] The ten-year-old who "died" in the judo accident said, "My pet dog Skippy was there. Skippy had died some years earlier and was the only 'person' that I had any real family connection with that was dead. I was overwhelmed with Joy and Love and embraced my dog."[21] I imagine dearly loved pets will be allowed in the Holy City because all love is of God.

Heaven will be a harmonious place where past relationships, all play, and even all work will thrive and fulfill God's purpose, free from earth's curse of decay and destruction. Dr. Atwater, a researcher, reports of a ten-year-old NDEr named Clara who observed people busy at work:

I seemed to be walking, but my feet didn't touch a floor. Suddenly I heard what sounded like a city-sized playground full of kids, laughing and playing. Hearing them calmed me. Another man came to meet us. . . . I was led up a sidewalk to a large building with large doors. I walked inside and saw people all around working and doing things. . . . [Jesus] was dressed in a white, long-sleeved, floor-length robe with a wide gold band around the mid-section. He wore sandals. His dark brown hair was shoulder length; he had a long face . . . and his eyes were as liquid love. He communicated by looking at me.[22]

Heaven's Parties

Heaven will be a thriving, joyful, festive place, where families and friends work together and then gather for feasts and parties to celebrate and enjoy life with the Giver of Life. It will give God great joy as we enjoy him together. You'll often see Jesus, the Highlight of Heaven, and he will even be an honored guest at your house when invited. Because he is both the first resurrected human and the omnipresent manifestation of the Father ("Anyone who has seen me has seen the Father," John 14:9), he can be on the throne, with the children, and with you all simultaneously.

A woman who had a heart attack later reported, "I went to a place that was beautifully lit—like the sunshine but much prettier and more golden. . . . [It] seemed like a *neighborhood*, and I was shown around to all the people I loved and missed, and they were all so happy."[23] Maybe you never thought about Heaven's neighborhoods and celebrations, but God enjoys us enjoying him and each other, and the prophets looked forward to Heaven's parties.

> The Lord Almighty will prepare
>   a feast of rich food for all peoples,
> a banquet of aged wine—
>   the best of meats and the finest of wines.

> On this mountain he will destroy
>> the shroud that enfolds all peoples,
> the sheet that covers all nations;
>> he will swallow up death forever.
> The Sovereign LORD will wipe away the tears
>> from all faces;
> he will remove his people's disgrace
>> from all the earth.
>> The LORD has spoken.

In that day they will say,

> "Surely this is our God;
>> we trusted in him, and he saved us." (Isaiah 25:6–9)

The night before his crucifixion, at the Last Supper, "[Jesus] took a cup of wine and gave thanks to God for it. Then he said, 'Take this and share it among yourselves. For I will not drink wine again until the Kingdom of God has come. . . . [And you will] eat and drink at my table in my Kingdom'" (Luke 22:17–18, 30 NLT). The City will be filled with celebration, and God himself will be at the center of it all!

Amazing thought—that all who live to serve the King while on this earth will one day experience the King serving us. Jesus told us, "The servants who are ready and waiting for [the King's] return will be rewarded. I tell you the truth, he himself [Jesus] will seat them, put on an apron, and serve them as they sit and eat!" (Luke 12:37 NLT).

You'll finally see how full of life and enjoyment God really is as you realize every good thing we ever enjoyed on earth was but a shadow of Heaven's wonders. Heaven will be a creative, artistic celebration of God. You've already heard how the music of Heaven amazes everyone. Some will write songs, some will dance dances, and others will bring gifts of creativity or discoveries that magnify the Creator. You'll never miss the cultural creativity, learning, or exploration of earth because this is merely a foretaste of Heaven. And as you explore the various cultural centers of learning, creativity, work, and enjoyment, you will eventually wind your way up to the center of it all—the throne of God.

The Throne of God

Imagine gathering with people from all nations in the great celebration John witnessed around the throne of God:

> After this I saw a vast crowd, too great to count, from every nation and tribe and people and language, standing in front of the throne and before the Lamb [Jesus]. They were clothed in white robes and held palm branches in their hands. And they were shouting with a great roar,
>
>> "Salvation comes from our God who sits on the throne and from the Lamb!" . . .
>
> Then [one of the twenty-four elders] said to me, "These are the ones who died in the great tribulation. They have washed their robes in the blood of the Lamb and made them white.
>
>> "That is why they stand in front of God's throne and serve him day and night in his Temple. . . .
>> He will lead them to springs of life-giving water.
>> And God will wipe every tear from their eyes."
>> (Revelation 7:9–10, 14–15, 17 NLT)

In the center of the City is the architectural wonder of the universe, amazing not just for its physical beauty, but for the mystery, wonder, and awe created by the very presence of the Father, Son, and Holy Spirit—there's no place imaginable you would rather be. The throne is the center of the most spectacular displays of human art, worship, dance, creativity—all presented to the Greatest Being in existence—celebrated before all humanity to glorify God.

Marv, the conservative bank president, peered through the gate. Far off in the distance, using telescopic vision, he "could see the throne, dazzling, brilliant white—it's hard to imagine in this dark world, but there my eyes could see so much clearer so much farther away. I saw huge white pillars surrounding the throne, and an enormous crowd of people, men and women, boys and girls, dancing and singing along in a mass choir of praise to the two Beings seated on it."

Coming from a Dutch Reformed tradition, Marv admitted he would never be one to even raise his hands in worship, but he said, "In Heaven, you won't be able to help yourself." The sights and wonders and emotions of God's presence make it impossible not to shout for joy. "Yes, I saw two Beings," Marv recalls, "indescribable images really, but they appeared to be two people sitting there. I've always assumed those two people were God and his Son, Jesus."[24]

Old Testament prophets Isaiah, Ezekiel, and Daniel describe seeing God on his throne with similarly vivid description: "Spread out above the heads of the living creatures was what looked something like a vault, sparkling like crystal, and awesome. . . . Above the vault over their heads was what looked like a throne of lapis lazuli, and high above on the throne was a figure like that of a man. . . . He looked like fire; and brilliant light surrounded him. Like the appearance of a rainbow in the clouds on a rainy day, so was the radiance around him" (Ezekiel 1:22, 26–28).

Richard recalls the sheer energy and beauty of God's throne:

> Everything in heaven flowed into and out of the Throne. It pulsed like a dynamo. . . . The Throne Building was huge—beyond my ability to understand . . . several hundred miles wide and at least fifty miles tall, and it had a domed roof. . . .

Thousands of steps led up to the Throne. . . . As we began to go up the stairway, I saw hundreds of thousands or perhaps millions of people going into and coming out from the Throne. They were worshipping and praising God. . . .

The entry area, or gateway, had columns. . . . The Throne was made out of some heavenly material. It was crystal clear, yet it consisted of what appeared to be gold and ivory and silver. . . . [It] was the most beautiful spot in heaven.[25]

Akiane, as a young child, noticed the same thing when she was taken to a "house of Light . . . so beautiful and so big. . . . God lives there. Walls like glass, but not glass . . . and many other colors I can't find here."[26]

As you come into this massive arena, charged with an energy beyond comprehension, you notice a huge area in front of the throne of God that looks like a huge crystal blue sea, but it's not. People are on it, dancing, performing, and worshiping—a giant concert of people enraptured in the glory and melody and awe of the One in front of them. "I saw a throne in heaven and someone sitting on it. The one sitting on the throne was as brilliant as gemstones—like jasper and carnelian. And the glow of an emerald circled his throne like a rainbow. . . . In front of the throne was a shiny sea of glass, sparkling like crystal" (Revelation 4:2–3, 6 NLT). Listen to how one person describes this crystal sea:

In front of the throne is a large oval area . . . made out of sapphire jewels. I found this also in Ezekiel [1:22–28], describing the sapphires underneath the throne of God and it's called a sea because it's blue and because it's shiny. It's called glass because it's actually made of sapphires that represent glass, so that's the term "sea of glass." In other words it's not water; it's not the flowing of the Spirit of God, it's a rather solid place to stand.[27]

Captain Dale Black recalls seeing people gathered on this crystal "sea" platform in the City center:

There was a huge gathering of angels and people, millions, countless millions. They were gathered in a central area that seemed over ten miles in diameter. The expanse of people was closer to an ocean than a concert hall. Waves of people, moving in the light, swaying to the music, worshiping God. . . . Somehow the music in heaven calibrated everything. . . . Music was everywhere. The worship of God was the heart and focus of the music, and everywhere the joy of the music could be felt. The deepest part of my heart resonated with it, made me want to be a part of it forever. I never wanted it to stop. . . . I had the feeling—and it was the most satisfying of feelings—that I was made for the music, as if each muscle in my body were a taut string of some finely tuned instrument, created to play the most beautiful music ever composed. I felt part of the music. One with it. Full of joy and wonder and worship. Perhaps this is what love sounds like when put to music. . . . I felt all this, every ecstatic moment of it. And I never wanted it to end.[28]

Never-Ending Life!

And the great news is . . . it never has to end. This is just the beginning. After your tour of Heaven's City, you will realize that all of the history of earth was merely the prelude to the first chapter of the real story of Life that's just beginning. And the present Heaven with all its wonders is merely chapter one of God's Story of Life. Greater things are yet to come with a new story of Heaven and earth renewed.

You will realize that all the struggle, all the suffering, all the painful challenges, every act of faith, service, and sacrifice done on this earth produced for us "an eternal glory that far outweighs them all" (2 Corinthians 4:17). The life you always knew you were meant to live—that Life is just beginning. The most wonderful experiences imaginable lie before you. Imagine Heaven! Live for it now!

"Look, I am coming soon! My reward is with me, and I will give to each person according to what they have done. I am the Alpha and the Omega, the First and the Last, the Beginning and the End.

"Blessed are those who wash their robes, that they may have the right to the tree of life and may go through the gates into the city. Outside are the dogs, those who practice magic arts, the sexually immoral, the murderers, the idolaters and everyone who loves and practices falsehood.

"I, Jesus, have sent my angel to give you this testimony for the churches. I am the Root and the Offspring of David, and the bright Morning Star."

The Spirit and the bride say, "Come!" And let the one who hears say, "Come!" Let the one who is thirsty come; and let the one who wishes take the *free gift* of the water of life. (Revelation 22:12–17, italics mine)

Appendix A

Reasons to Believe

AS A SCIENCE-MINDED, SKEPTICAL ENGINEER, I used to wonder, *How can you know if Jesus is really the Messiah/Son of God?* I just didn't know what I didn't know! I have since discovered many verifiable reasons to support faith. I believe these reasons actually provide outside evidence for how NDEs should be interpreted. While NDEs add confirmation to life after death and Christian claims, it goes the other way too. If God has actually intersected history in verifiable ways through the life, death, and resurrection of Jesus, this gives a rational basis for NDE accounts to be expected. I'll share a few lines of evidence that I find most compelling.

Many people make ridiculous claims about God, gods, or being a god. God tells us how we can know it's truly the Creator: "'Present your case,' says the LORD. . . . 'Declare to us the things to come, tell us what the future holds, so we may know that you are gods'" (Isaiah 41:21–23). God claims only he can tell what the future holds, and so he used prophets to foretell Messiah's coming, so we could know he is the One true God. "I am the first and I am the last; apart from me there is no God. Who then is like me? Let him proclaim it. Let him declare and lay out . . . what is yet to come—yes, let them foretell what will come. . . . Did I not proclaim this and foretell it long ago?" (Isaiah 44:6–8; ~680 BCE). Most skeptics will claim any prophetic foretelling must be a scam—that editors who came after Jesus made the text "look" like Jesus fulfilled prophecy. Yet history and the Dead Sea Scrolls tell a different story if you look closely.

In the Dead Sea Scrolls, we found a complete copy of the book of Isaiah predating Jesus by 150 to 350 years, so we know these prophecies were written before the fact (not later altered to make them look like Jesus fulfilled them). The *Arizona Daily Star* reported, "New radiocarbon measurements of the Dead Sea Scrolls [have been] made by scientists at the National Science Foundation. . . . Radiocarbon dated the famous Book of Isaiah scroll at between 335 BCE and 122 BCE. Paleographers had dated this scroll at between 150–125 BCE."[1] Isaiah foretells when, where, and why God will send this Messiah, so we would know when he arrives. History outside the Bible verifies what Isaiah foretold.

In Isaiah 9, God tells us where he will reveal himself. He will come to Galilee in the form of a son of man:

In the future [God] will honor Galilee of the nations, by the Way of the Sea, beyond the Jordan—

> The people walking in darkness
>   have seen a great light;
> on those living in the land of deep darkness
>   a light has dawned. . . .
> For to us a child is born,
>   to us a son is given,
>   and the government will be on his shoulders.

318

> And he will be called
>> Wonderful Counselor, Mighty God,
>> Everlasting Father, Prince of Peace.
> Of the greatness of his government and peace
>> there will be no end. (Isaiah 9:1–2, 6–7; ~680 BCE)

Isaiah says the infinite God will reveal himself in the form of a son of man, come to Galilee, be called "Mighty God," and establish eternal peace between God and every willing human. He wrote this 680 years before Jesus walked and taught along the Sea of Galilee—the New Testament writers and extrabiblical history (outside the Bible) affirm Jesus conducted most of his ministry in Galilee.

The Suffering Servant

God told us over six hundred years in advance what his Arm, his servant Messiah, would do to bring peace to humanity:

> To whom has the arm of the LORD been revealed?
> He grew up before him like a tender shoot . . .
> He was despised and rejected by mankind . . .
> Surely he took up our pain and bore our suffering . . .
> . . . he was pierced for our transgressions,
>> he was crushed for our iniquities;
> the punishment that brought us peace was on him,
>> and by his wounds we are healed.
> We all, like sheep, have gone astray,
>> each of us has turned to our own way;
> and the LORD has laid on him
>> the iniquity of us all. (Isaiah 53:1–6; ~680 BCE)

Isaiah goes on to say that Messiah would die for our sins, but "after he has suffered, he will see the light of life and be satisfied; by his knowledge my righteous servant will justify many, and he will bear their iniquities" (Isaiah 53:11). Jesus's life in Galilee, his death, and his resurrection were all written down centuries before he came.

Even the timing of Jesus's coming was foretold. For instance, Daniel foretold that Messiah would be killed, then Jerusalem and the temple would be destroyed (see Daniel 9:24–26). Again, the Dead Sea Scrolls show that Daniel was written before Jesus's time. God would demonstrate how much he loves us—enough to pay for all our willful, wayward sins—so he could be just and righteous if he forgives us and takes us back. He loves you so much, he paid the greatest price you can imagine. God removed every barrier between us and God except one—our pride! All he requires is a willing, humble heart wanting his forgiveness and guidance offered through Christ.

Crucifixion Foretold

Jesus's hands and feet were nailed to a Roman cross, and he was hung between two thieves. Why? Because he claimed to be God revealed, the Messiah, and he called out the corruption of the religious leaders who were only interested in their own power and position. Isaiah 53 foretold this too: "He was led like a lamb to the slaughter, and as a sheep before its shearers is silent, so he did not open his mouth. . . . For he was cut off from the land of the living; for the transgression of my people he was punished. He was assigned a grave with the wicked, and with the rich in his death, though he had done no violence, nor was any deceit in his mouth" (Isaiah 53:7–9).

Every Passover for 1,500 years prior to Jesus, each Jewish family was required to bring a sacrificial lamb to the temple in Jerusalem. It had to be male and unblemished, offered as a substitute payment to forgive the past year's sins (trusting God would one day pay to forgive all debts). All these sacrifices were a cosmic drama, foreshadowing God's great sacrifice.

Consider this: the Talmud, the historical commentaries of the religious leaders who crucified Jesus, says, "On the eve of Passover, they hanged Yeshu the Nazarene [Jesus] . . . because he practiced sorcery and led Israel astray" (*Talmud, Sanhedrin* 43a). Jesus's enemies could not deny that he was healing people and doing miraculous deeds, but due to their fear of losing power, they claimed his power came from demonic sorcery rather than from God. "The man who had been mute spoke. The crowd was amazed and said, 'Nothing like this has ever been seen in Israel.' But the Pharisees said, 'It is by the prince of demons that [Jesus] drives out demons'" (Matthew 9:33–34). So they convicted Jesus of blasphemy (claiming equality with God as the Messiah) and had Pontius Pilate hang him on a cross—exactly on the eve of Passover.

Jesus was the final Passover sacrificial Lamb. All sacrifice ended about forty years after Jesus's crucifixion. Think about this: every year for 1,500 years, every Jewish family would sacrifice a lamb for sins of the previous year, and then it just stops! I found a website called Judaism 101 that answers why: "For the most part, the practice of sacrifice stopped in the year 70 CE, when the Roman army destroyed the Temple in Jerusalem. The Torah specifically commands us not to offer sacrifices wherever we feel like it. . . . [We can offer them only] in the Temple in Jerusalem, but the Temple has been destroyed."[2]

All sacrifices stopped because they were only a cosmic drama foretelling God's great sacrifice—once for all people. This is why Jesus is called the Lamb of God. The day he was crucified, Jesus hung between two thieves. One thief demanded Jesus prove himself by doing what the thief wanted. "'So you're the Messiah, are you? Prove it by saving yourself—and us, too, while you're at it!' But the other criminal protested, 'Don't you fear God even when you have been sentenced to die? We deserve to die for our crimes, but this man hasn't done anything wrong.' Then he said, 'Jesus, remember me when you come into your

Kingdom.' And Jesus replied, 'I assure you, today you will be with me in paradise'" (Luke 23:39–43 NLT).

Two people, two free-will responses. Which reflects your heart? This God who revealed himself through Jesus is exactly the God of compassion NDErs describe. When a woman caught in adultery was brought to Jesus by the religious leaders who wanted to condemn her and stone her to death, Jesus said to them, "Let any one of you who is without sin be the first to throw a stone at her." They all dropped their rocks and left. "Has no one condemned you?" Jesus asked her. "No one, sir," she said. "Then neither do I condemn you," Jesus declared. "Go now and leave your life of sin" (John 8:2–11). Like Jesus said to Khalida, "Just believe in me, trust me, and know I love you." Will we love him? Will we admit we need his forgiveness and leadership? That's all he needs.

A Sign for the Nations

One sign of indisputable evidence occurred the week before Jesus was crucified when he foretold the destruction of Jerusalem, the temple, and the scattering of the Jewish people globally: "As [Jesus] approached Jerusalem and saw the city, he wept over it and said, 'If you, even you, had only known on this day what would bring you peace—but now [your enemies] . . . will not leave one stone on another, because you did not recognize the time of God's coming to you. . . . [Israel] will fall by the sword and will be taken as prisoners to all the nations. Jerusalem will be trampled on by the Gentiles until the times of the Gentiles are fulfilled" (Luke 19:41–44; 21:24; written before 64 CE).

Jesus foretells that not only would Jerusalem and the temple be wiped out because the Jewish people rejected him and crucified him, but the Jewish people would be scattered among the nations, having no homeland until the "time of the Gentiles" (which could refer to the time of Gentile occupation of Israel or the time for non-Jewish people to turn to God) was fulfilled.

How could Jesus have predicted in 32 CE that in 70 CE, forty years after his crucifixion, Rome would level Jerusalem and the temple, ending 1,500 years of sacrifice—then for nearly 2,000 years the Jewish people would have no homeland, no government, and would be scattered across the globe?

When my parents were born, Israel was still scattered and not a nation, and Palestine was barren compared to today. But the prophets Isaiah, Jeremiah, and Ezekiel also foretold the miraculous event that happened in 1948 (the year the Dead Sea Scrolls were unearthed). Isaiah, writing in 680 BCE, saw the 1948 events: "In that day the Root of Jesse [Messiah] will stand as a banner for the peoples; the nations will rally to him, and his resting place [Jerusalem] will be glorious. In that day the Lord will reach out his hand a second time. . . . He will gather the exiles of Israel; he will assemble the scattered people of Judah from the four quarters of the earth" (Isaiah 11:10–12).

Isaiah writes that the Messiah's "place of rest" (Jerusalem) will be known and the nations will rally to the Messiah, Jesus. Then a second time the Jewish exiles will be regathered from all over the earth. Isaiah wrote this before Israel was regathered a first time (when Babylon destroyed the first temple and deported the Jews in 586 BCE). Jesus said this second regathering would be a sign that the time of the Gentiles is fulfilled. Think about this: right after the satanic Holocaust that killed six million Jews in 1945, German Jews, Russian Jews, Ethiopian Jews, American Jews, and European Jews returned to the land they had been exiled from for nearly 2,000 years! Just as God foretold through Isaiah.

In 1948, a nation was born overnight! The *New York Times* announced, "The declaration of the new state by David Ben-Gurion, the first Premier of reborn Israel, was delivered during a simple and solemn ceremony at 4 PM."[3] God foretold all this through Isaiah as a sign to the world: "Can a country be born in a day or a nation be brought forth in a moment? Yet no sooner is Zion [Jerusalem] in labor than she gives birth to her children . . . they will bring all your people, from all the nations, to my holy mountain in Jerusalem" (Isaiah 66:8, 20; ~680 BCE).

How do you explain world history in our day, spoken by Isaiah as a sign from God in 680 BCE, foretold by Jesus in 32 CE, yet fulfilled in 1948? This is not mythology, this is not religion, this is history—His-story of a relentless love for you and me. Religion is our attempt to reach God. Jesus the Messiah is God's attempt to reach us—all of us! All he needs is a humble, willing heart saying, "I want your forgiveness and love, come lead my life."

Jesus fulfilled about sixty major prophecies written over 1,500 years. For more historical verification of Jesus's life, death, and resurrection showing evidence that he did reveal the unseen God, check out these books:

Lee Strobel, *The Case for Christ*
Gary Habermas, *The Case for the Resurrection of Jesus*
Gary Habermas, *The Historical Jesus*

Appendix B

Alternate Explanations for NDEs

OVER THE YEARS, many alternate hypotheses have been proposed and studied to explain NDEs as other than an actual experience of life after death. Since many research doctors and others have written whole chapters or entire books dealing with these explanations in depth (which I've listed below), I will mention the ones dealt with by Dr. Pim van Lommel and share his conclusion. For further research, I've included the books and chapters below.

Dr. van Lommel discusses each of these possible explanations for some or all of the NDE experience: oxygen deficiency (the fighter-pilot syndrome); carbon dioxide overload; chemical reactions in the brain; psychedelics (DMT, LSD, Psilocybin, and Mescaline); electrical activity of the brain (epileptic seizures and electrode brain stimulation); fear of death; depersonalization; dissociation; fantasy and imagination; deceit; memory of birth; hallucinations; dreams; and delusion brought on by medication.

After discussing the merits and problems of each of these alternate hypotheses, Dr. van Lommel concludes that "a near-death experience is a special state of consciousness that arises during an impending or actual period of physical, psychological, or emotional death. Demographic, psychological, and physiological circumstances fail to explain why people do or do not experience an NDE."

Multiple explanations have been suggested for each of the various elements of NDEs, but, argues Dr. van Lommel, although "various physiological and psychological factors could all play a role, none can fully explain the phenomenon. The theories on NDE set out above fail to explain the experience of an enhanced consciousness, with lucid thoughts, emotions, memories from earliest childhood, visions of the future, and the possibility of perception from a position outside and above the body."

These theories also fail to explain why experiences in an NDE seem more vivid and real than experiences that occur during ordinary consciousness. The fact that an NDE is accompanied by greater awareness and knowledge also cannot be explained, nor can science explain how this awareness, knowledge, and other elements of the NDE can even be possible when, in many people, the brain is not functioning normally. As Dr. van Lommel notes, "There appears to be an inverse relationship between the clarity of consciousness and the loss of brain function."

The fact that people from all cultures and across all demographics have conveyed similar experiences cannot be explained, nor can scientists determine why some people have an NDE while most people cannot recall anything from the period they were unconscious after a life-threatening crisis (if they don't have an NDE). Also, it's been shown that induced experiences usually do not completely replicate an NDE, primarily because certain hallmarks of the NDE are rarely mentioned after drug use or brain stimulation, but also because these experiences are never followed by personal transformation or a major life change.[1]

Below is a list of chapters and books for more in-depth analysis by other doctors or researchers. They explain why alternate hypotheses do not fully account for the common experience they have studied:

Carter, Chris. *Science and the Near-Death Experience*. Rochester: Inner Traditions, 2010.

van Lommel, Pim. *Consciousness Beyond Life*. New York: HarperCollins, 2010. Pages 105–35.

Miller, J. Steve. *Near-Death Experiences as Evidence for the Existence of God and Heaven: A Brief Introduction in Plain Language*. Wisdom Creek Press, LLC. Kindle Edition, 2012. Chapter 1.

Moody, Raymond A. *Life After Life*. San Francisco: HarperSanFrancisco, 2001. Pages 162–65.

Sabom, Michael B. *Recollections of Death*. New York: Harper & Row, 1982. Pages 151–78.

Sartori, Penny. *The Near-Death Experiences of Hospitalized Intensive Care Patients*. Lewiston, Queenston, Lampeter: The Edwin Mellen Press, 2008. Pages 59–120.

Acknowledgments

A BOOK IS NEVER A SOLO EFFORT, and I owe much thanks and gratitude to so many people who have contributed in some way. First, my amazing, supportive, loving wife, Kathy, who continues to be chief "bounce-this-off-you" officer of all my writing, plus a fantastic editor—thanks for helping make this happen. Ashley and Justin, you're both such encouragers, and I'm so excited to partner with my kids to help people *Imagine Heaven*—I love you both more than words can say.

Chris Coleman has functioned as my volunteer CMO and project manager—I can't tell you how grateful I am to be shoulder to shoulder in this with you. Michael Warden has once again brought his enormous wisdom to bear reading and editing the entire manuscript—thanks again—I thank God for your friendship and help. Kayla Covington read and edited the manuscript and caught things four of us missed—thanks for your diligence and caring attention. Theresa, who has tirelessly assisted me for well over ten years now, helped bring order to a complicated permissions process—you bring order to my chaos so well, thanks. Debra Evans also helped me with permissions—I so appreciate the many ways you serve others! JP Moreland read the manuscript and gave great feedback and encouragement—I so respect your wisdom. Thank you, Don Piper, for the time discussing these topics, reading the manuscript, and writing such an encouraging foreword.

I'm especially grateful to the folks at Baker Books. Jack Kuhatschek, you've been a great friend and champion of my writing for over a decade now—I so appreciate your encouragement and excellent editing insights. Thank you, Dave Lewis and Mark Rice, for coming to Austin to hear the book concept and believing in it so wholeheartedly. Barb Barnes and Julie Davis were so helpful in editing. I'm also grateful to Lauren Carlson, Brianna DeWitt, and Ruth Anderson for all you're doing to get people to *Imagine Heaven*—it wouldn't happen without such a great team.

Notes

Chapter 1 If You Only Knew What Awaits You!

1. George G. Ritchie and Elizabeth Sherrill, *Return from Tomorrow* (Grand Rapids: Spire, a division of Baker Publishing Group, 1978), 36. Used by permission.
2. Ibid., 36–55.
3. Ibid., 86.
4. Ibid., 93.
5. Ibid., 20.
6. Raymond Moody Jr., *Life After Life* (New York: HarperCollins, 2001), 5.
7. Ibid., 21–22.
8. "Hazeliene M's NDE," NDERF.org, http://www.nderf.org/NDERF/NDE_Experiences/hazeliene_m_nde.htm.
9. C. S. Lewis, *Mere Christianity* (San Francisco: HarperSanFrancisco, Harper edition, 2001), 134–35.

Chapter 2 Skeptical Doctors and the Afterlife

1. Kenneth Ring and Sharon Cooper, *Mindsight: Near-Death and Out-of-Body Experiences in the Blind* (Bloomington, IN: iUniverse, 2008), 14.
2. British Broadcasting Company, *The Day I Died: The Mind, the Brain, and Near-Death Experiences*, film (2002), http://topdocumentaryfilms.com/day-i-died/ (last accessed April 28, 2015).
3. Ring and Cooper, *Mindsight*, 27.
4. Ibid., 15.
5. British Broadcasting Company, *The Day I Died*, http://topdocumentaryfilms.com/day-i-died/.
6. Ring and Cooper, *Mindsight*, 16.
7. Ibid.
8. British Broadcasting Company, *The Day I Died*, http://topdocumentaryfilms.com/day-i-died/.
9. Ring and Cooper, *Mindsight*, 16.

10. Ibid.

11. Ibid., 17.

12. Ibid., 36.

13. Ibid., 17.

14. Direct quotes and paraphrase of this portion of Vicki's story from Ring and Cooper, *Mindsight*, 17.

15. Pim van Lommel, *Consciousness Beyond Life: The Science of the Near-Death Experience* (New York: HarperCollins, 2010), Kindle edition, 26.

16. Ring and Cooper, *Mindsight*, 36.

17. Ibid., 37–38.

18. Ibid., 35–36.

19. Ibid., 136.

20. "Near-Death Experiences Illuminate Dying Itself," *NYTimes.com*, October 28, 1986, http://www.nytimes.com/1986/10/28/science/near-death-experiences-illuminate-dying-itself.html (last accessed April 28, 2015).

21. Van Lommel, *Consciousness Beyond Life*, 9.

22. Michael Sabom, *Light and Death* (Grand Rapids: Zondervan, 2011), Kindle edition, locations 110–21.

23. Ibid., locations 83–90, 122–25.

24. Penny Sartori, *The Near-Death Experiences of Hospitalized Intensive Care Patients: A Five-Year Clinical Study* (Lewiston, NY: Edwin Mellen Press, 2008), 212–15.

25. Jeffrey Long and Paul Perry, *Evidence of the Afterlife: The Science of Near-Death Experiences* (New York: HarperCollins, 2009), Kindle edition, 26.

26. Ibid.

27. Synopsis of Sheila's NDE (including direct quotes) from Long and Perry, *Evidence of the Afterlife*, 26–30.

28. Long and Perry, *Evidence of the Afterlife*, 44.

29. Ibid., 72–73.

30. *The Lancet* article cited in *Journal of Near-Death Studies* 27, no. 1 (Fall 2008): 48 (online reference: http://netwerknde.nl/wp-content/uploads/jndsden-tureman.pdf).

31. J. M. Holden, "Veridical Perception in Near-Death Experiences," in J. M. Holden, B. Greyson, and D. James, eds., *The Handbook of Near-Death Experiences* (Santa Barbara, CA: Praeger/ABC-CLIO, 2009), 185–211.

32. J. Steve Miller notes *The Index to NDE Periodical Literature* collects these articles: http://iands.org/research/index-to-nde-periodical-literature.html; *Near-Death Experiences as Evidence for the Existence of God and Heaven: A Brief Introduction in Plain Language* (Acworth, GA: Wisdom Creek Press, 2012), Kindle edition, 8.

33. Holden, Greyson, and James, eds., *The Handbook of Near-Death Experiences*, 7.

Chapter 3 The Common NDE Experience

1. Miller, *Near-Death Experiences as Evidence*, 46–47.

2. Van Lommel, *Consciousness Beyond Life*, 72.

3. Long and Perry, *Evidence of the Afterlife*, 6–7.

4. Ibid., 57–58.

5. Van Lommel, *Consciousness Beyond Life*, 164.

6. Ibid., 71–72.

7. Ibid., 74.

8. Maurice Rawlings, *Beyond Death's Door* (Nashville: Thomas Nelson, 1978), 2–5.

9. Ibid., 8.

10. R. C. Sproul, *Now, That's a Good Question!* (Wheaton: Tyndale House, 1996), 300.

11. Crystal McVea and Alex Tresniowski, *Waking Up in Heaven: A True Story of Brokenness, Heaven, and Life Again* (New York: Howard Books, 2013), Kindle edition, locations 263–67.

12. Gary Wood, *A Place Called Heaven* (New Kensington, PA: Banner Publishing, Whitaker House, 2014), Kindle edition, location 430.

13. Van Lommel, *Consciousness Beyond Life*, 32.

14. Miller, *Near-Death Experiences as Evidence*, 86–87.

15. Moody, *Life After Life*, 26.

16. Miller, *Near-Death Experiences as Evidence*, 47.

Chapter 4 A Better Body

1. From transcript of interview with Dr. Mary Neal by John Burke, October 2015.

2. Ibid.

3. Mary C. Neal, *To Heaven and Back: A Doctor's Extraordinary Account of Heaven, Angels, and Life Again: A True Story* (Colorado Springs: Waterbrook, 2012), Kindle edition, 57.

4. Neal, *To Heaven and Back*, 68.

5. Interview transcript with Dr. Mary Neal.

6. Neal, *To Heaven and Back*, 70–72.

7. Marvin J. Besteman and Lorilee Craker, *My Journey to Heaven: What I Saw and How It Changed My Life* (Grand Rapids: Baker, 2012), Kindle edition, 12–14. Used by permission.

8. Lee Strobel, *The Case for Faith: A Journalist Investigates the Toughest Objections to Christianity* (Grand Rapids: Zondervan, 2000), 47.

9. Bill Wiese, *What Happens When I Die? True Stories of the Afterlife and What They Tell Us about Eternity* (Lake Mary, FL: Charisma House, 2013), Kindle edition, 59–60, 79–80.

10. Randy Alcorn, *Heaven* (Carol Stream, IL: Tyndale House Publishers, 2004), 45.

11. Moody, *Life After Life*, 50.

12. Ibid.

13. "Valerie R.'s NDE," NDERF.org, http://www.nderf.org/NDERF/NDE_Experiences/valerie_r_nde.htm.

14. Richard Eby, *Caught Up into Paradise* (Old Tappan, NJ: Revell, 1978), 203–4.

15. Besteman and Craker, *My Journey to Heaven*, 75.

16. Interview transcript with Dr. Mary Neal.

17. Sid Roth and Lonnie Lane, *Heaven Is Beyond Your Wildest Expectations: Ten True Stories of Experiencing Heaven* (Shippensburg, PA: Destiny Image, 2012), Kindle edition, 2–3.

18. Ring and Cooper, *Mindsight*, 37.

Chapter 5 You'll Be Yourself . . . Finally!

1. Synopsis of Crystal McVea's NDE, including direct quotes, from McVea and Tresniowski, *Waking Up in Heaven*, locations 117–32, 500–535.

2. Quoted from CBN interview of Crystal McVea, January 12, 2014, http://www1.cbn.com/700club/nine-minutes-heaven.

3. This section of Crystal McVea's NDE, including direct quotes, from McVea and Tresniowski, *Waking Up in Heaven*, locations 250–62.

4. Van Lommel, *Consciousness Beyond Life*, 46.

5. Ritchie and Sherrill, *Return from Tomorrow*, 58–65.

6. Roth and Lane, *Heaven Is Beyond Your Wildest Expectations*, 146–49.

7. Dean Braxton, *In Heaven! Experiencing the Throne of God* (Chambersburg, PA: Divine Design Publishing, 2012), Kindle edition, locations 427–29.

8. Roth and Lane, *Heaven Is Beyond Your Wildest Expectations*, 86.

9. Long and Perry, *Evidence of the Afterlife*, 24–25.

10. "Geralyn AS NDE," NDERF.org, http://www.nderf.org/NDERF/NDE_Experiences/geralyn_as_nde.htm.

11. "Mark H.'s DNE," NDERF.org, http://www.nderf.org/NDERF/NDE_Experiences/mark_h's_nde.htm.

12. Howard Storm, *My Descent into Death: A Second Chance at Life* (New York: Doubleday, 2005), Kindle edition, 33–34.

13. Steve Sjogren, *The Day I Died* (Bloomington, MN: Bethany House, 2006), Kindle edition, locations 1126–33.

14. Synopsis and direct quotations from McVea and Tresniowski, *Waking Up in Heaven*, locations 239–78.

15. Jeff Olsen, *I Knew Their Hearts: The Amazing True Story of Jeff Olsen's Journey Beyond the Veil to Learn the Silent Language of the Heart* (Springville, UT: Plain Sight Publishing, © 2012), Kindle edition, locations 484–87.

16. Bodie Thoene and Samaa Habib, *Face to Face with Jesus: A Former Muslim's Extraordinary Journey to Heaven and Encounter with the God of Love* (Bloomington, MN: Chosen, 2014), Kindle edition, locations 2157–65. Used by permission.

17. Don Piper and Cecil Murphey, *90 Minutes in Heaven: A True Story of Death & Life* (Grand Rapids: Revell, 2006), Kindle edition, locations 387–91. Used by permission.

Chapter 6 With Friends and Loved Ones

1. Olsen, *I Knew Their Hearts*, locations 442–523.

2. Piper and Murphey, *90 Minutes in Heaven*, locations 233–75.

3. Besteman and Craker, *My Journey to Heaven*, 151.

4. Neal, *To Heaven and Back*, locations 752–55.

5. Moody, *Life After Life*, 55.

6. E. W. Kelly, "Near-Death Experiences with Reports of Meeting Deceased People," *Death Studies* 25 (2001): 229–49.

7. Erlendur Haraldsson and Karlis Osis, *At the Hour of Death* (Guildford, Great Britain: White Crow Books, 1977), 184.

Chapter 7 The Family You Never Knew

1. Taken from Todd Burpo, Sonja Burpo, and Colton Burpo, *Heaven Is for Real: A Little Boy's Astounding Story of His Trip to Heaven and Back* (Nashville: Thomas Nelson, 2010), Kindle edition, locations 1339–48.

2. Ibid., locations 1810–11.

3. Ibid., locations 1442–81.

4. Wood, *A Place Called Heaven*, locations 305–14.

5. Besteman and Craker, *My Journey to Heaven*, 76–77.

6. Ibid., 146.

7. "Bob L.'s NDE," NDERF.org, http://www.nderf.org/NDERF/NDE_Experiences/bob_l_nde.htm.

8. Ibid., (last accessed July 17, 2016).

9. Van Lommel, *Consciousness Beyond Life*, 33.

10. Dale Black and Ken Gire, *Flight to Heaven: A Plane Crash . . . A Lone Survivor . . . A Journey to Heaven—and Back* (Minneapolis: Bethany House, 2010), Kindle edition, 107–8. Used by permission.

11. From transcript of interview with Howard Storm by John Burke, October 18, 2015.

12. Storm, *My Descent into Death*, 28.

13. Miller, *Near-Death Experiences as Evidence*, 80.

14. "Brian T's NDE," NDERF.org, http://www.nderf.org/NDERF/NDE_Experiences/brian_t's_nde.htm.

15. McVea and Tresniowski, *Waking Up in Heaven*, locations 586–92.

16. Braxton, *In Heaven!*, locations 535–44.

17. Betty Malz, *My Glimpse of Eternity* (Bloomington, MN: Chosen, 2012), Kindle edition, locations 925–37, 931–35. Used by permission.

18. Black and Gire, *Flight to Heaven*, 109–10.

19. Olsen, *I Knew Their Hearts*, locations 548–57.

20. Piper and Murphey, *90 Minutes in Heaven*, locations 425–30.

21. Eben Alexander III, *Proof of Heaven* (New York: Simon & Schuster, 2012), Kindle edition, 45–46.

22. Black and Gire, *Flight to Heaven*, 109.

23. Olsen, *I Knew Their Hearts*, locations 1160–208.

Chapter 8 The Most Beautiful Place Imaginable!

1. Black and Gire, *Flight to Heaven*, 28–29, 98–106.

2. Alcorn, *Heaven*, 54.

3. Van Lommel, *Consciousness Beyond Life*, 291.

4. James Jeans, *The Mysterious Universe* (Whitefish, MT: Kessinger Publishing, 2007), 137.

5. Moody, *Life After Life*, 31.

6. Ibid., 32–33.

7. The summary of Brad Barrows's NDE, including direct quotes, from Ring and Cooper, *Mindsight*, 18–21 and 38–45.

8. Miller, *Near-Death Experiences as Evidence*, 10–11.

9. Besteman and Craker, *My Journey to Heaven*, 56.

10. Taken from Mally Cox-Chapman, *The Case for Heaven: Near-Death Experiences as Evidence of the Afterlife* (Windsor, CT: Tide-mark, 2012), Kindle edition, locations 433–94.

11. Eby, *Caught Up into Paradise*, 204–5.

12. Richard Sigmund, *My Time in Heaven* (New Kensington, PA: Whitaker House, 2009), Kindle edition, locations 225–59.

13. Jenny Sharkey, *Clinically Dead—I've Seen Heaven and Hell* (Gospel Media, 2013), Kindle edition, 32–33.

14. Besteman and Craker, *My Journey to Heaven*, 116.

Chapter 9 Alive in New Dimensions

1. Synopsis of Eben Alexander's NDE, including the direct quotes, from Alexander, *Proof of Heaven*, 8–9, 29–32, 38, 48–49, 143.

2. "Eben Alexander: A Neurosurgeon's Journey through the Afterlife," Youtube interview transcript, published August 27, 2014, https://www.youtube.com/watch?v=qbkgj5J91hE.

3. Ibid.

4. Synopsis of Eben Alexander's NDE, including the direct quotes, from Alexander, *Proof of Heaven*, 8–9, 29–32, 38, 48–49, 143.

5. Ibid.

6. Piper and Murphey, *90 Minutes in Heaven*, locations 283–91.

7. Dallas Willard, *The Divine Conspiracy* (San Francisco: HarperSanFrancisco, 1998), 392.

8. Long and Perry, *Evidence of the Afterlife*, 59–60.

9. Moody, *Life After Life*, 51–52.

10. "Ray K.'s NDE," NDERF.org, http://www.nderf.org/NDERF/NDE_Experiences/ray_k's_nde.htm.

11. "Leonard NDE," NDERF.org, http://www.nderf.org/NDERF/NDE_Experiences/leonard_nde.htm.

12. Ibid.

13. Roth and Lane, *Heaven Is Beyond Your Wildest Expectations*, 151.

14. Black and Gire, *Flight to Heaven*, 101–2.

15. Burpo et al., *Heaven Is for Real*, locations 1587–92.

16. Braxton, *In Heaven!*, locations 507–23.

17. Black and Gire, *Flight to Heaven*, 99.

18. Van Lommel, *Consciousness Beyond Life*, 23.

19. Besteman and Craker, *My Journey to Heaven*, 55–57, 60–61, 65–66.

20. "John S. NDE," NDERF.org, http://www.nderf.org/NDERF/NDE_Experiences/john_s_nde_3876.htm.

21. "Andrew P.'s NDE," NDERF.org, http://www.nderf.org/NDERF/NDE_Experiences/andrew_p's_nde.htm.

22. Patrick Doucette, *Is Heaven for Real? Personal Stories of Visiting Heaven* (Kindle Publishers, 2013), Kindle edition, 124–25. (Available on Amazon: www.amazon.com/dp/B00BXKG41U.) Rebecca Springer, in *Intra Muros,* written in 1898, also discusses a kind of twilight rest.

23. Roth and Lane, *Heaven Is Beyond Your Wildest Expectations,* 139.

24. Scientists propose eleven dimensions in string theory, including multiple dimensions of time.

25. McVea and Tresniowski, *Waking Up in Heaven,* locations 243–50.

26. Hugh Ross, *Beyond the Cosmos: The Extra-Dimensionality of God: What Recent Discoveries in Astronomy and Physics Reveal about the Nature of God* (Colorado Springs: NavPress, 1996), 169.

27. Burpo et al., *Heaven Is for Real,* locations 1561–67.

28. Roth and Lane, *Heaven Is Beyond Your Wildest Expectations,* 149–50.

29. Doucette, *Is Heaven for Real?,* 121.

30. Braxton, *In Heaven!,* locations 490–91.

Chapter 10 A Love You'll Never Want to Leave

1. Jenny Sharkey, *Clinically Dead: I've Seen Heaven and Hell* (Gospel Media, 2013), Kindle edition, 16.

2. Ibid., 16–17.

3. Ibid., 25–31.

4. Long and Perry, *Evidence of the Afterlife,* 130.

5. Haraldsson and Osis, *At the Hour of Death,* 37.

6. "Simran W NDE," NDERF.org, http://www.nderf.org/NDERF/NDE_Experiences/simran_w_nde.htm (last accessed April 29, 2015).

7. Haraldsson and Osis, *At the Hour of Death,* 176.

8. Ibid., 190–91.

9. Ibid., 152–53.

10. Ibid., 50.

11. Ibid., 181.

12. Ibid.

13. Miller, *Near-Death Experiences as Evidence,* 83–85.

14. Bruce Greyson, quoted in Long and Perry, *Evidence of the Afterlife,* 169.

15. Faisal Malick, *10 Amazing Muslims Touched by God* (Shippensburg, PA: Destiny Image, 2012), Kindle edition, 81–82.

16. Moody, *Life After Life,* 78.

17. Alexander, *Proof of Heaven,* 70, 96.

18. Moody, *Life After Life,* 62–63.

19. Ibid., 58–59.

20. Miller, *Near-Death Experiences as Evidence,* 11–12.

21. Eben Alexander, "Proof of Heaven: A Doctor's Experience of the Afterlife," *Newsweek,* October 8, 2012, http://www.newsweek.com/proof-heaven-doctors -experience-afterlife-65327.

22. Synopsis and direct quotations from Alexander, *Proof of Heaven,* 46–48.

23. Malick, *10 Amazing Muslims Touched by God,* 81, italics mine.

24. Sabom, *Light and Death,* locations 1673–78, 1664–72, italics mine.

25. Nancy Botsford, *A Day in Hell* (Mustang, OK: Tate Publishing, 2010), Kindle edition, locations 201–8, italics mine.

26. Sjogren, *Day I Died*, locations 255–59, 250–52, italics mine.

27. Thoene and Habib, *Face to Face with Jesus*, locations 2157–65, italics mine.

Chapter 11 God Is Relational

1. The synopsis of Jack's NDE, including direct quotes, from Moody, *Life After Life*, 96, 100–101.

2. Braxton, *In Heaven!*, locations 1254–58.

3. Roth and Lane, *Heaven Is Beyond Your Wildest Expectations*, 136–37.

4. "Lisa's NDE," NDERF.org, http://www.nderf.org/NDERF/NDE_Experiences/Lana's_nde.htm.

5. Miller, *Near-Death Experiences as Evidence*, 83–84.

6. Ibid., 86–87.

7. C. S. Lewis, *The Abolition of Man* (New York: HarperCollins, 2009), Kindle edition, 81.

8. "Alexa's NDE," NDERF.org, http://www.nderf.org/NDERF/NDE_Experiences/Alexa'a%20NDE.htm.

9. Thoene and Habib, *Face to Face with Jesus*, 176–80.

10. Jaya sent this to me to explain where in the Vedas he came across these ideas:

The main theme in the Rg Veda and the Upanishads is the nature and purpose of only one supreme sacrifice known as the Purush Prajapati. This name is translated from Sanskrit as "the Lord of all creation who became Man" (Sathpathbrahmana 10.2.2.1_2; Rg Ved Purushasukta 10:19). . . .

This Purush Prajapati is the one and only way to eternal life (". . . Nanyah pantha vidyate-ayanaya": Yajur Ved 31:18). This Supreme Creator took a perfect human body (Nishkalanka Purusha) and offered it up as a self_sacrifice (Brihad Aranyak Upanishad 1.2.8). He was symbolized by a spotless lamb which was the animal most commonly sacrificed in those days (Maddyandiniya Sathpathbrahmana III). He is the only sinless human being, and only in knowing Him does one obtain immortality (Chandogya Upanishad 1.6:6, 7). Acknowledging the sacrifice of the perfect Purush Prajapati imparts eternal life (Kathopanishad 1, 3.8, 11). After giving Himself as the supreme sacrifice, He resurrected (not reincarnated) himself (Brihad Aranyak Upanishad 3.9.28.4_5; Kathopanishad 3:15). By his resurrection, the Purush Prajapati conquered death and released sin's stranglehold on mankind. He will return to earth only once more. At this point in its account, the Vedantic history of Purush Prajapati ends. . . .

To summarize, the only purpose of the Purush Prajapati is to sacrifice His lifeblood to pay our penalty for sin and to impart to us eternal life. It is the only way to Heaven and the only way of escape from eternal Hell (Rg Ved 9:113.7_11; Rg Ved 4.5.5; 7.104.3). [Author's note: use of underline instead of hyphen in original text.]

"From Darkness into the Glorious Light," Global Evangelical Missionary Society, 2004, http://www.gemsworld.org/Literature/For_Hindu_Friends/for_hindu_friends.html (last accessed May 5, 2015).

11. Neal, *To Heaven and Back*, 149.

Chapter 12 Light of the World

1. Akiane Kramarik and Foreli Kramarik, *Akiane: Her Life, Her Art, Her Poetry* (Nashville: Thomas Nelson, 2006), 7–12, 34, 37.

2. Roth and Lane, *Heaven Is Beyond Your Wildest Expectations*, 2–4.

3. This idea comes from a book by Edwin Abbott called *Flatland: A Romance of Many Dimensions* (New York: Classic Books, 2009).

4. Van Lommel, *Consciousness Beyond Life*, 18.

5. In the Dead Sea Scrolls, copies of the book of Daniel were carbon-dated before Jesus's birth, indicating Daniel's writings were not edited after the fact to look like Jesus fulfilled them.

6. "Muhammad A Probable NDE," NDERF.org, http://www.nderf.org/NDERF /NDE_Experiences/muhammad_a_probable_nde.htm (last accessed May 1, 2015).

7. "Katie A's NDE," NDERF.org, http://www.nderf.org/NDERF/NDE_Experi ences/katie_a_nde.htm.

8. A. J. Ayer, "What I Saw When I Was Dead," *National Review* (October 14, 1988): 38–40.

Chapter 13 The Highlight of Heaven

1. Braxton, *In Heaven!*, locations 409–19.

2. Ibid., locations 728–33.

3. Ring and Cooper, *Mindsight*, 36–37.

4. "Cynthia Y. NDE," NDERF.org, http://www.nderf.org/NDERF/NDE_Ex periences/cynthia_y_nde.htm.

5. Taken from Burpo et al., *Heaven Is for Real*, locations 200–201, 1069–72.

6. Rita Bennett, *To Heaven and Back* (Grand Rapids: Zondervan, 1997), 44–46, italics mine.

7. Roth and Lane, *Heaven Is Beyond Your Wildest Expectations*, 84–85, italics mine.

8. Ibid., 118.

9. Haraldsson and Osis, *At the Hour of Death*, 177.

10. Alexander, *Proof of Heaven*, 85–86.

11. Malick, *10 Amazing Muslims Touched by God*, 82–83.

12. Ring and Cooper, *Mindsight*, 35.

13. Braxton, *In Heaven!*, locations 561–64.

14. Thoene and Habib, *Face to Face with Jesus*, locations 2206–8.

15. Roth and Lane, *Heaven Is Beyond Your Wildest Expectations*, 147, 150.

16. Cox-Chapman, *The Case for Heaven*, locations 488–90.

Chapter 14 No More Mourning, Crying, or Pain

1. Synopsis of Crystal's story and NDE, including direct quotations, from McVea and Tresniowski, *Waking Up in Heaven*, locations 540–59, 574–600, 820–50, 1257–1301, 2079–84.

2. Ibid.

3. Quoted from CBN interview of Crystal McVea, http://www1.cbn.com/700 club/nine-minutes-heaven.

4. I heard this insight in December 2014 from Steve Stroope, pastor of Lake Pointe Church in Rockwall, Texas.

5. Taken from Burpo et al., *Heaven Is for Real*, locations 1030–67, 1100–10.

6. Roth and Lane, *Heaven Is Beyond Your Wildest Expectations*, 84–85.

7. Sigmund, *My Time in Heaven*, locations 824–25.

8. Alexander, *Proof of Heaven*, 48, 83–84.

9. Storm, *My Descent into Death*, 38.

10. Black and Gire, *Flight to Heaven*, 12–14.

Chapter 15 Angels

1. Adapted from "Jennifer V.'s NDE," NDERF.org, http://www.nderf.org/ NDERF/NDE_Experiences/jennifer_v_nde.htm.

2. Besteman and Craker, *My Journey to Heaven*, 31.

3. Black and Gire, *Flight to Heaven*, 98.

4. Besteman and Craker, *My Journey to Heaven*, 31.

5. Jeffrey Burton Russell, *The Prince of Darkness: Radical Evil and the Power of Good in History* (Ithaca, NY: Cornell University Press, 1988), 7.

6. Ibid., 260.

7. Storm, *My Descent into Death*, 140–141.

8. Chapter 7 of Sabom's *Light and Death* gives great insight into what Sabom claims to be biased research among some of his early colleagues.

9. Sabom, *Light and Death*, locations 2107–9.

10. Michael Sabom, *Recollections of Death: A Medical Investigation* (New York: HarperCollins, 1981), 129–30.

11. Sartori, *The Near-Death Experiences of Hospitalized Intensive Care Patients*, 244.

12. Sabom, *Light and Death*, locations 2161–62.

13. Quoted from CBN interview of Crystal McVea, http://www1.cbn.com/700 club/nine-minutes-heaven.

14. McVea and Tresniowski, *Waking Up in Heaven*, 164–65.

15. Quoted from CBN interview of Crystal McVea, http://www1.cbn.com/700 club/nine-minutes-heaven.

16. Braxton, *In Heaven!*, locations 394–95, 737–46.

17. C. S. Lewis, *The Problem of Pain* (New York: MacMillan, 1962), 93.

Chapter 16 What about Hell?

1. The following quoted material, aside from that which is cited with endnotes, is from the transcript of John Burke's interview with Howard Storm.

2. Storm, *My Descent into Death*, 20.

3. The last paragraph of this quoted material from Storm, *My Descent into Death*, 21.

4. The last two sentences in this paragraph from Storm, *My Descent into Death*, 25.

5. The last four sentences in this paragraph from Storm, *My Descent into Death*, 26.

6. All preceding quoted material is from the transcript of John Burke's interview with Howard Storm, with the exception of that which is cited with endnotes.

7. Moody, *Life After Life*, 92.

8. Van Lommel, *Consciousness Beyond Life*, 29–30.

9. Sartori, *The Near-Death Experiences of Hospitalized Intensive Care Patients*, 18.

10. Storm, *My Descent into Death*, 94.

11. Holden, Greyson, and James, eds., *Handbook of Near-Death Experiences*, 70, cited in Miller, *Near-Death Experiences as Evidence*, 170. Miller gives many other studies on hellish NDEs in notes 30–31 on p. 170.

12. Rawlings, *Beyond Death's Door*, 8.

13. Ibid., 94–95.

14. Haraldsson and Osis, *At the Hour of Death*, 90.

15. Ibid., 90.

16. Ibid., 67.

17. Nancy Evans Bush, *Dancing Past the Dark: Distressing Near-Death Experiences* (n.p.: Nancy Evans Bush, 2012), Kindle edition, locations 605–19.

18. Ritchie and Sherrill, *Return from Tomorrow*, 68, 73–76.

19. Ibid., 76.

20. Bush, *Dancing Past the Dark*, locations 676–79.

21. Ibid., locations 682–88.

22. Sharkey, *Clinically Dead*, 24–25.

23. Lewis, *Problem of Pain*, 127.

24. Storm, *My Descent into Death*, 51–53.

25. Alexander, *Proof of Heaven*, 69.

26. Summary and direct quotes from ibid., 29–31.

27. Bush, *Dancing Past the Dark*, locations 706–35.

28. Ibid., locations 706–7, 743–44.

Chapter 17 The Life Review

1. All quoted material in this section about Howard Storm's NDE, aside from that which is cited with endnotes, is from the transcript of John Burke's interview with Howard Storm.

2. The last sentence of this paragraph is taken from Howard Storm, *My Descent into Death*, 35.

3. The preceding four sentences are taken from Howard Storm, *My Descent into Death*, 36.

4. The last paragraph in this section from Howard Storm, *My Descent into Death*, 36, 51, 52.

5. Wood, *A Place Called Heaven*, 209–13.

6. From transcript of interview with Dr. Mary Neal by John Burke, October 2015.

7. Neal, *To Heaven and Back*, 57.

8. Ally Breedlove, *When Will the Heaven Begin?* (New York: Penguin, 2013), 185.

9. Van Lommel, *Consciousness Beyond Life*, 35–36.

10. "Mark J's NDE," NDERF.org, http://www.nderf.org/NDERF/NDE_Ex
periences/mark_j's_nde.htm (last accessed May 5, 2015).
11. Miller, *Near-Death Experiences as Evidence*, 83–85.
12. "Rene Hope Turner NDE," NDERF.org, http://www.nderf.org/Experiences
/1rene_hope_turner_nde.html (last accessed May 5, 2015).
13. Ritchie and Sherrill, *Return from Tomorrow*, 58–61.
14. Moody, *Life After Life*, 51–52.
15. Long and Perry, *Evidence of the Afterlife*, 111.
16. Sjogren, *Day I Died*, locations 280–308.
17. Van Lommel, *Consciousness Beyond Life*, 207.
18. Long and Perry, *Evidence of the Afterlife*, 113.
19. "Hillary H.'s NDE," NDERF.org http://www.nderf.org/NDERF/NDE_Ex
periences/hillary_h's_nde.htm.
20. "Ron A.'s NDE," NDERF.org, http://www.nderf.org/NDERF/NDE_Ex
periences/ron_a's_nde.htm.

Chapter 18 Rewards and Judgments

1. Wood, *A Place Called Heaven*, locations 226–62.
2. Besteman and Craker, *My Journey to Heaven*, 103.
3. "Barbara J NDE," NDERF.org, http://www.nderf.org/NDERF/NDE_Ex
periences/barbara_j_nde.htm (last accessed May 5, 2015).
4. "Mark's NDE," NDERF.org, http://www.nderf.org/NDERF/NDE_Experi
ences/mark_nde.htm (last accessed May 5, 2015).
5. Haraldsson and Osis, *At the Hour of Death*, 190–91.
6. Ibid., 152.
7. Ibid., 181.
8. "Anita_M's NDE," NDERF.org, http://www.nderf.org/NDERF/NDE_
Experiences/anita_m's_nde.htm.
9. Ring and Cooper, *Mindsight*, 58.
10. Quoted from transcript of John Burke's interview with Howard Storm.
11. Sharkey, *Clinically Dead*, 32–34.
12. Long and Perry, *Evidence of the Afterlife*, 14, 110–11.

Chapter 19 Exhilarating—Not Boring

1. Black and Gire, *Flight to Heaven*, 109–10.
2. Jonathan Edwards, *The Works of Jonathan Edwards*, vol. 2 (Bath, Avon,
UK: The Bath Press, 1974), 902.
3. Black and Gire, *Flight to Heaven*, 104–5.
4. Rebecca Springer, *Intra Muros* (Elgin, IL: David C. Cook Publishers, 1898), 3–7.
5. Burpo et al., *Heaven Is for Real*, locations 1156–62.
6. Ritchie and Sherrill, *Return from Tomorrow*, 80–83.
7. Malick, *10 Amazing Muslims Touched by God*, 81.
8. Wood, *A Place Called Heaven*, location 695.
9. Thoene and Habib, *Face to Face with Jesus*, locations 2147–54, 2199.
10. Van Lommel, *Consciousness Beyond Life*, 34.
11. Mickey Robinson, *Falling to Heaven* (Cedar Rapids, IA: Arrow, 2003), 97.

12. Moody, *Life After Life*, 50.

13. Ritchie and Sherrill, *Return from Tomorrow*, 84–86.

14. This portion of Howard Storm's NDE (with the exception of the cited quotations taken from John Burke's interview with Howard Storm) is paraphrased from Howard Storm, *My Descent into Death*, 26–28.

15. Quotes, including block quote, from interview transcript with Howard Storm.

16. Doucette, *Is Heaven for Real?*, 168.

17. Ibid., 166–67, 165–66.

Chapter 20 Paradise Found

1. Scientists' observations indicate that hidden dimensions in our space-time fabric could explain the discrepancies between quantum physics and general relativity. They've also found that most of our universe is composed of "dark matter." We can't see it, but science knows it's there.

2. Ed Gaulden, *Heaven: A Joyful Place* (n.p.: Ed Gaulden Publishing, 2013), Kindle edition, locations 381–481.

3. Doucette, *Is Heaven for Real?*, 118.

4. Ritchie and Sherrill, *Return from Tomorrow*, 84.

5. Storm, *My Descent into Death*, 26.

6. Gary Wood, cited in Roth, *Heaven Is Beyond Your Wildest Expectations*, 78, italics mine.

7. Black and Gire, *Flight to Heaven*, 99, italics mine.

8. Gaulden, *Heaven*, locations 517–42, 630–39.

9. Moody, *Life After Life*, 30.

10. Gaulden, *Heaven*, locations 552–56.

11. Ibid., locations 563–72.

12. If Ed's estimation is correct, 20 New Jerusalems x 1,400 mi. = radius of Paradise = 28,000 mi. Area = 3.14 x 28,000 x 28,000 = 2,460,000,000 square miles. Earth's land area = 57 million square miles. Paradise is about 43 times the size if mostly land. Of course this may all be totally off, but one day we will know.

13. Roth, *Heaven Is Beyond Your Wildest Expectations*, 78, italics mine.

14. Rawlings, *Beyond Death's Door*, 102–3, italics mine.

15. Malz, *My Glimpse of Eternity*, 97, italics mine.

16. The summary of Brad Barrows's NDE, including direct quotations, from Ring and Cooper, *Mindsight*, 20, 44.

17. "Michelle M's NDE," NDERF.org, http://www.nderf.org/NDERF/NDE_Experiences/michelle_m's_nde.htm.

18. "Don C's NDE," NDERF.org, http://www.nderf.org/NDERF/NDE_Experiences/don_c_nde.htm.

19. Black and Gire, *Flight to Heaven*, 105–7.

20. Malz, *My Glimpse of Eternity*, 97.

21. Ibid., 97–99.

22. Piper and Murphey, *90 Minutes in Heaven*, 38–39.

Chapter 21 The City of God (Pets Allowed)

1. Piper and Murphey, *90 Minutes in Heaven*, locations 416–27.
2. Doucette, *Is Heaven for Real?*, 108.
3. Black and Gire, *Flight to Heaven*, 106–7.
4. Neal, *To Heaven and Back*, locations 795–803.
5. Ring and Cooper, *Mindsight*, 45.
6. Doucette, *Is Heaven for Real?*, 110–11.
7. Ibid., 121.
8. Malz, *My Glimpse of Eternity*, 98–99.
9. Sigmund, *My Time in Heaven*, locations 236–59.
10. Ibid., 113–15.
11. Kramarik and Kramarik, *Akiane*, 10.
12. Alcorn, *Heaven*, 426.
13. Wood, *Place Called Heaven*, locations 249–75, 297–301.
14. Black and Gire, *Flight to Heaven*, 105.
15. Wood, *Place Called Heaven*, locations 267–74.
16. Doucette, *Is Heaven for Real?*, 112.
17. Gaulden, *Heaven*, locations 697–708.
18. Springer, *Intra Muros*, 9–10.
19. Wood, *Place Called Heaven*, locations 305–16.
20. Van Lommel, *Consciousness Beyond Life*, 74.
21. "Ray K's NDE," NDERF.org, http://www.nderf.org/NDERF/NDE_Experiences/ray_k's_nde.htm (last accessed May 5, 2015).
22. Clara, Near-death.com. Clara's NDE (age 10) is cited from the book by permission on http://www.near-death.com/children.html#a02 (last accessed May 5, 2015).
23. "Robin_M's NDE," NDERF.org, http://www.nderf.org/NDERF/NDE_Experiences/robin_m_nde.htm.
24. Besteman and Craker, *My Journey to Heaven*, 185–86.
25. Sigmund, *My Time in Heaven*, locations 1133–52, 1326.
26. Kramarik and Kramarik, *Akiane*, 10.
27. Doucette, *Is Heaven for Real?*, 157.
28. Black and Gire, *Flight to Heaven*, 101–3.

Appendix A Reasons to Believe

1. The original *Arizona Daily Star* article is inaccessible, but here is the data referenced: https://journals.uair.arizona.edu/index.php/radiocarbon/article/viewFile/1537/1541 (last accessed May 5, 2015).
2. Tracey R. Rich, "Qorbanot: Sacrifices and Offerings," *Judaism 101*, http://www.jewfaq.org/qorbanot.htm.
3. "May 15, 1948: Israel Declares Independence," The Learning Network, *New York Times*, http://learning.blogs.nytimes.com201205/14/may-14-1948-israel-declares-independence/?_r=0.

Appendix B Alternate Explanations for NDEs

1. Van Lommel, *Consciousness Beyond Life*, 132–33.

The author gratefully acknowledges the permission of the following authors and publishers:

Reprinted with the permission of Simon & Schuster, Inc. from *Proof of Heaven* by Eben Alexander, MD. Copyright © 2012 Eben Alexander, MD.

Besteman, Marvin J., and Lorilee Craker. *My Journey to Heaven: What I Saw and How It Changed My Life*. Grand Rapids: Baker, a division of Baker Publishing Group, 2012. Used by permission.

Black, Dale, and Ken Gire. *Flight to Heaven: A Plane Crash . . . A Lone Survivor . . . A Journey to Heaven—and Back*. Minneapolis: Bethany House, a division of Baker Publishing Group, 2010. Used by permission.

Braxton, Dean. *In Heaven! Experiencing the Throne of God*. Chambersburg, PA: Divine Design Publishing, 2012. Used by permission.

Bush, Nancy Evans. *Dancing Past the Dark: Distressing Near-Death Experiences*. Nancy Evans Bush, 2012. Used by permission.

Thanks to Patrick Doucette for permission to quote his book *Is Heaven for Real? Personal Stories of Visiting Heaven*. Available on Amazon: www.amazon.com/dp/B00BXKG41U.

Quotes used by permission from Ed Gaulden, *Heaven: A Joyful Place*, retitled *Heaven Is*.

Haraldsson, Erlendur, and Karlis Osis. *At the Hour of Death*. Guildford, Great Britain: White Crow Books, 1977. Used by permission.

Quotes from pp. 40–41, 46, 62, 75, 94, 125, 141, 161, 183, 264 from *Evidence of the Afterlife* by Jeffrey Long, MD, with Paul Perry. Copyright © by Jeffrey Long. Reprinted by permission of HarperCollins Publishers.

Malz, Betty. *My Glimpse of Eternity*. Bloomington, MN: Chosen, a division of Baker Publishing Group, 2012. Used by permission.

Reprinted with the permission of Howard Books, a division of Simon & Schuster, Inc. from *Waking Up in Heaven* by Crystal McVea and Alex Tresniowski. Copyright © 2013 Crystal McVea and Alex Tresniowski.

Thanks to J. Steve Miller for permission to use quotes from his extensive research in *Near-Death Experiences as Evidence for the Existence of God and Heaven: A Brief Introduction in Plain Language*. Acworth, GA: Wisdom Creek Press, 2012.

Quotes from pp. 25–26, 51, 87, 109, 125, 148, 149, 221, 246, 276, 288 from *Life After Life: The Investigation of a Phenomenon: Survival of Bodily Death* by Raymond A. Moody Jr. Copyright © 2001 by Raymond Moody. Reprinted by permission of HarperCollins Publishers.

Excerpts from *To Heaven and Back: A Doctor's Extraordinary Account of Her Death, Heaven, Angels, and Life Again: A True Story* by Mary C. Neal, M.D., copyright © 2011, 2012 by Mary C. Neal. Used by permission of WaterBrook Multnomah, an imprint of the Crown Publishing Group, a division of Penguin Random House LLC. All rights reserved.

Olsen, Jeff. *I Knew Their Hearts: The Amazing True Story of Jeff Olsen's Journey Beyond the Veil to Learn the Silent Language of the Heart*. Springville, UT: Plain Sight Publishing, 2012. Used by permission of Cedar Fort, Inc. Available on Amazon and Booksandthings.com (email contact@booksandthings.com for 20% off Booksand things.com coupon code while available).

Piper, Don, and Cecil Murphey. *90 Minutes in Heaven: A True Story of Death & Life*. Grand Rapids: Revell, a division of Baker Publishing Group, 2006. Used by permission.

Ring, Kenneth, and Sharon Cooper. *Mindsight: Near-Death and Out-of-Body Experiences in the Blind*. Bloomington, IL: iUniverse, 2008.

Ritchie, George G., and Elizabeth Sherrill. *Return from Tomorrow*. Grand Rapids: Spire, a division of Baker Publishing Group, 1978. Used by permission.

Heaven Is Beyond Your Wildest Expectations: Ten True Stories of Experiencing Heaven by Sid Roth and Lonnie Lane, copyright © 2012. Reproduced by permission of Destiny Image.

Sharkey, Jenny. *Clinically Dead—I've Seen Heaven and Hell*. 2013. Used by permission.

Excerpts from *My Descent into Death: A Second Chance at Life* by Howard Storm, copyright © 2005 by Howard Storm. Used by permission of Doubleday, an imprint of the Knopf Doubleday Publishing Group, a division of Penguin Random House LLC. All rights reserved.

Thoene, Bodie, and Samaa Habib. *Face to Face with Jesus: A Former Muslim's Extraordinary Journey to Heaven and Encounter with the God of Love*. Bloomington, MN: Chosen, a division of Baker Publishing Group, 2014. Used by permission.

Quotes from 35, 47, 48, 51, 94, 127, 174, 222, 243, 249, 276, 308, 326 from *Consciousness Beyond Life* by Pim van Lommel, MD. Copyright © 2010 by Pim van Lommel. Reprinted by permission of HarperCollins Publishers.

Excerpts from *A Place Called Heaven* by Dr. Gary L. Wood. Copyright © 2008, 2014 by Dr. Gary L. Wood. Used by permission of Banner Publishing and Whitaker House. www.whitakerhouse.com.

John Burke is the author of *Unshockable Love*, *No Perfect People Allowed*, and *Soul Revolution*, and the lead pastor of Gateway Church in Austin, Texas, which he and his wife founded in 1998. Since then, Gateway has grown to over 4,500 members, made up mostly of unchurched people who began actively following Christ at Gateway. John is also the founder and president of Gateway Leadership Initiative (GLI), a non-profit organization working to help church planting pastors and ordinary Christians "raise the church out of the culture." John has spoken in fifteen countries to over 200,000 people. Follow him at Johnburkeonline.com.

Daily Encouragement to Deepen Your Faith

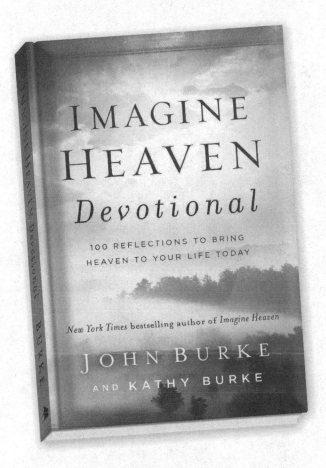

Each of these 100 devotions includes near-death stories from the bestselling book, Scripture, a prayer, as well as brand-new stories and content that helps readers apply heavenly promises to how they live life today.

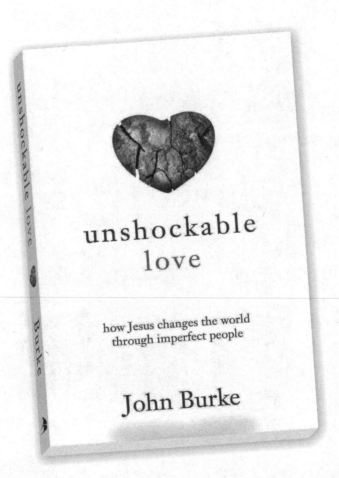

TO CONNECT WITH

JOHN | **BURKE**

—— VISIT JOHNBURKEONLINE.COM ——

- — BLOG
- — SPEAKING EVENTS
- — BOOKS
- — CONTACT
- — OTHER FREE RESOURCES

For more information on *Imagine Heaven*, including an audiobook, visit

IMAGINEHEAVEN.NET